The Rise and Fall of the Arab Empire
And The Founding of Western Pre-eminence

THE RISE AND FALL
OF THE ARAB EMPIRE

AND THE FOUNDING OF WESTERN PRE-EMINENCE

Rodney Collomb

SPELLMOUNT

British Library Cataloguing in Publication Data:
A catalogue record for this book is available
from the British Library

Copyright © Rodney Collomb 2006

Cartography by Pierre Alexaline
Pictures from Library of Congress except 19, Courtesy of the University
of Birmingham Collections, Birmingham

ISBN 1-86227-327-8

First published in the UK in 2006 by
Spellmount Limited
The Mill, Brimscombe Port
Stroud, Gloucestershire. GL5 2QG

Tel: 01453 883300
Fax: 01453 883233
E-mail: enquiries@spellmount.com
Website: www.spellmount.com

1 3 5 7 9 8 6 4 2

Printed in Great Britain by
Oaklands Book Services
Stonehouse, Gloucestershire GL10 3RQ

Contents

1

Arabia and Mohammed the Prophet

6th-Century Mecca – The Prophet – Sharia Law – Charlemagne and the
Separation of Church and State

6th-Century Mecca:

Although there is little documentary evidence, legend has it that after
about 500 AD, while Europe fell deeper into anarchy following the
breakup of the Roman Empire, the town of Mecca in the western
Arabian hill country, the Hejaz, became an important commercial and
cultural centre. The town, at an elevation of about 2,000 ft, lay on the
1,500-mile caravan trail from the Levant to Yemen linking the prosperous Christian trading centres of the eastern end of the Mediterranean
– Alexandria, Gaza, Tyre, Jerusalem, Damascus, Antioch – with frank-
incense- and myrrh-producing Yemen and Somalia, the clove-islands
of Zanzibar, and the luxuriant coastal lands of India and Malaya.
In contrast to Mecca, much of the Arabian peninsula at this time
was impoverished, over-populated, inhospitable, a largely waterless
wilderness. Mecca, a town with no agricultural resources of its own,
had acquired the status upon which its prosperity depended from a
favourable combination of other factors. Intermittent warfare after
about 502 AD between the (Greek) East Roman and the (Persian)
Sasanian empires interrupted the more practical caravan routes from
the Mediterranean Sea to the Indian Ocean through Egypt and the
Red Sea, and along the Euphrates into the Persian Gulf, to Mecca's

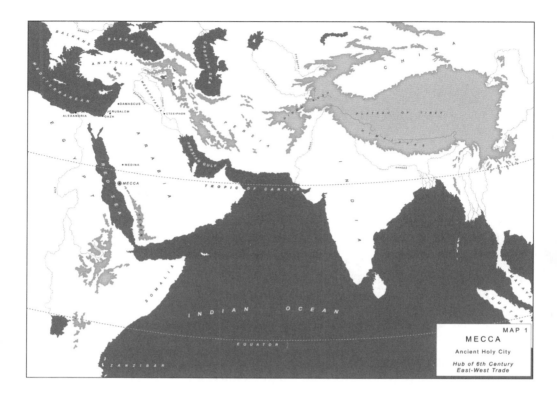

MAP 1
MECCA
Ancient Holy City
Hub of 6th Century
East-West Trade

advantage. Mecca was also served by the harbour of Jedda, forty-five miles away on the Red Sea.

Oral tradition indicates that for centuries Mecca had been a place of pilgrimage, the site of the Kaaba, the hallowed repository of the great Black Stone believed by some to have been given to Abraham (c. 2100 BC?) by the angel Gabriel. The Kaaba, thought also to have been built by Abraham, was said by some to mark the spot where Adam first appeared after the Fall of Man. For the pagan tribesmen, worshipping a multitude of graven images, the Black Stone inspired the greatest awe. People from the several Jewish tribes around the town of Medina on the trail 250 miles north of Mecca also recognized the sanctity of Mecca because of its Abrahamic roots.

Mecca maintained its prominence by obtaining agreement among the distant cousins of the town-dwellers, the nomadic tribesmen of the arid steppelands and desolate lava-fields who fought constantly over grazing land, to keep the peace around the city. Still, trade caravans had to pay tolls to cross tribal lands. But from Mecca's identity as a place of security, there emerged a further understanding between the town-dwelling and nomadic peoples that at certain times of the year caravans could move freely without harassment anywhere in the peninsula. Everyone benefited from these agreements, the Meccan Peace, but especially the prosperous oligarchs of the city, most of them members of the pagan Koreish (Quraish) tribe. This twelve-clan tribe had occupied Mecca since the early 500s, from pastoral origins. Mecca might be described at the time as a city-state run by a syndicate of well-to-do merchants with a strong sympathy for nomadic independence and ancient custom, and guided by the gods.

The Prophet:
In about 572, a boy, Mohammed bin Abdullah, was born in Mecca to a poor though notable family of the Hashemite clan of the Koreishis, the clan named after Hashim, Mohammed's great-grandfather. Mohammed, orphaned in infancy, was brought up in poor circumstances at first by a grandfather, later by an uncle. Legend indicates that in adulthood while working as a merchant-trader Mohammed, by nature contemplative and mystical, turned to holy pursuits, retiring periodically to a cave in Jebel (Mt.) Arafat near Mecca to meditate. Immemorial Muslim conviction maintains that in about 610 the archangel Gabriel appeared to Mohammed while meditating in this cave and in a stream of appearances over a period of time revealed to him the will of God, the all-encompassing faith that would be the guide for all aspects of life for all mankind, forever. Broadcasting Gabriel's revelations in lyrical prose, the charismatic Mohammed condemned the widespread polytheism, declaring as did the People of the Book (*dhimmis* in Arabic) – the Jews and Christians – that there was only one god, Allah, the Compassionate, the Merciful, who had ordained him, Mohammed, His last Messenger on Earth before the Day of Judgement.

Muslim tradition affirms that Mohammed the Prophet, fired by moral indignation at the sinfulness around him, preached of social, economic, political equality for all people. He called for peace and forbearance, mercy and compassion, charity, fortitude, temperance, loyalty. He denounced the high living of the ruling elite, the oligarchs of Mecca, the subordination of women, female infanticide, the "blood laws" and feuds of the tribes. Calling upon the will of God revealed

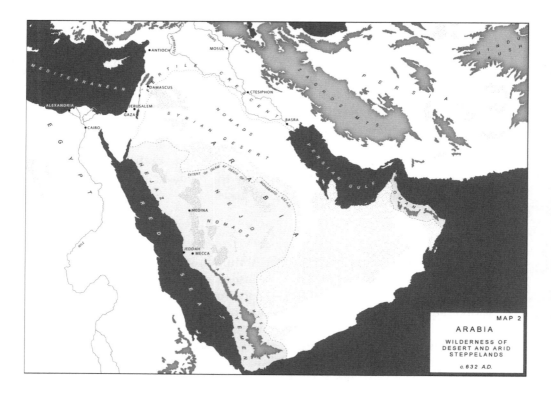

MAP 2
ARABIA
WILDERNESS OF
DESERT AND ARID
STEPPELANDS
c. 632 A.D.

to him by Gabriel and employing his own spellbinding powers of persuasion coupled with the sword, in the decade before his death in 632 Mohammed and what were his mainly urban followers unified many of the partly settled and partly nomadic tribes of western Arabia, the 4,000-8,000-foot high Hejaz province bordering the Red Sea, into a confederation steeped in the new faith.

The great appeal of the religion that Mohammed named "Islam", meaning "submission", submission to the will of Allah, was that the simplicity and tangibility of its ideas satisfied the spiritual needs of the times. In establishing Islam, the Prophet created an authoritarian monarchy dominated by that religion and its unchangeable laws. Unlike the quasi-democratic tribal leaders of the time who were generally *primi inter pares*, in a society built upon the "eternal truths" that had been revealed to him, Mohammed ruled autocratically, led prayers, promulgated laws, dispensed justice, levied taxes, and decided on whom to make war and when.

Over time Gabriel's revelations, as voiced by Mohammed, were embodied in the 6,219 verses of the Koran, the holy book. And accounts of Mohammed's teachings and doings were assembled in the "Traditions" – the *Hadith*. These works together with *ijma*, consensus of the faithful tested over a lengthy period of time, and *ijtihad*, a sincere attempt to discover the proper meaning of the Koran through debate, form the principles of Islam and of Sharia law. But like the clergy of both of the other Abrahamic religions, Judaism and Christianity, from earliest times Islam's ministers demanded unquestioning submission to God's laws, as interpreted by them.

Sharia Law:
Unlike Western codes of law, now based on modified Roman Law, English Common Law, the systematic collection of customary rules of European communities governing the inter-actions of their people, or the mainly secular constitutions written in the 18th and 19th centuries, Sharia, to paraphrase S.E.Finer, covers not only law but also liturgy for public worship and every-day private behaviour. Unlike Western codes which generally determine the must-do and the must-not-do, infallible, divinely ordained Sharia law stipulates the obligatory, the recommended, the issues over which the law is indifferent, the disapproved, the forbidden, and the lawful. Still, much Islamic law was based on pre-Islamic Arab custom.

Islam is more than a religion. It is a complete closed ethical and behavioural system, admitting no innovation or improvement. It is already perfect; it is beyond question, and no room exists for minority or eccentric opinion. The individual of the 7th century owed total obedience to Allah. This was his first, last and only duty in life. There was no question of separation of matters of faith from worldly affairs, no question of social rules evolving with the needs of the times. Government was forever to be by God's laws as had been revealed to Mohammed.

Charlemagne and the Separation of Church and State:
In direct contrast to the doctrines of Islam, the Christian Gospel according to Mark, 12:17, commands: "Render unto Caesar the things that are Caesar's and to God the things that are God's." Such is a Biblical basis for secular government, for the separation of church from state, even if

Christian philosophers had to struggle against the Church through the Middle Ages and afterwards to explain as well as justify the separation. In Baghdad on Christmas Day in the year 800, the leader of the Arabs, Caliph Harun al-Rashid, ruled with little-challenged power over the Islamic empire, its beliefs and behaviour. On that same day in Rome, Pope Leo III placed the Imperial Crown of the Holy Roman Empire on the head of Charlemagne, the illiterate King of the Franks, and proclaimed him "Caesar", explicitly acknowledging that Charlemagne's authority in worldly affairs was separate from and paralleled his own in spiritual matters.

Although the old Roman Empire had perished, its religion, Christianity had survived. To establish a balance of power between the heavenly and the earthly in the new one, Leo III had agreed to a new order based upon the allied but separate authority of the Latin Church and the Christian Emperor. This covenant was very much a product of the threatening rise of Islam. By this time Arab forces had conquered the Middle (Near) East, north Africa and most of Spain and Portugal. They had, even more troublingly, established bridgeheads on the Mediterranean coast of France. These events had compelled the Pope in the face of the alienation of the Greek Orthodox Patriarch of eastern Europe, Byzantium, then ruled by the daunting Empress Irene, to seek partnership with the most powerful political leader of the West, Charlemagne (with whom she had, before being overthrown, proposed a marriage alliance). It was the looming menace of Islam that propelled Charlemagne from local king to emperor of much of western Europe. His imperial seal bore the device *"Renovatio Imperii Romani"*.

2

The Rise of the Arab Empire; the Years of Conquest

The Prophet's Successors, the Caliphs – Expanding the Kingdom – the Murders of Early Caliphs – The Umayyads – The Earlier Caliphs, Successors of the Prophet 632-750 – Future Extinction of Umayyad Dynasty in Iraq – Governance

The Prophet's Successors, the Caliphs:
Scarcely any contemporary account of the early Arab conquests has survived. The progress of empire-building has had to be reconstructed from anecdotal material preserved by chroniclers, in some cases a century or more after the events. Mohammed seems to have made no formal provision for a successor to lead the Faith after him, and upon his death dispute over succession to the leadership arose immediately. Abu Bakr, one of Mohammed's fathers-in-law, father of the Prophet's second or third wife, Aisha (of about eight wives), was chosen by the elders to succeed the Prophet, but only over the objections of Mohammed's cousin, Ali bin Abi Talib, who claimed the leadership, and of Ali's wife, Fatima, Mohammed's daughter by his first wife, Khadija. Fatima was the only one of the Prophet's several children to reach adulthood. She died at the age of twenty-seven leaving two sons, Hassan, the elder and Hussein whose memory would become the mainspring of Shiism. Mohammed's youngest widow, Aisha, who reportedly had been given by her father in marriage to him before her eighth birthday (or several years older according to other sources),

7

was childless. Mohammed had married her in his fifties. (At this time the Church of Rome sanctioned marriage at the age of fourteen for "men", twelve for "women".) Dispute over the legitimate succession of the Prophet was not resolved upon his death, nor ever afterwards.

There were four close companions of Mohammed, all deemed worthy of leading the Faith after him: Abu Bakr, his father-in-law, a member of the Ta'im (Tamim) clan of the Koreish tribe, was a prosperous merchant; Ali, Mohammed's cousin and son-in-law; Omar bin al-Khattab, a member of the Beni Adi clan of the Koreishis; and Uthman bin Affan, a member of the Beni Umayya clan, descendants of the founder of the tribe called Qusayy. This clan is known to English-speaking historians as the "Umayyads". The Umayyads were the leading merchant family of Mecca. When Abu Bakr was elected successor of the Prophet he made the Arabian town of Medina his administrative capital. Abu Bakr died, apparently of natural causes, within two years of his accession after campaigning to subdue those parts of the Arabian peninsula that had held out from the will of God during Mohammed's life time, and to bring them into the fold.

Expanding the Kingdom:
Following the Prophet's death in 632, Islam spread like wildfire, revealing widespread need in the region for spiritual guidance. At this time in the Middle East and North Africa an enfeebled Persian empire covering today's Iran and Iraq, living under the divided leadership of the Sasanian dynasty, and the remnants of the Roman Empire in the west and north in the form of Byzantium and its client states, existed in effect in a power vacuum where Roman imperial order had once stood. Byzantium's capital was Constantinople, now Istanbul. Persia's capital was Ctesiphon, now an ancient ruin in Iraq a few miles from Baghdad.

While we talk of the Byzantine empire, its inhabitants called themselves Romans (*Romaioi*). As they were Greek speaking, the Arabs called them Greeks. If the Romans ever had a name for their empire, it may well have been "Romania". The term "Byzantium" was coined from the Greek language by Western scholars in the 16th century, named after a Greek colony founded on the site of Istanbul in the 7th century BC.

In Byzantium, Christian like much of the Roman Empire since Constantine the Great founded his new capital on this ancient site in 330 AD, the Emperor and the Patriarch of the Greek Orthodox Church shared power as secular and spiritual pillars of authority. The Emperor's court was the centre of an army of professional bureaucrats administering the empire. The high officers of the court were all eunuchs (as indeed they were in the imperial court of China at the time.) In atmosphere at this time the Byzantine court was oriental, devious, sycophantic and authoritarian. Government edicts governed all aspects of commercial life and craft production. Nevertheless, as the scion of Graeco-Roman culture, Byzantium, the guardian of Classical scholarship in its great cities of Constantinople and Alexandria, incorporated a diverse population which in the towns was educated as nowhere on earth outside China, with schools, universities, female education and arts studies. In the arts, particularly in mosaics and the architecture of the 7th and 8th century, Byzantium was unequalled in Eurasia.

In contrast, Sasanian Persia, which had finally been subdued inconclusively by the Greeks allied with migrating Turkic tribesmen, and which had been a highly centralized kingdom with provinces kept under tight control, had broken down into rival military dictatorships. But Persian society still remained rigidly organized under a caste system of priests, soldiers, scribes and commoners. The kings claimed divinity within the embrace of their religion, Zoroastrianism, where the Universe was the field of conflict between light with goodness and darkness with evil, (theological "dualism"). Good supported by Man would eventually triumph over Evil.

The two lately powerful empires of Byzantium and Persia were exhausted by 628 after a century of intermittent warfare. Both were faced with financial crisis. To economize, the Byzantines under Emperor Heraclius I had ceased paying the mainly Christian Arab tribes of Syria for maintaining security on their eastern frontier facing the Persians in Mesopotamia. However, many of the Byzantine military forces were not Greek-Byzantine nationals at all, but foreign mercenaries, Turks, Armenians and Arabs owing little loyalty to the Empire. In such frail political circumstances the disciples of the Prophet Mohammed rallied the fierce bedouins newly converted to Islam and swept out of peninsular Arabia in 635-38 to capture Syria. Iraq (Mesopotamia), a province of the Persian empire for the previous 700 years, with its ribbons of agriculture along the Tigris and Euphrates rivers and its largely Semitic population under Aryan Persian domination, was also quickly overcome, "islamized" and "arabized" by the invaders. A significant

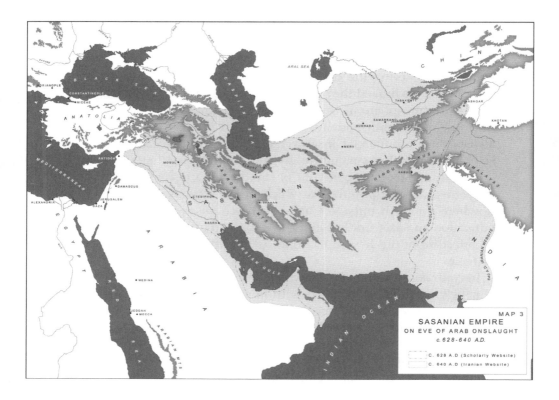

MAP 3
SASANIAN EMPIRE
ON EVE OF ARAB ONSLAUGHT
c. 628-640 A.D.

C. 628 A.D (Scholarly Website)
C. 640 A.D (Iranian Website)

number of the common folk of Iraq seem to have surrendered willingly. Still, bloody battles were fought against Persian military forces. And obstinate resistance was encountered in eastern Persia which was not fully subdued until the last Sasanian king, Yezdegird III, was murdered near the easterly provincial capital of Merv in 651-2.

In 638, the largely Christian city of Jerusalem had fallen to the Arabs under Omar bin al- Khattab who had succeeded Abu Bakr as caliph in 634. Upon accession Omar had taken the title "Commander of the Faithful", a style adopted by all later caliphs. The Prophet's cousin Ali had again unsuccessfully claimed the throne. Omar kept Medina as his capital, and in 639 a general of his at the head of 3000 Arabian Yamami cavalrymen attacked the Byzantine forces of Egypt, defeating them by 641. Alexandria with its seven centuries also of Graeco-Roman-Coptic culture held on for a year before falling. It was briefly retaken by the Greeks before finally giving way. Ancient records indicate that the majority Nestorian Christians (who believed that Christ existed as two beings, a human and a divine – another dualistic belief) of Mesopotamia and western Persia, and the Monophysite Christians of Egypt (who believed that Christ had a single divine nature) all of whom had been persecuted for heresy by the Orthodox Byzantines, often welcomed the Muslim Arabs as men come to free them from injustice. By 656, the Muslims had taken the rest of the Middle East and North-east Africa.

(Nestorians, now united with the Roman Church and known as Chaldeans, form the largest of the many small Christian communities in present-day Iraq. Other Christians of Nestorian heritage in Iraq who do not recognize the primacy of Rome are called Assyrians, of which there exist about eight sub-denominations. The Coptic Christians of today's Egypt are close doctrinally but not identical with the former Monophysites. In Syria the Monophysites are known as Jacobites. The Maronites of today's Lebanon and Syria are Catholics of the Eastern rite, but then there are some twelve different Christian confessions in today's Lebanon.)

At the beginning of the 7th century, the Arabic language was a minor language confined to the Arabian peninsula. To the north, Syriac, an Aramaic dialect, was spoken widely by the common people west of the Euphrates River. (Jesus Christ is likely to have spoken Aramaic or one of its several dialects.) Greek and Latin were spoken by the Byzantine governing classes. It was only in 630 however that the Byzantine Emperor Heraclius had exchanged Latin for Greek as his official language. East of the Euphrates, Aramaic, in Syriac or Assyrian dialect, was commonly spoken in what is now Iraq. Persian and some Greek were spoken by the rulers. But then, the Arab conquerors quickly spread their own language and replaced the native tongues.

Arabic, a language that some have argued lends itself easily to overstatement, to polemic, is a major unifying factor in the present-day Arab world, and a key to identity. Along with the religion, the language was historically a crucial element in the process of advancing Islamic culture. Then, as now, the manner of expression, as much as the meaning, was a distinctive Arab characteristic. And in the language lies much of today's Arab spirit of unity.

(In his 1980 essay "Learning to Think Like an Arab Muslim", Edward V. Badolato, the American military scholar, wrote: "The Arabs place a high value on the Arabic language, and it exerts an overpowering psychological influence over their behaviour...English cannot even challenge Arabic for its sheer power and ability to impact on the emotions of the listener...Arab orators are prone to be carried away in verbal exaggeration when speaking before an audience...Speakers are admired not so much for what they say but how they say it...Arabs are forced to over-assert in almost all types of communication, as otherwise they stand a good chance of being gravely misunderstood". Also, for the past decade or more, the Egyptian writer and businessman, Tarek Heggy, has deplored what in English he calls the "big talk" Arab culture: "Our public discourse is drowning in a sea of hyperbole...The use of superlatives is rampant in our media...We sink into grandiloquent rhetoric which drowns the truth in a welter of words...We pay dearly for our gift of the gab". And the Lebanese philosopher, Nizar Qabbani is reported to have said in the 1990s: "We have donned a thin veneer of civilization while our soul remains mired in the Dark Ages.")

Interestingly, while the people of Iraq, Syria and Palestine soon dropped their Greek and Aramaic languages for Arabic, the ordinary Egyptian people kept their own language, Coptic, for another six hundred years before it was suddenly abandoned. Coptic, like Latin and Aramaic, eventually became little more than a liturgical language. The word Copt is derived from the Greek word for Egyptian.

The Murders of Early Caliphs:
In 644, the Commander of the Faithful, Omar bin al-Khattab, who had conquered Mesopotamia and Egypt and about whom few contemporary accounts survive, was murdered by a Christian slave in a mosque in Medina, reportedly because the Caliph refused to reduce the artisan slave's taxes. The powerful Meccan trader oligarchy, bulwark of the Umayyad clan, then arranged for the elderly, but notably god-fearing Uthman bin Affan to be elected caliph. About the early days of nation-building there is an immense literature of heroic legends usually failing to distinguish between fact, speculation and fiction. Much will never be known, but by mid-century, victorious generals under Uthman's command had seized all the lands from what is now eastern Libya to Persia, a span of 2,500 miles.

Despite the lack of historical certainty, a reasonable explanation can be given for the astonishing military success of the Arab tribesmen in the 7th century. Before Islam, as with most nomadic herdsmen, intertribal raiding was their chosen means of increasing food supply and raising status. Mohammed's unification of the Arabs focused much of this combative energy. The warlike bedouins provided the expansionist dynamic, and the lasting authority of Mohammed, the compelling word of God, channeled their energy through religious fervour into overcoming the armies of the neighbouring Byzantine and Persian empires. At the same time, while accommodating the conquests of Omar and Uthman, the Arab kingdom internally was in ceaseless turmoil, riven by ferocious tribal feuding, clan jealousies and militant sectarianism growing out of disputes over the right to lead Islam. Fanatical, puritanical cults soon began to destabilize the community.

With the weak, aging and nepotistic Uthman as caliph, resentment against the Meccan régime grew as the oligarchs gathered in most of the spoils of conquest for themselves. The pious Uthman is believed by some scholars to have issued an official text of the Koran and to have ordered others to be destroyed, arousing more hostility. Again, in 650 he seems carelessly to have lost the Prophet's signet ring causing widespread discontent to begin to focus on him personally. In the second half of his twelve-year reign there arose a mass movement of resistance leading to his murder, also in Medina, by a gang of mutinous soldiers from the Arab army of Egypt led by Mohammed, son of the deceased Caliph Abu Bakr (and brother of Aisha, widow of the Prophet.) The assassins were supporters of the Prophet's cousin, Ali, pretender to the throne. This murder in 656 brought discredit to both the supporters of Ali, who personally was above reproach, and the Meccan oligarchy whose behaviour had stirred up such fervent opposition. After this killing the Arabs were never again able to unite across sectarian boundaries. Civil war erupted.

When peace was restored, Ali was proclaimed caliph by those who were likely behind the murder of Uthman. (Ali's early supporters are known as "Alids". After the 8th century, they are called "Shias", the term being derived from the Arabic for "members of the party of Ali".) Ali moved his capital out of Medina, Arabia, to Kufa on the Euphrates in today's south-central Iraq where he was welcomed by the populace for his known piety. Ali was however still fiercely opposed by his rivals represented by the Prophet's young widow Aisha and by the Umayyads. Dispute over the lawful succession to the caliphate was not over with the appointment of Ali. It is the basis for the division of Islam into Sunni and Shiite branches. Then, after months of fighting, truces, negotiations, treachery, Ali too was killed in a mosque in Kufa at the age of about sixty- one in 661. He was killed by a former supporter, a fanatical "Kharijite" – separatist – named Abd ar-Rahman bin Muljam al-Sarimi, incensed it is said by Ali's having arbitrated his dispute over the succession to the caliphate with the Umayyad, Mu'awiya, governor of Syria, nephew of the murdered Caliph Uthman. For fear of desecration of his grave, Ali was buried secretly by his followers, probably in the nearby village of Najaf, where a shrine to his memory was built.

Ali was succeeded provisionally by his eldest son, Hassan, then aged thirty-seven; but Hassan lacked support, and abdicated. (Some accounts though say he was murdered by the Umayyads; others maintain that Mu'awiya bribed him into a life of indulgence, many wives – sixty to ninety, it was said – together with a stable of three hundred concubines.) And the Umayyads engineered the appointment of their most eminent personage, Mu'awiya, to the throne. This Meccan merchant clan which is believed to have been reconciled to Islam mainly by financial incentive – the booty of conquest due to "God's chosen on Earth" – then ruled the state for the next ninety years.

The Umayyads:
Mu'awiya set up his capital in Damascus, Syria, where he had been the well regarded governor. With the support of the *ulema* – the religious scholars who had quickly risen to positions of influence in the kingdom – the Umayyads assumed the leadership of what would become the mainstream branch of Islam, the Sunni. For all that, the murdered Ali's followers still held that it was only the Hashemite clan and Ali's line of descent through Hussein and Hassan who could be successors of the Prophet. They condemned the Umayyads as corrupt secular usurpers, and in the name of Ali who had been the leader of the movement of dissent they founded the zealous Shiite branch of Islam. This was a primal event in the history of the religion, as profound or more so than the Great Schism of 1054 dividing the Roman Catholic and Greek Orthodox churches. Not only in both ruptures were dynastic and doctrinal differences at issue, but also power politics and the laying of hands upon the spoils of power were matters of great moment.

With their usurpation, the Umayyads claimed divine right, demanding unquestioning obedience. And whereas the four earlier caliphs, the "rightly guided" companions of the Prophet, had been elected by their peers, the Umayyads introduced hereditary succession. The ruler would appoint a successor-to-be with the agreement, tacit or otherwise, of senior members of the family. A son, nephew, brother or cousin could be selected.

The temporal foundations of the Arab civilization were laid during the first half-century of Umayyad rule. The factors that had bonded the early conquerors together were religion and loot. Under the Umayyads the bonding factors appear more to have been Arab ethnicity and the continuing quest for loot, land and slaves. And soon, the new régime revealed that it cared little for the spiritual life of Islam. With the move of the capital to Damascus they set about unabashedly enriching themselves while the conquest of distant lands continued.

The collection and evaluation of the Caliph's entitlement of a large portion of the plunder from captured territories, the payment and sharing out of the spoils of victory for the bedouin cavalrymen, the gathering of taxes and the management of governmental expenditures were all unfamiliar responsibilities for the warrior caste. Few of Mohammed's followers had the experience competently to manage these tasks; alone among the Arabs, the Meccan oligarchs had. Great fortunes were then amassed by the oligarchs and the Arab military aristocracy from plunder, tribute and the monopoly of trade.

The Earlier Caliphs, Successors of the Prophet, 632-750 AD

The Prophet's Rightly Guided Companions:

Abu Bakr	632-34	Overran Arabia. Died of natural causes
Omar	634-44	Extended empire, Egypt to Iraq. Murdered.
Uthman	644-56	Extended empire, Libya to Persia. Murdered.
Ali	650-61	Keystone figure of Shiism. Murdered.

The Umayyads:

Mu'awiya	661-80	Empire reaches Tunisia, Afghanistan.
Yazid I	680-83	Beset by turmoil. Shiism takes root.
Mu'awiya II	683	Infant, deposed.
(Interregnum)	684	Turmoil, civil war.
Marwan I	684-85	Civil war.
Abdul Malik	685-705	Built Dome of the Rock, reorganized government.

Walid	705-15	Extended empire, Spain to India.
Suleiman	715-17	Abdicated after military defeat.
Omar II	717-20	Restructured tax system.
Yazid II	720-24	Faced organized religious opposition.
Hisham	724-43	Empire reached point of overextension.
Walid II	743-44	Murder and mayhem.
Yazid III	744	Religious struggles. Died in months of appointment.
Marwan II	744-50	Internecine warfare. Assassinated.

Future Extinction of Umayyad Dynasty in Iraq:

Gathering local tribal recruits eager for booty as they rode along, by 720 the bedouin warriors had pushed back the boundaries of the empire from Libya in the west and Persia in the east to their maximum historical extent in Morocco and Spain on the Atlantic, to the Syr Darya river (the Iaxartes) in today's Kazakhstan, and to the Indus River, in what is now Pakistan, 5,000 miles from the Atlantic. The Kingdom of Kabul would be taken in 664. Probing forays in search of more spoils continued, particularly into France, the land of the Franks (the Germanic tribe that had conquered Gaul in the 6th century). But communications with the Arab heartland were so tenuous that except for towns near the Mediterranean coast few of these later advances succeeded in holding territory north of the Pyrenees for very long. The Arab empire would become over-extended and most militarily unsustainable ambitions had to be abandoned. A campaign into central France in 732 would lead to defeat at the hands of Charlemagne's grandfather, Charles Martel, Duke of the Franks, at Poitiers, a few days' ride from Paris. But this failure was in the future, and not at all obvious to the conquerors in 720. In this broad sweep of territory marked by wide stretches of desert separating the fertile areas, the Arabs, though still bent unwaveringly on plunder, created a brilliant civilization the peer in cultural achievement of the contemporaneous T'ang Empire of China. The Arab empire outshone Byzantium, the survivor of the Byzantine-Sasanian conflict, confined then to the mainly Greek speaking Anatolia, the Balkans and the foot of Italy. The Persian Sasanian Empire was gone, transformed into Arab-governed provinces.

Governance:
At first, governance of the conquered lands was simply military rule with Arab tribal headmen imposed arbitrarily upon humbled populations. The establishment of the Islamic empire can be seen as an unusually stark example (though there are others in history) of the conquest of ancient civilizations by the uncivilized. The conquered lands included deeply-rooted traditions, Greek, Roman, Egyptian, Syrian, Persian, Hindu. The conquering bedouin warriors lacking any civilized culture of their own – with the remarkable exception of matchless poetry and powerful rhetoric – chose not to destroy or deliberately to transform the cultures they overran. For a time the conquered lands were even permitted to keep their own laws and customs. But then, and not even by design, the Arabs islamized and arabized the indigenous peoples while they themselves inherited and adopted the sophisticated Roman and Persian bureaucracies that were in place.

Mu'awiya, the first Umayyad caliph, governed with intelligence and generosity. He had nonetheless at his command a disciplined army manned largely by the most powerful tribe of Syria, of which a wife of his was a member. As governor of Iraq he installed his illegitimate half-brother, Ziad, whom he publicly recognized. During Ziad's authoritarian though righteous ministry Iraq remained peaceful. Ziad had previously been a supporter of Ali and was in tune with the widespread Alid sentiment of the country. (Some accounts though describe Ziad's rule as harsh.) After Ziad's death in 673, not unexpectedly, as old tribal tensions reemerged with passionate religious divisions, the zealotry of the majority Alids of Iraq became deeper and more troubling.

Mu'awiya died in his seventies in 680. His son, Yazid, inherited the title. Months later, the Prophet's grandson, Hussein, second son of Caliph Ali and Fatima, and then already fifty-four years old, arrived in Iraq from Mecca at the urging of Iraqi Alids. Expecting widespread support he challenged Yazid for the caliphal throne. But before support could arrive Hussein with most of his family and only a small group of his followers, fifty or so (though other accounts give numbers up to six hundred), were set upon by a superior Iraqi force loyal to Yazid near the town of Karbala and were all killed. They cut Hussein's head off. His son, Ali Zain al-Abidin, absent from the field of battle through sickness, was later caught but was eventually released. The martyrdom of Hussein rather than the failures and assassination of his father, Ali, is at the heart of Shiism. The martyrdom is now observed each year by a day of communal grieving, *Ashura*, and the ancient Sumerian tradition of bloody self-flagellation symbolizing the persecution of the Shiite community and the beheading of Hussein. Alid determination to establish the caliphal succession through Ali and Fatima rather than through a line of usurping Meccan merchants had been the cause of this disaster. It cast a cloud over the Umayyads from which they never escaped.

In 683, Caliph Yazid died while his Syrian army was besieging rivals in Mecca. Yazid's son Mu'awiya II succeeded him but died within four months at age twenty-three, poisoned it was said. Revolts in which rival fanatics were prominent broke out everywhere. Marwan, of another branch of the Umayyads (and one of the earliest Arab chess players), was then declared caliph. He died within a year and, following another outbreak of civil war and an interregnum, was succeeded by his eldest son, Abdul Malik.

The first years of Abdul Malik's reign were occupied with further uprisings, with restoring order by force among the feuding Arabs, and with negotiating peace with Byzantine Emperor Justinian II "the Slit-nosed". Offence is said to have been taken by Shia-majority Iraq to the imposition of Caliph Uthman's fifty-year-old "official" Sunni version of the Koran. Grievances moreover arose because public finances were based on the principle that relatively few "pure" Arabs paying few taxes would govern a majority of heavily taxed infidels.

Palestine was more peaceful, and Abdul Malik initiated an important cultural development of the Umayyad term, the building of mosques for communion with Allah. The Dome of the Rock, the first outstanding example of Islamic architecture, built possibly as a substitute for the Kaaba and as a new focus for Islam, was completed in Jerusalem c. 692. It is there today, untouched except for resplendent tilework commissioned by the Ottoman Turk sultan, Suleiman "the Magnificent", some 850 years later. Abdul Malik also started building the Al-Aqsa mosque (now a focus of conflict between the Israelis and Palestinians) near the Dome of the Rock, on Temple Mount, the site of a wooden mosque built seventy years earlier by Caliph Omar. This latter edifice itself was erected on the site of an ancient shrine, Solomon's temple. The Prophet had dreamt he was miraculously brought to this holy place by night on a winged horse, *al-Buraq*, and raised to the Seven Heavens, the threshold of Eternity. (The Al Aqsa mosque was rebuilt after an earthquake in 746. It was repaired again after a fire in 1969, by Osama bin Laden's multi-millionaire father, Mohammed Awad bin Laden, who was once a labourer in the docks.)

With peace established in Iraq during the last few years of his life, Abdul Malik was able to extend the western frontiers of his empire to Tunisia, overcoming and expelling the Greeks from Carthage. More importantly, he reorganized the government and improved the bureaucracy, setting up a regular postal service from his capital Damascus to the provincial capitals. Abdul Malik was the first caliph to have government matters conducted in the Arabic language rather than in Greek or Persian, as before. To replace the still circulating Greek and Persian coinage, he issued new Islamic coinage with gold dinars and silver dirhams.

As the Arabs consolidated their hold on conquered lands their age-old quasi-democratic tribal organization transformed itself along autocratic lines. What made the caliphate different however from any previous autocratic bureaucratic empire was that it was a theocracy, government by God, under an unchallengeable sacred law. (Pharaohnic Egypt, sometimes described as a theocracy, was in fact caesaro-papist, where the worldly ruler was in charge of religion.) At the same time, from the beginning, the defeated peoples were with few exceptions permitted to continue practising their own religions under their own religious leaders – Christians of several rites, Judaist, Zoroastrian, Manichaean, Hindu, Buddhist, Shamanist – and to pursue their economic activities in security in return for paying (humiliating) poll tax on top of tribute, as acknowledgement of their inferiority to Muslims. Leaders of the subjugated peoples were often allowed to continue administering their own communities under governors and military commanders appointed by the caliph. A notable exception to the tolerance of infidels was a number of communities of Persian Zoroastrians who, being persecuted, fled *en masse* to India where they form today's Parsee minority.

If the non-Muslim minorities (majorities also in many instances) were discriminated against – which they were – they were often better treated under the relatively tolerant Arabs of the day than Jews, non-conformist Christians and heretics were usually treated in Christendom. The Christian religion in Western Europe and in the Byzantine empire in the 7th and 8th centuries was the faith of uncompromising, unforgiving rulers and prelates. And woe betide the Christian apostate or doubter who questioned his baptism.

The expansion of the empire with the arabization of the conquered lands changed the conquerors. It even changed the meaning of the word Arab. To the Meccans and other town-dwellers "Arab" was a term of disdain applied in the early days to the bedouins. Later, without the prejudice, the term was extended to include the ethno-linguistic "Semitic" peoples (a term coined by August Schlozer in 1781 from Noah's first son, Shem) of Iraq, Syria and Palestine, the "Hamito-semitic" Egyptians (from Ham, Noah's second son) and the mixed peoples of northwest Africa. Even so, Persians kept their own identity together with their own languages.

From early days the Arabs, particularly the military aristocracy, married or took as slaves many non-Arab girls. Fair-haired, blue-eyed European girls were much prized. Consequently, in a few generations many of the generals and hereditary administrators in the provinces had little Arab blood. At the same time, men of good Arab stock were reproached by their ethnocentric peers for choosing to marry women converts to Islam, for were these women not "God's spoils of war as were their lands and properties"?

After the death of Caliph Abdul Malik in 705, his son, the pedigreed al-Walid, ruled for ten notably successful years. His reign has been described as the most brilliant in all the history of the Caliphate. Under him, the empire was extended westwards, taking Morocco and Spain, and eastwards to India where the grand city of Multan (where the game of chess may well have originated) was captured with immense booty. Transoxania, today's Uzbekistan (Özbekistan), with its ancient towns of Samarkand and Bukhara, were added to the list. And in 711, Tariq bin Ziad, a former slave, then governor of Tangiers, crossed the Straits of Gibraltar with a Berber army and defeated the Gothic king of Spain, an epoch-making event in European history.

Caliph al-Walid built the great mosque of Damascus in 705-15. He reopened the canals that irrigated the Tigris-Euphrates plain – a key to the prosperity of Mesopotamia since Sumerian times. He supported agriculture, excavated new water ways, dug wells, drained marshes. He also completed building the Al-Aqsa mosque in Jerusalem, much of the cost being covered by booty.

During the two-year reign of al-Walid's successor, his reputedly self-indulgent brother, Sulaiman, revolts, assassinations and failed attacks on the Byzantines shook the empire. Several of Caliph Sulaiman's rivals as well as three of his generals were arbitrarily tried and exe-cuted; other notables were furtively murdered on his orders. And the victorious Syrian army, the mainstay of the Umayyads, was beaten by the Byzantines led by the newly enthroned Leo III "the Isaurian" in Anatolia and on the walls of Constantinople. This campaign in 717 was a turning point of Arab imperial ambitions, the last Arab military undertaking in the grand style. After this date, Arab military success consisted mainly of raids and short-lived occupations of land in territories with indistinct boundaries that are now known as France, Anatolia and Pakistan.

After defeat at the hands of the Greeks, Sulaiman abdicated and nominated his cousin, Omar bin Abdul Aziz, entitled Omar II, to succeed him. Omar's widely recognized spirituality made for a time of peace in the empire. He spoke out against frontier raiding in search of booty. His main concern was the reform of taxation including the lifting from converts to Islam of the burden of poll tax. A census showed that apart from Alexandria and a few other towns in the Nile delta, the population of Egypt was still largely Christian and Jewish. But then the Caliph went on to sack non-Muslim employees from the administrative services and to impose severe restrictions on them. The result was mass voluntary conversion of Christians and Jews to Islam and the resultant crippling of the poll tax-reliant public finances at a time when the flow of booty was slowing markedly. This was offset only partially by the economy of the empire expanding through increased agricultural production and the widening of trade.

Conversion to Islam and marriage with Muslims brought such advantages as relief from the payment of the poll tax and heightened social and political rank, to say nothing of the unquestionable certainties and consolations of the religion, so that the process of islamization was rapid following the remission of some of the taxes on converts. In the early days only three or four per cent of the empire had been Muslim, but by about the middle of the 8th century, fifty to ninety per cent of the empire was converted. For all that, native Arabs continued for generations to be considered socially superior. And this remained true until the end of the Umayyad period.

After Caliph Omar II died he was venerated publicly for his integrity. His successor, however, his brother Yazid II, was faced with serious difficulties. The state of public finances after the tax reforms and other fiscal changes called for measures that caused widespread discontent. Organized religious opposition to the Umayyads reappeared, stigmatizing them as ungodly and tyrannical. Clan rivalries re-surfaced giving rise to rebellion, disrupting Yazid's reign until his death. In the chronicles he is depicted, perhaps unfairly, as another hedonist. Yazid II had nominated his brother, Hisham, to succeed him, the fourth of Abdul Malik's sons to become caliph. Hisham was miserly, harshly conservative, well-meaning if stubborn, honourable yet maladroit.

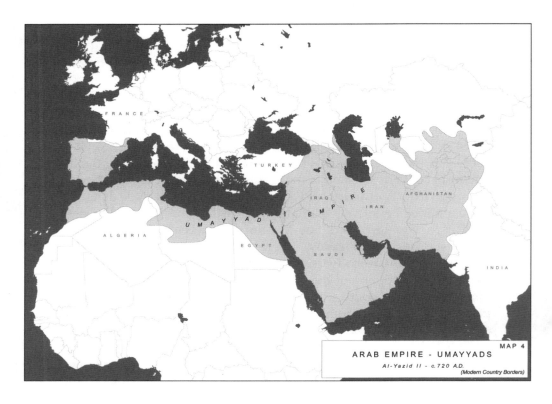

MAP 4

ARAB EMPIRE - UMAYYADS

Al-Yazid II - c.720 A.D.

(Modern Country Borders)

It was during his reign (724-43) that the Arab empire reached Paul Kennedy's "point of overextension" where, like a soap bubble, it was destined to burst. Successful advances were still being made by the Moors into southern France. But, in 730 (while the Venerable Bede who introduced the date of Christ's birth as the commencement of the Christian calendar, was writing his seminal history of the English in his Northumbrian monastery) the Caliph's forces were decisively defeated by the Uzbeks in Transoxania. They were beaten again by the Byzantine Emperor Leo III in Anatolia. Simultaneously, Arab armies were destroyed by the Khazars in Azerbaijan; reverses were suffered in India; and in 732 Charles Martel put a final stop to Arab ambitions in France. Some lost territory was regained by a reconstituted Syrian army, and the Khazars were eventually beaten and made to pay tribute. Then the Berbers rose again in Morocco and the day was only just saved by fresh Syrian troops. Soon afterwards, however, another Berber mutiny broke out in Spain. Syrian troops were sent, overcame the mutineers, but were allowed to remain in the country where they and their sons would become an unforeseen and crucial element in the political make-up of what would be an independent Spain after 755. Victory and defeat followed each other in quick succession around the boundaries of Hisham's empire until his death in 743 when, albeit beleaguered, the caliphate's heartlands were still relatively prosperous and secure.

The Khazars were an improbable confederation of Western Turkic, Caucasian and Slav tribes together with Jewish communities along the Black Sea coast. For reasons that are not clear, the Shamanist, mainly Turkic, nobility and part of the general population adopted Judaism as their state religion between 740 and the mid-800s. By the mid-900s Judaism had become widespread among them, while they remained tolerant of other religions.

The Khazars held lands from the Caspian Sea to the Ukraine until much of their territory was overrun by the Russians, Ukrainians and Byzantines c. 970. It was the Khazars who prevented the Muslims advancing in force north of the Caucasus, although Islam seeped into and over the mountains from the 16th to the 18th centuries. (In writing *The Thirteenth Tribe* in 1976, Arthur Koestler claimed that these Judaists – of whom he may have been a descendant – became the mass of Ashkenazy population in Russia and eastern Europe. Recent mitochondrial DNA research work suggests however derivation of many of the Ashkenazy from Palestine, probably in the 1st-2nd century expulsion by the Romans, and others, also with original Middle Eastern provenance, in medieval migrations from western Europe.)

It has been calculated that at its maximum extent under Caliph Hisham the Arab empire covered 12.6 million square kilometres. By comparison, the United States now covers 9.4 million square kilometres, and China 9.6 million. Historians are even now debating the question of how a few tens of thousands, perhaps not more than 100,000, wild horsemen and simple camel drovers spread between the far west (Spain), the north (along the border with Byzantium), and the far east (Pakistan and Afghanistan), could have done all this in so little time against, in many instances, larger, battle-hardened armies from established cultures. But, they did.

Then, within the space of a year of murder, mayhem and endless religiously inspired rebellion by Taliban-like Salafist extremists, Hisham was followed in quick succession by al-Walid II, Yazid III and Marwan II. Factional struggles flared which Marwan II, son of a cherished Kurdish slavegirl (the first caliph of such parentage), was not able to resolve, and the Umayyad era was embroiled for its last six years under his leadership in inter-communal fighting. Finally, in 747, in what appears to have been political unrest intensified by an ancient tribal quarrel, a full-scale rebellion with extensive Alid sectarian support for the revolutionary side broke out in Persia, turning into a civil war ending in a bloodbath on the Great Zab river in northeastern Iraq. The Umayyad dynasty of Mecca was overthrown and the 13th Umayyad Caliph, Marwan II, and most of his family were hunted down and slaughtered. Marwan escaped at first to Egypt. There, however, he was later caught and killed. The Meccan merchant connection was at last broken. Still, the dominance of the Koreish tribe remained, and in 750 these events brought to power another Koreishi clan, the Abbasids, named after an uncle of the Prophet, Abbas bin Abd al-Muttalib who had died in his eighties in 652. (Interestingly, he is believed not to have been a Muslim.) The clan was led at first by this uncle's great-great grandson, Abul-Abbas, who took the caliphal title of Al-Saffah, "the Butcher", "the Spiller of Blood".

The defeat of Caliph Marwan's forces was due at least in part to the widely held conviction that the Alid movement was divinely inspired. The supplanting of the Sunni Umayyads by the Sunni Abbasids was a turning point in the history of Islam. The alliance of the many different interests that had overthrown the Umayyads had been secured by the common determination for régime change but was destined to disintegrate into competing forces once the battle was won. It is noteworthy that Alid sentiment (Shiism) with its strong appeal to the common people in Iraq and Persia through its opposition to the Umayyads whom it viewed as illegitimate, was widely held among these forces. It is noteworthy also that the Sunni minority of Iraq always believed it was their birthright to rule this Shia-majority country.

In spite of its shortcomings the Umayyad caliphate had spread Islam through the Arabic language to an unprecedentedly wide community. This first caliphate laid the foundations for a cultured fellowship from which there would be lasting benefits.

3

The Abbasids and the Golden Age
of the Caliphate

*The Abbasids – The Wealth of the Empire – Natural Resources –
Baghdad – Scholarship*

The Abbasids:

The new Commander of the Faithful, the Butcher, shifted his seat
of power from Damascus, Syria, to the historic site of the cradle of
civilization, the centre of the old Sumerian and Babylonian empires.
As his capital he built the new town of Hashimiya – named after the
Prophet's clan – seventy miles south of present-day Baghdad, in the
irrigated flatlands between the two great rivers. Hashimiya lay close
to the ruins of ancient Babylon.

As al-Saffah failed to abide by his promises to grant some political power to the Alids, the radical climate that had raised him to
the caliphate remained, with uprisings by different parties across the
empire from Libya to Persia. The rest of his life was consequently
filled with campaigns against these rebels. Perhaps the most important
event during his reign, just after his accession to power, was the victory
by his forces and his Persian and Turkic tribal allies over the Chinese
on the Talas river (in today's Kazakhstan), putting an end to Chinese
expansion to the west. Among the prisoners they took, the triumphant Arabs discovered artisan paper-makers whom they sent back to
Samarkand where the skills of these craftsmen would help quickly to
spread the new civilization.

25

Upon al-Saffah's death in 754 his half-brother who adopted the title al-Mansur ("the divinely aided one"), son of a Berber slavegirl named Salamah, succeeded. Al-Mansur, soon becoming known for his cunning and ruthlessness, had to fight for the throne against an uncle whom however he was able to lure to his court to have assassinated. The consequence was another round of bloodshed. At the same time the twenty-five-year-old Abd ar-Rahman, grandson of Caliph Hisham and the sole Umayyad prince to have escaped the slaughter of his family in the revolution, arrived in Spain. There, in 756, he founded an independent emirate with its capital in the old Roman city of Córdoba on the then navigable Guadalquivir River.

As mentioned above, fifteen years earlier Berber troops in Spain had taken up arms against their Arab allies with whom relations had often been strained, causing Umayyad Caliph Hisham to send his mainly Syrian army to put the revolt down. When the Syrian troops had defeated the rebels they had been rewarded with land and permanent residence in Spain – a standard solution for a resource-poor homeland. Many of these Syrians were supporters of the Umayyads whose seat of power had been in Damascus, so when Abd ar-Rahman arrived in 755, although he met opposition loyal to the Abbasids, many of the immigrant ex-military Syrians and their sons had supported him. Thereafter, Prince Abd ar-Rahman had been able to resist all attempts by Abbasid Caliph al-Mansur to unseat him through support for local rivals. And from the time of Abd ar-Rahman II (r. 822-52), during whose reign the country was brought largely under control, Spain was independent of the rest of the Muslim world while remaining culturally united with it. This revived Meccan dynasty, with some questions of lineage, was to reign in Spain for 275 years.

It was during the rule of al-Mansur that the Iraqi caliphate's phase of near continuous warfare ended and settled down to raiding and counter-raiding across the borders. In 762, al-Mansur, having succeeded in many of his campaigns against domestic enemies and having laid the foundations for a durable state, shifted his capital to Baghdad. This was the site of an old Persian village on the Tigris river twenty miles from the former Persian capital of Ctesiphon (in ruins since the Arab conquest) and located on a key caravan route, the 1000-year-old Silk Road to China. Building stone was brought from the ruins of Ctesiphon for use in the construction of Baghdad. Baghdad was also the starting point of a vital thirty-five mile long navigable canal excavated by the ancient Persians linking the Tigris with the Euphrates.

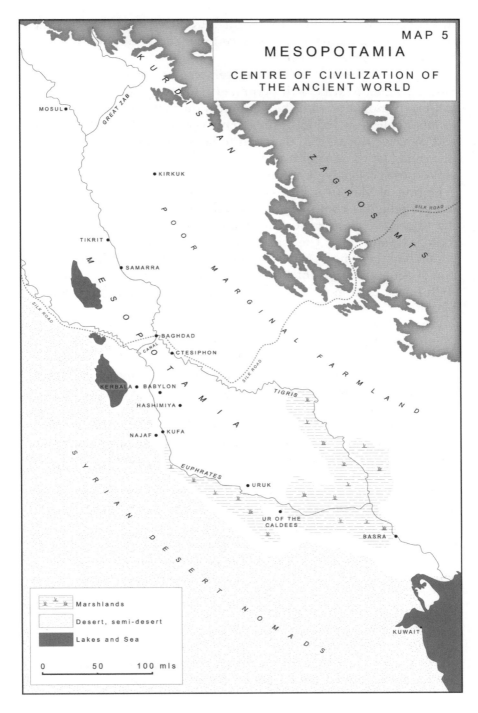

MAP 5

MESOPOTAMIA

CENTRE OF CIVILIZATION OF
THE ANCIENT WORLD

MOSUL

GREAT ZAB

KURDISTAN

ZAGROS MTS

SILK ROAD

KIRKUK

POOR MARGINAL FARMLAND

MESOPOTAMIA

TIKRIT

SAMARRA

SILK ROAD

CANAL

BAGHDAD

CTESIPHON

SILK ROAD

KERBALA

BABYLON

TIGRIS

HASHIMIYA

NAJAF

KUFA

EUPHRATES

URUK

SYRIAN DESERT NOMADS

UR OF THE
CALDEES

BASRA

KUWAIT

Marshlands

Desert, semi-desert

Lakes and Sea

0   50   100 mls

In his new capital Caliph al-Mansur introduced the office of vizier, prime minister, reorganized the government and built his "House of Wisdom", a centre of learning.

The early Abbasid caliphs, who reemphasized strict observance of Sunni Islamic doctrine, still permitted religious pluralism. For these caliphs, compliance with the Scriptures did not preclude adherence to other beliefs by infidels. Alids, however, presented such doctrinal and dynastic threats that they had to be denied any political power. So, having failed as a political party, the Alids regrouped as rebellious sects known collectively as Shias.

During al-Mansur's bloody reign, Shiism, in an atmosphere of intense religious controversy, gave birth to an offspring steeped in the Kharijites' early radicalism, the Ismailis, who in turn split into more, extreme cults. The Ismailis took their name from Ismail who would have become the seventh "Imam", descended through the male line of Ali and Fatima, had he not disappeared before his father, the sixth Imam, died, poisoned in 785 reportedly by al-Mansur's son, al-Mahdi.

When al-Mahdi had succeeded his father in 775 as 3rd Abbasid caliph, Shias in east Persia had risen in revolt. Fighting had broken out again with the Byzantine Emperor Leo IV "the Khazar" and later with Constantine VI, though al-Mahdi's father had generally enjoyed peaceful relations with his northern neighbour. Caliph al-Mahdi, known for his brutality and addiction to erotic poetry, persecuted all who questioned his conservative Sunni views of Allah's will, condemning them as heretics. He was criticized too for having abandoned the thrifty ways of his two predecessors, emblazoning his court with luxury, and for having failed to come to terms with the Shias. He died at forty-three, after a hunting accident (or, it was rumoured, by poisoning), but by the time of his death his vanquishing of many of his internal enemies and the assurance of taxes from the provinces, together with several good harvests, had enabled him, in the last quarter of the 8th century, to found what would quickly become a brilliant civilization.

Al-Mahdi's cruel, despotic son al-Hadi lived only a year after his accession in 785, dying also under suspicious circumstances. It was whispered that he had been poisoned by his mother, a strong-willed Yemeni slavewoman named Khayzuran.

In the new régime, Arabs as such were no longer accorded their privileged social status. Even so, the caliphs were still Arabs, if only in the male line. In contrast, the mothers of their children – wives, concubines, slavegirls – came from every corner of the empire. The new régime was a blend of many elements in which the old welded force of Arab tribal confederations, the bedouin military aristocracy and the remains of the Meccan oligarchy, was replaced by a range of Abbasid loyalists, ambitious self-seekers and talented Persians, particularly Arabic-speaking Persians, triumphant soldiers, poets and scholars. The governing community soon acquired a distinctly Aryan image.

In the caliphal court as of the end of the 8th century, Persian (Farsi) replaced Arabic as the primary written language. Overturning Umayyad Caliph Abdul Malik's century-old edict, it became the language of government, literature and scholarship. Arabic was retained for religion, law and the natural sciences. While adopting Persian as the primary written language the court replaced the 900-year-old Pahlavi alphabet of Persian with Arabic script. (The Iranians today write in Arabic script modified to accommodate particular sounds.)

The Abbasid court was more cosmopolitan than the Umayyad had been, and while not colour-blind and owning slaves of all colours, the Abbasids established a principle of racial egalitarianism among Muslims. In place of Arab ethnicity the acceptance of Allah's will became the identifying quality of the rulers, the affluent, the righteous people. At the same time, the Abbasid dynasty increased its own political power by adopting the traditions of the ancient Persian Empire. They became rulers by divine right, remote, magnificent paradigms of virtue, grace and power, attended by servile flatterers, approachable only through trains of lackeys. The caliphs were no longer the mortal successors of Mohammed. Immodestly, they had become the shadows of God on Earth.

Even though it was the Umayyads who had built the empire, it was the Abbasids who were to enjoy its golden age. The cessation of the wars of conquest and the lessening of internal conflict gave impulse to profitable activity. In these conditions Baghdad rapidly became the centre of a brilliant intellectual and material civilization which spread over the Muslim world. In Baghdad the Abbasids reigned through these golden times, about sixty years, c.780-840, the cultural height of the empire, its acme of power and prestige. Contemporaneously, however step by step through the empire's political dismemberment, came the decline of Arab overlordship and the humiliation of the caliphs.

Some writers (Hugh Kennedy among them) put the golden age earlier, at 763–809. For the Muslim world as a whole, on the other hand, the high point of Islamic civilization was reached later, in about

900–1050, with the rise to pre-eminence of Moorish Spain and "Arab" Egypt.

The heyday of the Iraqi caliphate was reached perhaps with Harun al-Rashid, a brother of the short-reigning al-Hadi. Harun, born in Persia, was enthroned in 786 at the age of twenty. He and al-Hadi were the sons of a slavegirl of unknown origin. The young caliph appointed his Persian tutor al-Barmaki as vizier with full powers over day-to-day government, and exchanged embassies with Charlemagne like whom he was troubled by the rise of Umayyad Spain. The al-Barmaki family guided the empire and the Abbasids to their pinnacle of power and wealth. But while Harun could enjoy the company of his 4,000 slave-girls, the people were made to bear heavy taxation.

The loss by the caliphate to the Umayyads of such a prize as Spain less than forty years after its conquest had been an omen of things to come. Intermittently though progressively during Baghdad's golden years the Arab empire was dismantled from the margins inwards, a process accelerated by the caliphs finding it necessary to award or farm out tax-raising powers to local governors and military command-ers, emboldening many of them. Until well into the 9th century even employing the tactic of rotating and replacing provincial governors every two years or so to thwart their ambitions often failed. Christian Georgia, on the south side of the Caucasus mountains overlooking Armenia, soon broke away into independence. Muslim northwest Africa from Tunis to the Atlantic Ocean seceded into self-govern-ing emirates. And once again the Khazars crossed the Caucasus into Armenia causing great damage. The empire had barely been patched together and it was already falling apart.

Tribal indiscipline in Egypt, bedouin raids in Syria, persistent Shiite insurrection accompanied the social restructuring of populations and changes in economic power among the peoples of the empire. Intrigue and conspiracy in Harun's court made matters worse. By the turn of the century while government revenues were not insubstantial, spoils from military conquest had long since dried up and taxes on important provinces – Spain, Georgia, Tunisia, Algeria, Morocco – had ceased. Revolt broke out again in Persia in 806 and was quelled by Harun. It reignited in 809. On his way to counter this latest rebellion Harun died, aged forty-three, at the same age as his father, al-Mahdi.

These were times of cultural accomplishment, riches for the rul-ing class, their fortunes founded in the years of conquest, but falling revenues for the state. These conditions persisted with Harun's eldest son, the cruel al-Amin, son of Queen Zubaydah, a cousin of Harun's. In his will Harun had misguidedly split the empire between his two favourite sons, one getting Iraq and the west, the other Persia and the east. After his father's death, al-Amin ruled from 809 to 813. His half-brother, al-Ma'moun, son of a Persian concubine, never accepted his sibling's authority. And when al-Amin was unwisely persuaded by his vizier to replace al-Ma'moun in the succession with his own son, contrary it appears to Harun's will, war between the brothers broke out. Al-Ma'moun won after besieging Baghdad for more than a year. He destroyed part of the city and many of its architectural treasures and had his brother executed. Dynastic strife often arose like this from the admixture of absolute monarchy, polygamy, multiple offspring and inheritance disputes among the many half brothers, ending with the victory of one of the deceased ruler's sons and the death of one or more of the rest.

The execution of al-Amin brought no end to the political conflict, which spread throughout the Middle East. Al-Ma'moun, in thrall to powerful allies, was unable to win control of the situation for years, during which he had to keep his capital at Merv (in today's Turkmenistan). In the end, control was achieved by subjecting some of his allies to "extreme sanction". Only in 819 was he able to return to and start rebuilding Baghdad.

After ten years of civil war, state coffers were severely depleted. Much diplomatic repair work had to be done to reconcile the many parties involved. Nevertheless, Caliph al-Ma'moun, *Emir al-Mu'minin* (Prince of Believers), came in time to be considered the equal of his father for his devoted patronage of the arts and science. And notwithstanding the civil war, the period beginning with the reign of al-Mahdi and continuing until the end of al-Ma'moun's were years of splendour and scholarly fulfilment, if also of continuing rebellion and loss of territory.

After regaining Baghdad, following precedent, al-Ma'moun launched several successful expeditions against the Greeks under Michael II "the Amorian", and later under Michael's teen-aged son Theophilus. Then, a joint Arab settler-Copt insurrection broke out in Egypt fomented by the continual raising of taxes. In the end, the insurrectionists were beaten. The surrendering men were butchered and their womenfolk sold into slavery. With perpetual undercurrents of discontent in Egypt, uprisings occurred repeatedly in the following years. The Christian Copts however were humbled and were seldom again able to make war against the Muslims.

The restive Khorasan province of eastern Persia broke away from the caliphate in 821 under an hereditary governorship. And soon after al-Ma'moun's accession to power the Persian peasantry rose once more in revolt and fought him and his successor, a half-brother, al-Mutasim (son of a Turkic slavegirl), for twenty years before being overcome. The revolutionaries, imbued with radical Ismaili spirit, had again preached that the Sunni caliphate of the Abbasids was illegitimate; only the natural issue of Mohammed could lawfully be caliph, descendants that is, of the Prophet's martyred grandson Hussein and his descendants. The word of God had been revealed to Mohammed, not to a brother of Mohammed's father. Descendants of an uncle had no more right to the caliphate than had a clan of Meccan merchants. The Ismaili brand of extremist Shiism which would shape Arab history for centuries had been strengthening since the time of al-Mansur, acquiring adherents and sending missionaries all around the Muslim world.

The Wealth of the Empire:
Just before its dissolution, with a population of about 30 million (compared with 50 million at the time in T'ang China), the Arab empire possessed two great assets. The first was Islam, unassailable, even if internally divided by sectarianism and rivalries. The second was wealth. From the 8th century, because of the irrigation system of Mesopotamia, the Northern Hemisphere climate then transiting from what scientists have named the Dark Ages Cold Period (the Euphrates had frozen in 608) to the Medieval Warm, nearing its most clement in the Middle East, harvests were good. And with war reparations, tribute and taxes streaming from the provinces, no place was wealthier. Gold and silver flowed from mines in Africa, Afghanistan and Persia. Under the Umayyads great wealth had been acquired in confiscated farmland, from estates of enemies, defeated rulers, in precious metals and stones, silks and spices, riverboats and wheeled carts, livestock, slaves, weapons. Stores had been seized from the granaries and storehouses of conquered lands, from palaces, temples and churches. The flow of plunder had generally ceased after the conquest of the rich Indian city of Multan and the Indus river valley in 713. Nevertheless, for the best part of a century after this, rivers of material tribute flowed to the later Umayyads and the early Abbasids.

The Arab empire formed a far-flung common market reaching from the Atlantic to the borders of China. Even after the loss of Spain, the

Maghreb and the Caucasus area from the empire, traders kept trading freely across the boundaries. Commercial ties between Europe and the East had been torn apart by the Umayyad conquests. Still, Jewish merchants had been quick to rebuild profitable links. The economic framework of the Roman Empire had been constructed on principles of free markets with few restraints, tolerable taxes and the encouragement of trade around and across the Mediterranean. The involvement of both the north and the south shores of the Sea was crucial for wealth creation. Free trade in the Arab empire, east to west, expanded in the 8th century creating more wealth and broadening and deepening the tax base, but it was not until the 9th century that trade with Europe was re-established. Peter Mansfield quotes the 9th-century geographer Ibn Khurradadbeh: "These Jewish merchants speak Arabic, Persian, Latin, Greek, French, Spanish and Slavonic. They travel from the West to India and China by land and sea. From the West they bring eunuchs, slave girls, boys, brocades, castor-skins, marten and other furs and swords, and from China they bring musk, aloes, camphor, cinnamon and other products of these parts." Notwithstanding the riches generated by trade, added to the spoils and tribute of conquest, the economy of the empire was basically agrarian. Agriculture was always precarious, and as in all medieval agricultural societies when the harvest failed the peasants starved.

Natural Resources:
Edible grains were the most important agricultural produce of Mesopotamia and the Nile – wheat, barley, rice. Textiles were the most important manufacturing, cottage industry product – cotton, flax, wool. After the incessant wars of the Umayyads, the early Abbasids at times established a measure of internal security, and in the periods of peaceful relations with neighbouring countries trade expanded.

There were on the other hand no major deposits in the Arab heartlands of the crucial metals needed for industry and weaponry – iron, copper, tin – nor any lead, zinc or nickel. Small deposits of gold, iron ore and copper existed in the Hejaz of Arabia, supporting the rise of Mecca as a commercial centre, and a small deposit of copper in Palestine. Egypt had some tin deposits and from ancient times imported copper to make bronze. Otherwise, the Arab Middle East was practically devoid of these important resources. For the needs of industry, agriculture and weaponry, metals had to be imported from the provinces. But before long, mines in the distant empire began to show signs of depletion. Bernard Lewis mentions that in the 10th century ten thousand silver miners worked in the Hindu Kush of eastern Afghanistan. But this was 1,500 miles overland from Baghdad, 2,000 miles by land and sea. Apart from limited areas of production in Kurdistan and Lebanon, the heartlands were also poorly provided with timber-producing forests.

These deficiencies were serious handicaps when supplies of raw materials were cut off for political reasons. For the economic welfare of the empire it was vital that politically peaceful conditions exist. The relative scantiness of fish stocks – due to paucity of land-derived organic nutrients in the southern Mediterranean and the northern Red Sea – was another handicap. Although the Arabian Sea and Indian Ocean coastal waters of Arabia, enriched by ocean currents, were well stocked with fish, as were the Atlantic coasts of Morocco and Portugal, fishing in the Mediterranean on a scale greater than that for satisfying local needs was mainly in the Levant and European waters. The northern was the only part of the Mediterranean fed by significant amounts of river-borne nutrients. Iberia, with its teeming Atlantic Ocean fisheries had become independent in 756, Morocco in 789. Much organic nutrient carried downstream by the Nile was spread by irrigation and flood over the farmlands of the valley and delta, and only sardines were fished in quantity in nearshore waters off the delta. Tuna, far offshore from Egypt, was difficult to catch in quantity. Enough organic material to satisfy local needs for fish reached the Persian Gulf, from the Tigris and the Euphrates. But no important rivers flowed into northern Red Sea waters, while nutrient-bearing ocean currents were far away. (Crayfish in the northern waters are *haram*, forbidden, for Muslims.) Fishing on a limited commercial scale took place in the southern Red Sea. And both the Nile and the Mesopotamian river courses had fresh water fish for local consumption.

Baghdad:
By the beginning of the 9th century the major cities of Islam were immense compared with their poverty-stricken equivalents in Europe. Baghdad was the largest and richest city in the world outside of China, with a population of 500,000. It included Jewish and Christian Arab communities. (Chang-an, capital of T'ang China, had upwards of 1,000,000 people at this time.) Within forty years of its foundation as

the capital, Baghdad became a triumph of town planning: municipal sanitation, street lighting, public supply of clean water, public baths and washing facilities, professional policing, comparable in public facilities with Rome at its height. Córdoba in Umayyad Spain and Alexandria and Damascus were to enjoy similar development.

In Baghdad they built a galaxy of mosques, palaces and government offices. Everywhere water flowed in ponds and gardens. The city, built in the form of a circle to the west of the Tigris, had three concentric walls two miles in diameter through which highways radiated from the Caliph's main palace. Along these the mounted postal service of couriers established by Caliph al-Mansur enabled the capital to receive news, taxes, treasure and journeying traders from the empire. A network of canals in the suburbs beyond the outer wall connected the city with the river close by to the east, and the canal connecting the Tigris with the Euphrates with an associated web of channels reaching westward made Baghdad a major hub of communication. This city in the periodically mild climate of the 9th century was like the later Venice, a city of architecture, boatmen, industry, poets, artistry and wealth.

Scholarship:
From the 5th to the 9th century Christendom, a mosaic of quarrelsome feudal fiefdoms engaged in ceaseless baronial and dynastic wars, lay benighted as the Roman Empire was dismembered – until, that is, Charlemagne rose, c. 800. Apart from the monasteries and a few towns in northern Italy, literacy had effectively disappeared in Europe. (But the first half of the 8th century was still the likely time of the writing of the highest achievement of Old English literature, the heroic poem *Beowulf*.)

Like most great revolutions the Islamic revolution began in carnage and afterwards became creative and artistic. Beginning in the 8th century the Arabs built a cultural universe of art, learning, literature and science spreading out across the Middle East and North Africa. The Arabs inherited Persian literature, poetry and statecraft, and were edified by Greek science and medicine. Many of the treasured works of antiquity were translated into Arabic and eventually transmitted to the West. A copy of the thirteen-book mathematics storehouse of knowledge, *Elements*, written and assembled by Euclid of Alexandria in about 300 BC, and which had set out to provide "proofs for all existing wisdom" in mathematics and science (and which remained the principal textbook of geometry in Europe until the 17th century) was given by Emperor Constantine V to Caliph al-Mansur, in about 770. Harun al-Rashid later sent men to the court of the young Constantine VI with whom he had rebuilt good relations to collect more Greek scientific works (before the youthful emperor was deposed and blinded on the orders of his mother, who succeeded him as Empress Irene.)

Nothing sustained the scholarship of Baghdad more than paper, the Chinese invention which the Arabs had come across upon their victory on the Talas River in 751. This Muslim victory had led to the wide production of books in the Arab empire, even if they had to be laboriously hand-copied. Government records and merchants' accounts came to be kept on paper. The great cities of Islam became a world of scribes, correspondence and bookshops, a book culture, even if mainly of poetry, religious works spreading the word of Allah, and history glorifying Arab deeds. Poets were held in the highest esteem. Many of these poets and writers were also translators of works from Greek, Sanskrit, Hindi and Persian and, together with the scientists they formed the secular cornerstones of the civilization.

The Victorian explorer and English translator of the *Arabian Nights*, Richard Burton (translator also of the *Kama Sutra* and the *Perfumed Garden* of Cheikh Nefzaoui), described Baghdad from his researches as a city of pleasure, "a Paris of the ninth century". To him, few exemplified this better than Abu Nuwas, the extravagantly mannered if outrageously misbehaving Persian friend and court poet to Caliph Harun al-Rashid. Abu Nuwas, an unrepentant bibulous bisexual, was described as wanting girls yet only if they looked "as much like boys as possible". Abu Nuwas (who has a main road in modern Baghdad named after him) gloried in debauchery and dissipation, yet was renowned for the quality of his verse, his poems laced with humour, irony and realism, and for his pursuit of wine and pederasty. The *Arabian Nights* relates that on occasions Harun lost patience with him.

(The *Arabian Nights*, the *Thousand and One Nights* – *Alf Layla wa Layla* – a composite work of likely Persian-Indian origin, comprises a collection of more than 200 popular tales passed on orally and developed over a period of several centuries after about 850. The work, assuming its final form and frame-story probably in 15th century Mamluk Egypt, was translated first into French by Jean Antoine Galland, over a period of years beginning in 1704, with some paraphrasing and adaptation to European taste, but in doing so lost much of its Arabic linguistic subtlety. The fascinating stories of the *"Nights"* nevertheless added

Aladdin, Ali Baba, Sinbad the Sailor and Sheherazade to Western mythology and echo much of the Persian atmosphere of Baghdad and the Golden Age Abbasid court. Some believe that certain of the stories were added by Europeans at a later date, Ali Baba for one.)

The wise men of early Abbasid times were interested in many spheres of knowledge, in alchemy, astrology, astronomy, botany, geology, mathematics, medicine, navigation, philosophy, zoology, the kingly art of horse breeding, the noble sport of falconry. But in the community at large the common man was usually ignorant and bigoted, and savants had to obtain the patronage and protection of liberal princes.

Science was dependent on and kept alive by the curiosity of caliphs and nobles. Most remarkably, for a time in the late 8th and early 9th centuries Middle Eastern governments and princes permitted such freedom of cultural activity that Jews oppressed in Europe and even some rebellious Christians fled Europe and sought refuge in Islam. Even the limited freedoms provided by the Arabs were greater than any available elsewhere in the world at the time.

In the late 8th and the 9th century, schools of higher learning were endowed in the great cities of the empire. The flow of revenue funded lavish building projects. Poets, doctors and scientists were sponsored by the rich and generously rewarded. Nestorian Christian geographers who had been persecuted by the Byzantines for their "deviant" religious beliefs found warm welcome in Muslim Baghdad where they found a place at the heart of academia.

In the *Canterbury Tales* Chaucer identifies several 10–13th century "Arab" physicians as making outstanding contributions to medicine. The Uzbek, Avicenna's, million-word *Canon of Medicine* was the standard European medical reference work from the 13th century to the 16th. In the *Inferno* Dante put him side by side with Hippocrates and Galen. In 1970 the World Health Organization paid tribute to the Persian, Rhazes, stating that his writings on smallpox and measles show originality and accuracy, and his essay on infectious diseases was the first scientific treatise on the subject. The Syrian, Ibn al-Nafis Damishqui, discovered the blood's circulatory system.

Science was rooted in astronomy and geography and in the allied sciences that these disciplines depended upon – mathematics, optics and physics. Scientific progress was driven by the requirements of maritime navigation, the need to locate the direction of Mecca to turn towards when praying and for laying the dead to rest. Public works, architecture, engineering and construction relied on mathematics, physics and mechanics. "Arabic" numerals and the place-valued decimal system were adopted from India by Caliph al-Mansur in about 760, including the concept of the zero, perhaps first envisioned by the Indian, Brahmagupta, a century earlier. Harun al-Rashid built the first hospital in the modern sense of the term in Baghdad. He also established a school of astronomy and had Euclid's *Elements* translated from Greek into Arabic. At a time when most Europeans believed that the Earth was flat, scholars at the House of Wisdom, which had been founded by al-Mansur (and expanded by the newly enthroned al-Ma'moun c. 825) felt certain it was spherical. (The classical Greek astronomer-mathematicians in Alexandria had also suggested it was spherical.)

In about 830, an Uzbek mathematician-astronomer, Mohammed bin al-Khwarizmi, methodized the use of symbols representing numbers to resolve linear and quadratic equations – algebra – the first systematic consideration of this ancient subject. For the revival of mathematics and astronomy this work was of unparalleled importance. (There are some doubts about Al-Khwarizmi's birthplace, possibly Baghdad.)

Tables for trigonometric functions were computed. Spherical trigonometry was advanced. Scholars then calculated the Earth's circumference – an essay involving astronomy, geography, advanced mathematics and accurate instrumentation – as 32,800 kms, a diameter of 10,400 kms. (It was not until the end of the 18th century that French geodesists, Delambre and Méchain, established the meridian circumference by definition as 40,000 kms, a diameter of 12,700 kms. Astonishingly, in about 235 BC the Libyan-Greek, Eratosthenes, chief librarian at Alexandria, had estimated the Earth's diameter as 12,600 kms.)

The Arab scholars also knew that the Earth rotated round the Sun – heliocentricism – not the other way round, as Europeans believed. (In about 250 AD, Aristarchus of Samos in the Aegean, an older contemporary of Archimedes, had advanced the hypothesis of heliocentricism for which, it must be remarked, he was threatened with prosecution for impiety, for everyone could see that the Earth was the centre of the Universe.) Abbasid astronomers measured the angle of inclination of the Earth's axis to the plane of rotation around the Sun. In about the year 830 they measured this angle as 23° 33'. It changes over time and today it is 23° 27'. They also calculated the solar year as 365 days, 5 hours, 46 minutes, 24 seconds. Today it is 365 days, 5 hours, 48 minutes, 47 seconds. It seems that many of the astronomical observations of the Arabs failed to reach the West or were disregarded or wilfully ignored, in order, it has been alleged, to belittle the achievements of the Arabs. Seven hundred years after Caliph al-Ma'moun's astronomers were at work, the Polish ecclesiastic, Copernicus (1473-1543), "discovered" the planetary motion around the sun. His theory was condemned by the Christian Church. Still, both the Abbasid astronomers and Copernicus must have relied to some extent upon the observations and theories of the ancient Greeks. After this early flourish of scientific discovery the five Islamic centuries from 900 to 1400 probably cannot be compared favourably with the most creative period of Hellenistic science from 300 BC to 200 AD.

Calligraphy and the rich, marvellously evocative styles of poetry and literature with their elegant word play were a central feature of Arab culture. With regard to sculpture and pictorial art, however, whereas some of the Umayyads had not been uncomfortable with artistic representation of the human form, under the Abbasids from the late 8th century, and particularly from the time of the holy man Ahmed bin Mohammed Hanbal (780-855), there arose the ban on anthropomorphic imagery that exists widely today. (Imagery of the human form had been condemned by the Prophet as idolatry, the worship of false gods that he had fought hard to suppress in Mecca, where legend suggests there had been images of some three hundred gods.) Pictorial art was then confined to imaginative calligraphy and repetitive geometric patterns, and the Mesopotamian tradition of sculpture of the human form perfected in classical Greece and carried over into Rome was lost to Arab civilization. There are no contemporary graphic or graven images of the early Muslim Arab leaders, no paintings, sculptures, carvings, icons or mosaics of them although illustrations of human form in the margins of Islamic texts began with the Baghdad School some hundreds of years later. Muslim India under the Moghuls and Safavid Persia rarely accepted these Arab strictures, and extended for themselves their own rich artistic heritage.

For their technical inventions and discoveries modern civilization has much to thank the Arabs for, in medicine particularly, together with astronomy, optics, botany and navigation. The Abbasid golden age was not an age of political or social advancement, nor of the development of pictorial art. (Although the very limitations on figurative art led to its own particular aesthetic and without those limits the abstract, geometric wonders of Islamic art we have would not have been created.) It was a time of abundance for the few, occasional comfort for the many, and memorable scholarly advances.

The Abbasid Caliphs of Baghdad, 750-1258 AD

Caliph	Ruled	Notes
Al-Saffah	750-54	Fought rebels ceaselessly. Paper-making discovered
Al-Mansur	754-75	Widespread violence. Built Baghdad
Al-Mahdi	775-85	Shia revolts. Laid foundations of Golden Age
Al-Hadi	785-86	Died in circumstances arousing suspicion
Harun al-Rashid	786-809	Celebrated in Golden Age and *Arabian Nights*
Al-Amin	809-13	Civil war with brother. Executed
Al-Ma'moun	813-33	After civil war, fostered science, arts, culture
Al-Mutasim	833-42	Moved capital to Samarra. Slave troops take power
Al-Wathiq	842-47	Bedouin uprising
Al-Mutawakkil	847-61	Extravagant, corrupt. Assassinated by his son
Al-Muntasir	861-62	Turkic military takes complete control. Poisoned
Al-Musta'in	862-66	Assassinated by the army
Al-Mutazz	866-69	Assassinated by the army
Al-Muhtadi	869-70	Assassinated by the army. Zanj revolt starts
Al-Mutamid	870-92	Regained control over army. Zanj revolt
Al-Mutadid	892-902	Maintained some order. Qarmation uprising
Al-Muqtafi	902-08	Qarmation activity. Recovered Egypt
Al-Muqtadir	908-32	Alternating tranquillity and turmoil. Died fighting
Al-Qahir	932-34	Deposed and blinded by military who had regained power
Al-Radi	934-40	Pious and well-meaning but ineffectual
Al-Muttaqi	940-44	Deposed and blinded by Turkic military
Al-Mustaqfi	944-46	Deposed and blinded by Buwaihids
Al-Muti	946-74	Subjugated by Buwaihids. Loses Egypt to Fatimids
Al-Ta'i	974-91	Deposed by Buwaihids looting his palace
Al-Qadir	991-1031	Hanbali caliph
Al-Qa'im	1031-75	Survived Buwaihid and Seljuk rule
Al-Muqtadi	1075-94	Seljuks permit caliphal recognition as leader of the Faith
Al-Mustazhir	1094-1118	Passive onlooker to conflict between Seljuk princes

Al-Mustashid	1118-35	Began forming independent army. Assassinated
Al-Rashid	1135-36	Deposed
Al-Muqtafi II	1136-60	Defeats Seljuk army in Mesopotamia in 1155
Al-Mustanjid	1160-70	Internal rivalries led to his assassination
Al-Mustadi	1170-80	Recognized by Saladin as head of Islam
Al-Nasir	1180-1225	Destroyed remnants of Seljuk régime in Mesopotamia.
Al-Zahir	1225-26	Father of first puppet caliph under Mamluks
Al-Mustansir II	1226-42	Founded university in Baghdad
Al-Mustasim	1242-58	Kicked to death by Mongols

Extinction of Caliphate in Mesopotamia 1258 AD

4

Islamic Spain and the Moors

The Invasion – Al-Andalus

The Invasion::
When the Umayyad prince Abd ar-Rahman escaped the slaughter of
his family in the Middle East and after adventures arrived in Moorish
Spain he quickly rallied support in a community where many people
welcomed him. But it took him seven years to overcome the last of the
Abbasid loyalists; while several regions sought to establish or maintain
their independence until the time of Abd ar-Rahman's great-grandson,
the best part of a century later. In the first quarter of the 9th century his
grandson, al-Hakam I, nevertheless succeeded in extending his lands
to the Balearic Islands and in establishing strategic bases on the islands
of Corsica and Sardinia.

In 711, Spain had been invaded by the Moors, an ethnographic mix
of Phoenicians, Carthaginians, Arabs, Greeks, Vandals, Alans and
indigenous Berbers under the Caliph al-Walid-appointed leader, Tariq
bin Ziad. (The Berbers, of unknown origin, appear to be pre-historic
migrants into northwest Africa.) Within a few years, the Moors had
taken from the ruling Visigoths the whole of the Iberian peninsula
except for Asturias and the Basque area in the far north – where they
were halted in 718. The Iberian branch of the Visigoths were Germanic
Christians who had invaded primitive Celtic tribal Spain in the late 5th
century, in part to escape the superior numbers and military power of

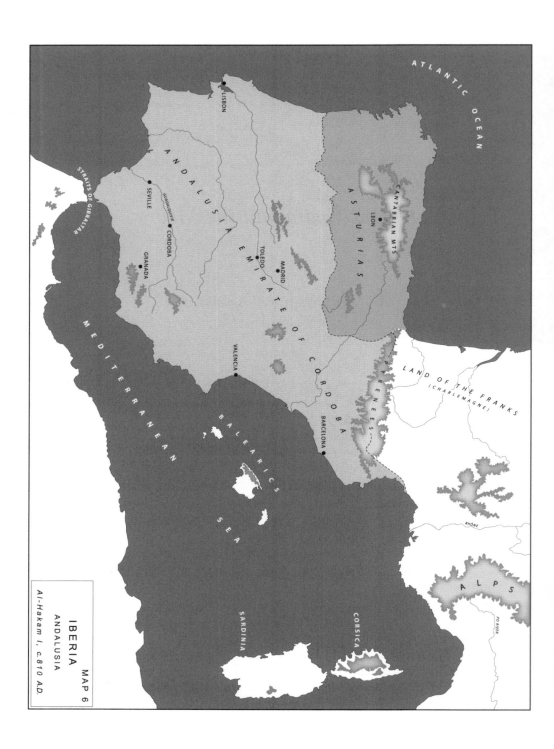

ATLANTIC OCEAN

LISBON

ANDALUSIA

SEVILLE

GUADALQUIVIR

CORDOBA

GRANADA

STRAITS OF GIBRALTAR

EMIRATE OF CORDOBA

TOLEDO

MADRID

ASTURIAS

LEON

CANTABRIAN MTS

PYRENEES

LAND OF THE FRANKS
(CHARLEMAGNE)

VALENCIA

BARCELONA

MEDITERRANEAN

BALEARICS

SEA

RHONE

ALPS

PO RIVER

SARDINIA

CORSICA

IBERIA

MAP 6

ANDALUSIA

Al-Hakam I, c.810 A.D.

the ascendant German tribe then dominating France, the Franks. For a while in the 600s, Visigoth Spain with its capital at Toledo had been the largest unified state in Europe, but by the time of the 711 Moorish invasion was in poor condition, torn apart by internal strife.

Al-Andalus:

After early difficulties, the Umayyads brought stability of sorts to the country and by the early 9th century, Muslim Spain, *Al-Andalus*, was beginning to introduce effective government and sovereignty under Sunni Sharia law. Abbasid Caliph Harun al-Rashid's exchange of envoys with Charlemagne, King of the Franks, was likely motivated by their shared concern over Spain's growing political power under Abd ar-Rahman's grandson, Hakam. Within a century of Abd ar-Rahman's arrival until as late as 1200 – though shrinking territorially at the end of the 10th century – confident, successful Muslim Spain became the most civilized place in the West. Córdoba was from the 9th to the 12th century Europe's largest city, its greatest centre of industry and scholarship, science and technology. The city became a major centre of textile production, with up to 13,000 weavers. Its Great Mosque, completed by Abd ar-Rahman's son Hashim in 796, was considered by some Muslims as third in sanctity in the Muslim world after the Kaaba and the Al-Aqsa mosque.

Córdoba was one of several areas existing in Spain of large-scale Jewish settlement. The Jews were long settled in Iberia and had come in great numbers both at the time of their expulsion from Israel by the Romans centuries before and in partnership with Phoenician and Greek traders in ancient times. While Abbasid Iraq began to deteriorate after the mid-9th century, *Al-Andalus* rose to become a place of renowned prosperity and repute, a country of open-mindedness and tolerance. In *Al-Andalus* Jewish culture flourished alongside Islamic culture in an atmosphere of joint enterprise, common objectives and mutual respect, to the benefit of the Spanish people and ultimately of the rest of Europe.

With the arrival of the Umayyads, the Jews who had been persecuted by the Visigoths had been encouraged to cooperate with the Christian community. As merchants, bankers, craftsmen, doctors and scholars, Jews played an important economic and cultural role. In Peter Mansfield's words, "whenever a Christian prince needed an architect, physician or musical director he applied to Córdoba. In 960, Queen Tota of Christian northern Spain brought her son, the vexing

Sancho "the Fat", who had been deposed from his principality in Léon on the grounds of his obesity, to Córdoba to be cured by a Jewish doctor." This was at the court of Abd ar-Rahman III.

In Europe, enlightened medical practice and health matters were considered an Arabo-Jewish art, and continued to be so until the 15th century. There is little mention though in the history of Muslim Spain of native Christian Spaniards being prominent among the scientists, writers and artists.

Abd ar-Rahman III (r. 912-961) is recognized as one of the great leaders of the Muslim world. He "subdued rebels, built palaces, gave impetus to agriculture, immortalized ancient deeds and monuments, and inflicted great damage on infidels to a point where no opponent or contender remained in *Al-Andalus*. People obeyed *en masse* and wished to live with him in peace." Beginning in about 936, a few miles from Córdoba, he built the satellite palace-city of Medina al-Zahra, a jeweled showcase of his wealth and cultural values.

In science and technology, in the last decades of the 10th century before factional struggles led to the breakup of the country, the ruthless but remarkable vizier of Andalusia, al-Mansur ("Almanzor"), could contact the Sultan of Egypt (another al-Hakim "the Wise") 2,000 miles away in Cairo by means of a chain of mirror relay stations and coded flashes across the Straits of Gibraltar and along the North African coast. And in the same realm of technology, the Iraqi scientist, Abu Ali Hasan Ibn al-Haitham ("Alhazen"), who had worked in Cairo for Sultan al-Hakim on engineering projects and later went to Spain, is considered the father of modern scientific optics. Alhazen discovered the properties of light and glass lenses which would lead in the 16th century to the invention by Europeans of the telescope and the microscope. (Modern Muslim writers argue that these were evolutionary improvements, not inventions.)

For four hundred years *Al-Andalus* was the industrial and scientific leader of the West and, arguably, the world's leader in non-technological progress during the later part of this period (while the Sung dynasty of China was under attack by the Mongols). The Córdoban aristocracy was, just as importantly, the arbiter of taste and fashion. It was the Moors who introduced agricultural irrigation to Spain. It was they who brought to the West oranges, lemons, spinach, asparagus, aubergines, artichokes, pasta and toothpaste! And when the Spanish now call out *Olé* or greet each other with *Hola*, not all of them realize they are voicing a plea to Allah. (The story of Muslim Spain picks up on page 89.)

5

The Koran

The Writing of the Koran – – Interpretation of the Koran – The Schools

The Writing of the Koran:
Difference of opinion exists among scholars as to how, when and by whom the words of Allah were first written and brought together in the Koran. Some Islamic scholars think that it was under the first caliph, Abu Bakr, in 632-34, that accounts from memory and contemporaneous records of Mohammed's preachings were assembled by disciples on parchment, flat stones, palm leaves or camel bone. Other scholars believe that it was under Caliph Uthman in 644-56 that such writings were collected and united with accounts from memory of some of those who had heard Mohammed's words decades before. No independent evidence to support either of these accounts is extant. Further, there have been suggestions that the first plausible written *surah* (chapter) of the 114 *surahs* of the Koran is dated about 691, under the fifth Umayyad caliph, Abdul Malik. But it has also been said that no mention of the Koran is to be found in any Arabic religious writings before about 750. Again, it has been suggested that notwithstanding the sophistication of the bureaucracy under the Umayyads, no attempt to derive law from Koranic texts was made before about 780-800, under Harun al-Rashid. And some serious scholars (e.g. John Wansborough) have questioned the basic tenet that the Koran records God's revelations to Mohammed, asserting that this remarkable piece of prose was

47

likely compiled by a series of writers in the 8th century to record the reported teachings of the Prophet.

Arab writing in the 8th century allows for a considerable range of interpretation. Unlike the modern Arabic alphabet, in the 8th century, alphabetic letters were more like memory aids for men who already knew much of the material they were reading. Vowel sounds were not indicated at all. With William R. Polk's example as a guide, a trans-literation of the Muslim profession of faith from modern Arabic into English, "There is no god but Allah, and Mohammed is His Prophet," now rendered as "*La ilaha illa'llah Mohammedu 'rasulu Allah,*" would have been written as something like, "*l lh ll llh mhmmd rsl llh.*" Today, vowel sounds are still not expressed by alphabetic letters, but are indicated by diacritic marks, dots, accents above and below the conso-nants, like Hebrew *nikkudim*.

Then again, no difference existed in the 8th century between the notation of several consonants, between the n, t, th, y, b phonemes, greatly increasing the difficulty of understanding written text. Written text could be interpreted differently, reflecting the pre-dispositions of the interpreters, thus raising the serious possibility of multiple or flawed interpretation. Moreover, as time passed many sects asserted that the Scriptures had occult meaning and therefore needed allegori-cal interpretation spiritually transcending the literal sense. Friedrich Ueberweg, the 19th century German historian of philosophy, concluded that as there were "7 or 70 or 700 interpretations for every Koranic text" the reader could always find one that suited him.

Interpretation of the Koran:
So varied were the interpretations that in orthodox Sunni Islam there arose not a clergy but a body of judicial scholars, the *ulema*, who spe-cialized from religious and linguistic points of view in interpreting the Koran and the Traditions.

Even though the *ulema* are often referred to in the West as clerics, there is in fact no clergy in the majority (85-90%) Sunni branch of Islam, in the sense of an organized hierarchical body of persons mediating between God and man. (Historically however, Sunni Ottoman Turkey had partly-hierarchical *ulema* who might be called a quasi-clergy.)

The *ulema* are male, expert-jurist-teachers. Theologians would per-haps be a better term for them than clerics. Still, informally hierarchical bodies of religious scholars, the *mullahs*, close to the Christian concept of clergy, do exist in the (10 -15%) Shiite branches of Islam. With the exception of 21st century, modernizing Morocco, all Muslim sects have the same ulema-imposed ban on the ordination of women into the "priesthood" – as do the Roman Catholic and Jewish faiths – the ban arising from ancient cultural roots in the Middle East.

The basic difference between the Sunnis and the Shias is that the Sunnis accept as Caliphs (the legitimate earthly leaders of the Faith) the first four companion successors of the Prophet and the heads of the two succeeding Koreishi clan-based dynasties, the Umayyads and the Abbasids. The Shias accept only Ali, the last of the first four leaders, as the first caliph, the first "Imam", and only his direct descendants through the male line as successors, both spiritual and temporal leaders of the Faith.

In 874, upon the death of his father at the age of twenty-seven, in Samarra, poisoned it is said, Mohammed bin Hassan al-Askari at the age of six became for the majority of Shias, the Twelfth Imam, the twelfth successor of the Prophet. For fear of the Sunnis (al-Mutamid was caliph and a great slave revolt was in progress) the young Shiite Imam had to be sheltered by his followers until the 940s when he disappeared into "occultation" (concealment), one account saying he went down a well to escape assassination by agents of the vizier of the time. This Twelfth Imam is widely believed to be alive today and still in concealment. The shrine in Samarra dedicated to this Mohammed and his father Hassan al-Askari, the 11th Imam, is the Golden Mosque that was destroyed by explosives in February, 2006. The majority of Shias, called "Twelvers", await the Hidden Imam's return as the *Mahdi* – the Messiah – the saviour of mankind, to deliver us all from our iniquitous ways.

In his speech to the United Nations in September, 2005, following his election as President of Iran, Mahmoud Ahmadinejad – who believes he was surrounded by a halo of heavenly light as he addressed the General Assembly – indicated that the return of the *Mahdi*, with whom he is in touch, is imminent.

The Schools:
Given all the divisions in early Islamic society and Muslims' enduring inability, arising out of differences of interpretation of the Scriptures, to agree on a number of core matters of doctrine, it is not surprising that the Sunni *ulema* developed four canonical schools of law, *fiqhs*, all

systematized in the 9th century, all valid today in one Muslim country or other, all differing in some important detail of dogma, interpretation or emphasis. These are the *Hanafi*, the *Maliki*, the *Shafii* and the *Hanbali* schools, named after scholars preaching and teaching between 750 and 850. The *Hanafi* has the most followers today. The unswervingly fundamentalist *Hanbali* (Wahhabi) code of Saudi Arabia has the fewest adherents, but is seen as the most threatening, or at least alien, by 21st-century Western eyes.

At the present time the *Hanafi* school, the predominant Islamic code of the Indian sub-continent, is divided between two main out of several sects. The minority, High Church, largely Pashtun *Deobandi* sect (named after the town where it originated in 1867) is the fundamentalist inspiration of Afghanistan's Taliban. The mainstream, mainly Punjabi *Barelvi* sect (named after a local dynasty) is Low Church.

Shiism has three well-followed *fiqhs*, by far the most important being the *Ja'afari*, the established "Twelver" code of Iran, which follows the teachings of the 6th Imam, Ja'afar as-Sadiq (d. 765, poisoned [?] by Caliph al-Mansur).

The Ismaili Shiites, known as "Seveners", hold that Ja'afar as-Sadiq's elder son, Ismail, who died or disappeared before his father died, is in fact the Imam in hiding, and is the legitimate 7th and last Imam who will reappear at the end of time to save mankind. Twelvers maintain that Ja'afar's younger son, Musa al-Kazim (who they say was poisoned by Harun al-Rashid in 799) was the 7th Imam, but not the *Mahdi*.

(The Sudanese boat builder's son, Muhammad Ahmad, who proclaimed himself the *Mahdi* and killed General Gordon at Khartoum in 1883, was not a Shia but a Maliki Sunni with strong Sufi beliefs, as doubtless his present-day descendants are.)

Reinterpretation of the Scriptures continued until the 10th century, during the collapse of the Abbasids, when juridical opinion hardened and it was declared that "The Gate of Interpretation (*bab al ijtihad*) is closed." (Some writers have said that this edict was promulgated centuries later by the Ottomans.) The closing, the denial of people's right in the mainstreams of Islam to re-examine the principles of their faith, is 21st century Islam's greatest challenge and obstacle to progress. There are signs, though, that steps in the right direction may one day be taken.

6

The Decline and Collapse of the Abbasid Empire

Turkic Slave Troops – Sufism – Extravagance and Corruption – Despotism – The Treatment of Women – Mediterranean Commerce – Reasons for the Collapse of the Empire – The Caliphate, Conclusion

Turkic Slave Troops:
Following the early Arab conquests, the caliphal armies of Iraq had changed from being manned by the most independent freeborn warriors anywhere – the bedouins – to armies composed of mercenary professionals, many of them from Persia's eastern province of Khorasan. Under Caliph al-Amin these forces were reinforced by companies of slaves because of shortage of "pure" bedouin Arab manpower. Such armies were not new. Bodies of trained and bonded warriors had existed for centuries in the Middle Eastern world. For his "slave-armies", Caliph al-Ma'moun turned to the combative nomadic peoples of south-central Asia – Transoxania (Transoxiana). From these Turkic tribes young boys were obtained as slaves, many of them originating as annual tribute payment to the caliph from provincial vassal chiefs. The recruits were brought up as Muslims, trained for total loyalty to the caliph, and emancipated upon completing their military training. At first these troops were invaluable since, as they were acquired young from outside the Muslim world and therefore lacked family ties, they were both rootless and more dependable than native Arabs or Persians.

It was Caliph al-Mutasim, al-Ma'moun's younger half-brother (son of a Turkic slavegirl), who took the fateful step of recruiting his entire 4000-man praetorian guard from these Turks. In 836, because of unrest in Baghdad, murderous rivalry between military units in the city and to signal a break with the past, al-Mutasim moved his court to Samarra on the Tigris seventy miles north of Baghdad where, unlike Baghdad, cheap land was available for his troops – a crucial concern. However, away from the constraints of the capital the Turkic regiments quickly encroached upon government, taking over the executive powers of the caliph and finally controlling succession to the throne. This was the consequence of an alien military force operating side by side with mainly unarmed civilians in a political environment where power was held in proportion to the possession of arms.

The rise to power of the Turkic military aristocracy was another turning point in the fortunes of the caliphate. Within no time the "slaves" were murdering caliphs and had enthroned and dethroned five caliphs successively. The caliphs had become mere pawns in court struggles. And Arab civilization with all its values and strengths, if also with its philosophical and economic feet of clay, began at this time to founder. With the death of al-Mutasim in his forties in 842 the Golden Age was essentially at an end. The empire was disrupted, insurrections occurring repeatedly, revenues falling drastically, and the caliphs' grip on the armed forces was broken. Both Córdoba and Alexandria, with their respective Moorish-Spanish-Jewish and multi-ethnic populations, came each in its own time to compete on terms of equality with Baghdad. Eventually, both overtook Baghdad, the first cultural capital of Islam.

Al-Mutasim's son, entitled al-Wathiq, ruled for five years. He is noted in the annals as the caliph who beheaded forty-two Byzantine military officer captives for refusing to forswear Christianity and accept Islam, and dumped their heads in the Tigris. His reign was marked by the resurgence of the bedouin tribes of central and western Arabia. It was only with prolonged effort over three years that the army led by a Turkic general, Bogha, was able to suppress them. This revolt is memorable in marking the point of complete and final disaffection of the bedouins from allegiance to the caliphate, although they remained devotedly Sunni. After this, periodic nomad lawlessness was added to constant unrest among the largely urban Shias in Iraq.

Caliph al-Wathiq died at the age of thirty-six in 847. His vizier then had the audacity to press the claim of al-Wathiq's infant son to succeed his father – so that he the vizier might manipulate the remains of caliphal power and wealth through the child. He should have been more circumspect. The army had other ideas. They secured the succession of al-Wathiq's brother, surnamed al-Mutawakkil. Among the new Caliph's first acts upon acceding to power was to seize all the possessions of the overthrown vizier and for his *lèse-majesté* to have him put to death most cruelly in a torture apparatus of his own design.

Al-Mutawakkil imposed severe restrictions on non-orthodox Sunni sects and persecuted the Jews, Christians and Shias alike. His reign was handicapped financially by giant military expenditures – a 70,000-man slave army – coping with uprisings, war with the Greeks and his private excesses. He in turn got his just deserts when he tried to murder his army-chosen heir-apparent, his eldest son, al-Muntasir, who conspired with the officers to have his father and his father's close counsellor, al-Fath, cut down while the two of them sat drinking.

It was at this point, in 861, two centuries after the murder of Caliph Ali, that power passed completely for a period of about fifteen years into the hands of the Turkic military aristocracy. The next caliph, al-Muntasir, lasted only six months before he was poisoned. And the following three were all murdered outright or locked up and starved to death. With anarchy reigning in Samarra, central government of the provinces collapsed and Yemen, Libya and Egypt departed the empire. Not satisfied with assuming the powers of the caliph, the generals' clans then turned their swords on each other. For all that, enthroned in 870 as al-Mutamid, one of al-Mutawakkil's sons aided by a brother, al-Muwaffaq (who would become the real power in the country), was eventually able to regain control over the army and its Turkic officer corps. Some lost land was then recovered, some rebels subdued, enemies destroyed, tribute renewed. But by 886 another province, Christian Armenia, had regained its independence.

During the forty years of hegemony of the Turkic mercenaries in Samarra, a time of chaos, deadly rivalry and further loss of national treasure, a trial of strength arose between the caliphs and the *ulema* in which the religious scholars were successful. Caliphal power for decades after this was constrained politically and administratively and limited on the whole to ceremonial matters and nominal leadership of Sunni Islam, while the *ulema* strengthened their hold on religion and education.

At this time the last of the four codes of Sunni Sharia law was established and systematized from the writings and teachings of the jurist, Ibn

Mohammed Hanbal. The code was fundamentalist, austere, unswerving from the word of God as Ibn Hanbal had understood it. While it was the code with the fewest adherents it was to loom large when in the 18th century, inspired by its principles, Wahhabism arose in Arabia.

From 858, during the time of al-Mutawakkil, all governors appointed to Egypt had been Turkic officers. In 868, during the primacy in Samarra of the general Bayikbeg (under the caliphate of al-Mutazz who was imprisoned and starved to death) regionalism took firm hold of the Arab world, Egypt being lost to Ahmed bin Tulun, Bayikbeg's thirty-three-year-old stepson who had been appointed originally as deputy governor. While continuing to acknowledge the Abbasids as caliph, Ibn Tulun created his own sovereign emirate, and invaded the Levant adding it to his possessions. When Ibn Tulun died and was succeeded by his twenty-year-old son, Khumaruya (Khamarawaih), the young successor's Abbasid uncle, al-Muwaffaq, tried to retake Egypt for himself, but failed. There then followed a period of expansion for autonomous Egypt, with Khumaruya extending his domains widely into Syria and to parts of Mesopotamia, reaching the Euphrates and reducing the Abbasid caliphate to little more than a local province. Khumaruya got to be very rich, but was strangled by a coterie of his eunuchs and estranged concubines. The killers were crucified. His son, Abul Askir Jaish, reigned for six months, but he too was murdered and replaced by another short-lived brother, Harun. Tulunid independence of this nature lasted thirty-seven years, until 906.

At the time in 869 that the young Shiite 12th Imam, the *Mahdi*-in-Hiding, was being hidden by his followers in Samarra, a great revolt had broken out among black slaves called the "Zanj" (after Zanzibar – *Zanjibar* in Arabic – the slave port) who had been brought in their thousands to drain the marshes and work the fields of Iraq. Unlike most slaves in the Arab world who were employed on domestic or military duties, these were labouring field slaves, chattel slaves. The revolt, certainly an attempt to escape from bondage but not to abolish slavery – which was believed with Koranic authority to be in complete harmony with the spirit of Islam – was messianic in spirit. Its leader, a veiled Arab calling himself Ali bin Mohammed, claimed to be the *Mahdi* come to free the slaves from oppression. Among the rewards he promised them was that they would be able to have slaves of their own once they were free.

In the 870s, with the revolt in full swing in Iraq and Persia, the Arab conquerors of the heavily populated plain of the Indus River and

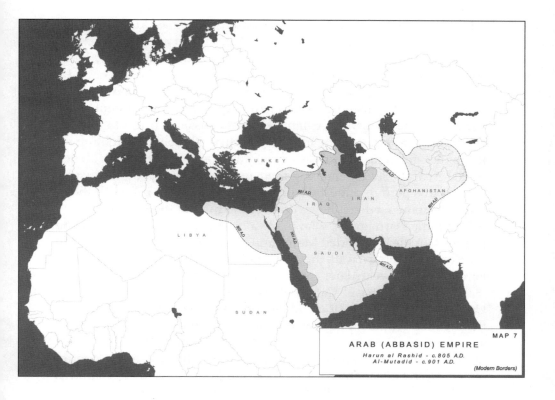

MAP 7
ARAB (ABBASID) EMPIRE
Harun al Rashid - c. 805 A.D.
Al-Mutadid - c. 901 A.D.
(Modern Borders)

their Turkmen and Uzbek vassals in Transoxania broke away from the Abbasid empire creating their own independent kingdoms. The slave revolt took fourteen years and all al-Muwaffaq's efforts to defeat, but the leader, Ali bin Mohammed, was finally slain, in 883, and his head taken back to Baghdad on a pike. The revolt finished, the now reassured caliph returned to Baghdad from Samarra, moving the centre of his restored capital from the west bank of the Tigris to the east. But Iraq had by this time been laid waste.

Al-Mutamid's nephew, al-Mutadid (al-Muwaffaq's son), succeeded as caliph in 892. The able al-Mutadid's main success was to retain control over the Turkic officer corps and gradually to renew Abbasid power. He placated the Tulunids in Egypt by adding a Khumaruya daughter to his train of wives. The girl was ten or twelve years old at the time. But in 899, once again, radical communistic Ismailis, or Qarmatians as they have been called (named after one Hamdan Qarmat), rose in rebellion, the most serious of all sectarian revolts in Arabia. Discontent with the caliphate was social and economic as well as doctrinal.

Although the revolt was crushed in Iraq, victory was won only at further great cost to the caliphate, leaving turmoil for many more years. Much of Peninsula Arabia escaped into independence, and a Qarmatian, Abu Said al-Jannabi, founded a kind of commonwealth in the Al-Hasa (Al-Ahsa) province of Arabia on the Persian Gulf coast, with its capital at Lahsa. Al-Jannabi was assassinated in 913, but his community lasted until the mid-11th century, all the while fighting for its politico-religious objectives. The Qarmation commonwealth owned 30,000 African slaves, enabling their masters to lead a life of luxury. During this period, other Ismaili zealots were able to establish themselves in Yemen, where they won over the ruler to their beliefs.

In 930 the Qarmatians, who made a business of robbing and taxing pilgrims on the hajj, raided Mecca and carried off the Black Stone from the Kaaba, keeping it until they were persuaded by influential Tunisian Ismailis twenty years later to return it, reportedly broken.

It had been Abbasid Caliph al-Mansur who had lost Spain to the Umayyads in the 750s (it could be argued rather that Tariq bin Ziad, the invader of Spain, had already made himself independent), Harun al-Rashid who had lost northwest Africa to independence in the last decade of the 8th century, and al-Ma'moun who lost direct control over eastern Persia. The rest of the empire from Libya to Pakistan was then lost to the Iraqis under the confused conditions prevailing in the period from 860 to 903. By the early 10th century, the empire of the Abbasid caliphs *sensu strictu* had been whittled away, replaced by a host of sovereign Muslim emirates on politically friendly terms or otherwise with each other. The Abbasids reigned only over Mesopotamia and the Hejaz while repeatedly losing and regaining parts of Syria and Egypt throughout the century, and generally only with religious, rather than temporal, authority. At the heart however there remained the overarching dominion of Islam, uniting spiritually all the elements of the erstwhile empire, now materially, politically and doctrinally disunited.

(At the same time, post-850, the T'ang empire of China was disintegrating, and for many of the same reasons: clan rivalry, heretical dissent, political and military overextension, population growth. But everywhere another cause can be identified – ruinous taxation supporting corruption and extravagance, and leading to lawlessness and rebellion. In China peasants sold their children into slavery to pay their taxes. In the last days of the T'ang it was written: "Outside the vermilion gates of the palace and the smell of wine and flesh, people are freezing and starving to death. In thousands of villages they harvest only weeds while women do the ploughing. The people of China can face any test if their leaders treat them humanely." This Chinese dynasty, which flourished from almost the same birth date as the caliphate – 618 – came to an end in almost the same year that the Arab caliphate lost the remains of its empire – 907. On the credit side however the T'ang empire was both peaceful and prosperous for much of its early existence, and it produced a professional bureaucracy, the Mandarins, based on merit principles, unequalled anywhere. Be that as it may, T'ang China was characterized also by the most hideous penalties for misdeeds.)

Taking advantage of weakness in the Tulunid House, Caliph al-Mutadid's son, al-Muqtafi, becoming the 17th Abbasid caliph, regained control over Egypt in 906 from the independent governor, Harun, Khumaruya's second son. This enabled the Caliph and his successor to appoint governors in Egypt for more than twenty years, marking a new high point of Iraqi caliphal power over Egypt, until the last of these governors would make another inherited viceroyalty for himself, creating the Ikhshid dynasty. (But the Fatimids, an Ismaili sectarian dynasty in Tunisia, would overthrow the Ikhshids in 969, after several unsuccessful earlier attempts. The Nile was a most desirable asset, and the city of Alexandria would be worth almost any risk and effort.)

The accession to power in Iraq in 908 of al-Muqtafi's brother at the age of thirteen with the satirical title of al-Muqtadir – meaning "the powerful through the indulgence of God" – occasioned the renewal of intrigue at court. The young caliph's advisors manipulated him. Governors in the provinces sought independence. Qarmation unrest increased, accompanying coups and counter-coups. These conditions weakened the control over Egypt which had just been re-established by Baghdad. Al-Muqtadir suffered another loss when Mosul, a Kurdish-Assyrian-Turkmen city on the Tigris in northern Iraq, cut loose from Baghdad under a bedouin named Hamdan bin Hamdoun who set up a brilliant if evanescent dynasty beyond the reach of the national forces. The homeland too was beginning to break up. This caliph, fabled for skulduggery and extravagance, was unseated from the throne and reinstated several times, surviving until 932 when he died at thirty-seven at the hands of his own military commander, General Mu'nis.

With weakness and disarray in Baghdad under the Sunni caliphs, a Shiite threat had arisen in the Maghreb of north Africa. Ismailis had come to power in Tunis at the beginning of the 10th century and had proclaimed their own caliphate rivalling in religious matters the widely recognized Abbasid caliphate of Iraq. By 929, this political and sectarian threat had prompted the 8th Emir of Umayyad Spain, the supremely confident seventeen-year-old Abd ar-Rahman III, to claim for himself the caliphal title that his ancestors had held two centuries before in the heyday of the Damascus Umayyad empire. With the approval of his religious advisors this Sunni emir had had himself entitled "Caliph" Abd ar-Rahman, Commander of the Faithful, true and legitimate successor of the Prophet, while the Ismaili "caliph" in Tunis was still occupied securing his own position.

After some decades with little power, the Turkic military, under General Mu'nis, won back their dominance over Iraq with the death of Caliph al-Muqtadir in 932. The depraved al-Qahir, a brother of al-Muqtadir's, succeeded him. Al-Qahir and the next caliph but one, al-Muttaki, soon angered the military who blinded and deposed them both. Being blind rendered them ineligible to rule and thus justified their dethroning. But while one mutilated caliph was being replaced by another, the Hamdanid separatists in Mosul branched out westwards to Aleppo taking this the largest city in northern Syria from the Ikhshids. This action, coincidentally, strengthened Arab defences in Anatolia against the Byzantines.

The Hamdanids, originally Twelver Shias, adopted the mysterious Ismaili heresy of the Alawites (Alawis) who regard Imam Ali, the Prophet's cousin, as an incarnation of God, celebrate Christmas and Easter, believe that women do not have souls, and drink wine. (The Alawites trace the origin of their beliefs to the 11th Imam, Hassan al-Askari. There is much more of course to them than this, but most of it is known by only an inner circle of the truest believers.) The politically powerful 10-15% Alawite minority of today's Syria are the rulers of that country.

Sufism:
Simultaneously with political chaos and caliphal decadence, at some time variously suggested as having been between 960 and 1160, in the Iraqi city of Basra or possibly in Bosra (Busra) Syria, a secret society of liberal-minded encyclopedist scholars known as the Brethren of Purity or the Sincere Brethren (*Ikhwan as-Safa*), and notably including both Sufi and Ismaili members, attempted to reconcile classical Greek

ideas with Islamic faith. In this endeavour they failed because whereas Plato argued that a ruler must be a philosopher guided by reason, the faithful Muslim must accept the truths, the certainties, revealed to Mohammed and agree that the caliph's legitimacy arises from the unquestionable Holy Law, the will of Allah.

The Brethren published some fifty-two lengthy epistles (*Rasa'il*) which have been described (although questionably) as a manifesto of Ismaili beliefs. The *Rasa'il* were distributed throughout the Muslim world. Even if later suppressed by the Sunni Abbasids, these writings formed a compilation of much of the scholarly wisdom that a cultured man of the times was supposed to acquire, covering mathematics, astronomy, medical science, biology and botany, geography, music, ethics and philosophy. The eighth *Rasa'il* includes a portrait of the ideal man which, in the light of today's clashes of civilizations and nations, is fascinating and somehow spine-tingling: "He should be Persian in origin, Arab by religion, Iraqi by culture, Hebrew in experience, Christian in conduct, Syrian in asceticism, Greek by the sciences, Indian by perspicacity, Sufi by way of life, angelic by morals, divine by his ideas and knowledge, and destined for Eternity."

Sufism was an important part of the spiritual life of Arab civilization. It remains so. Sufism advocated a departure from Sharia-based, *ulema*-led orthodoxy in Islam to a more direct personal relationship with the Almighty. It arose as an ascetic mystical movement believing in union with God by means of contemplation and self-surrender with the resulting acquisition of knowledge inaccessible to intellect. It seems to have first appeared in the town of Kufa, Iraq, in the 8th century. Although not formally anti-orthodox, as were the Ismailis, Sufis held a personal view of Allah opposed to Sunni transcendentalism with its belief in the supernatural and the primacy of the spiritual over the material. Sufism's roots were in ancient oriental mysticism and, during his time, in the perception of mystical qualities in the life and teachings of the Prophet. These ideas germinated in the social and economic conditions prevailing in the caliphate following Mohammed's death.

The growth of Sufism coincided with and was reinforced by the tide of classical Greek learning streaming into the Islamic world in the 8th and the first part of the 9th century. It was through the Nestorian Christians of Iraq and Persia that Greek influences had entered the Muslim world. During the late 8th century until the mid-9th, Sufism helped to reinvigorate orthodox Islam bringing it closer to the common people. Inevitably, the *ulema* became alarmed at its success and its gnostic aspects and rose in opposition. But by 900, Sufism had become an organized belief system with its own prayer leaders, to the even greater concern of the orthodox *ulema*.

The destructive civil wars, the ruthless military dictatorship arising in Iraq, the extravagant life-styles of the ruling classes contrasting with the poverty and suffering of the masses (exacerbated by corruption and heavy taxation), together with the influence of Platonic rationalism – suggesting that reason should be the guiding principle in life, questioning the need for reliance on any form of religious belief – all encouraged the spread of Sufism. Soon after 900, together with contemplative mysticism, there sprang up an inquiring current in Sufism that was both counter-Sunni and anti-Shia, as Sufism permeated both Sunni and Shiite creeds. Sufis became proselytizing missionaries. Sufi fraternities later gave rise to dancing dervish orders performing religious exercises leading to rapture through song, dance, drugs and hypnotic suggestion – to the even greater alarm of the orthodox Sunni authorities. Their response was to deepen their conservatism, tightening their control over people's thinking, erecting further religious barriers to change.

The celebrated Persian Sufi mystic, Mansur al-Hallaj, sixty-four years old at the time, was condemned in 922 to 1,000 lashes, parts of him first to be cut off, and decapitation; (other accounts say crucifixion). The Caliph al-Muqtadir's *Hanbali* court condemned him for, while in a state of ecstasy, uttering the words *"Ana al Haqq"* – "I am Truth" – apostasy in Islam where Truth is a name for Allah. The saintly al-Hallaj is said to have forgiven his tormenters as they tortured him to death.

Extravagance and Corruption:
By 900, as climate change began to subject the people to enervatingly high temperatures, the Abbasid caliphate had fallen financially into a very poor state. While the currency of the arts, science and letters had not been debased, trade patterns and wealth generation had been seriously disrupted. William R. Polk calculates that Iraqi government revenue for the year 900 was only 3 to 4% of what it had been in 800. The Umayyad and early-Abbasid "rivers of tribute" had run dry. Prior to 800, after direct taxes on the people, tribute from the provinces had been the main financial pillar of the state. By this date, plunder was

no longer there for the taking. By 900, the gravely reduced income came almost exclusively from taxation of the peasants and extortion of workers and merchants.

Lack of political power and national beggary did not however mean that the caliphs themselves lived in penury. With the accession to power of al-Amin, graft in the Abbasid world had been institution- alized. The fiscal system consisted of arrangements permitting and inciting officials at every level – and there were many bureaucratic levels – by every means to wrest money from the people. There was no sense of right and wrong, of proper public purpose. Corruption per- vaded every process of public administration, officials making illicit gains as if it were their natural right, as no doubt they thought it was, passing on part to their superiors. They were in it for the money. A vast proportion of the taxes exacted from the suffering peasants and artisans, whatever the state of the harvest or trade, found its way into the pockets of officialdom.

The hundreds of courtiers and servants, the multitude of eunuchs, the rich raiments and jewelry and harems and zoological gardens and works of art, the battalions of bodyguards, the royal craftsmen and artisans, the Koran readers, the storytellers, the cup bearers, the food tasters, the patronage of the arts and science could be supported only by a well practised system of embezzlement and expropriation. S.E. Finer calculated that under Caliph al-Muqtadir, admittedly one of the most corrupt caliphs in the whole of the disastrous 10th century, one- half or more of government revenues went to the caliphal household. The government and its agents did not care how the money was raised so long as it rolled in.

Despite the poverty of the country, cultural life and scholarship which relied much less on government support and more on pri- vate charity remained less impaired. One reason why the caliphs maintained much of their luxurious lifestyle was because they were permitted by their Turkic military masters to continue plundering the populace, so that the colonels could maintain the fiction in the Muslim world of honouring the Prophet's successors.

Much of the revenue of the state was spent in the most outlandishly wasteful way. Caliph al-Mutawakkil was described in 855 as having a harem of 12,000 women. (Other accounts offer different numbers down to a meagre 400.) Later, Caliph al-Mutamid was able to exercise some judicious control of the finances of the caliphate. Nonetheless, in 917 the Byzantine ambassador could report to his Emperor, Constantine

VII Porphyrogenitus, that in the twenty-two-year-old Caliph al-Muqtadir's twelve palaces in Baghdad 38,000 tapestries adorned the walls, 22,000 carpets were piled on the floors, and in the grounds sparkling brooks ran and fountains played. In the main palace, guarded by "10,000 gilded breastplates", on a pond of glistening mercury there sailed ships of gold. And mechanical birds sang as artificial trees rose out of the floor to bedazzle guests.

By the mid-9th century, corruption, the failings of the empire, and the cessation of the flow of plunder had exacerbated the effects of ruinous taxation. Peasants in the hinterlands were driven off the land into poverty; irrigation works fell into disrepair; where order had once prevailed bandits and beggars abounded. Still, some aspects of the Arab empire were little changed. Baghdad remained a pivotal point on the Silk Road between the Orient and the Occident, bringing in revenue for the government from journeying traders – even though trade along this network had diminished in favour of maritime routes. And while Baghdad's aura as the cultural heart of Islam persisted for several more eventful centuries, Mecca remained its soul.

The Arab potentates of this era were not to be outdone by their peers. When in 949 Ambassador Liutprand of Cremona was sent by King Berenger II of Italian Piedmont to the court of the same Emperor Constantine VII Porphyrogenitus in Constantinople, his report included the following:

> In front of the Emperor's throne stood a tree of gilded metal of which the branches were filled with birds of various kinds also made of gold-leafed iron which gave forth a variety of bird-song. The throne itself was so cunningly constructed that at one moment it looked low … and a moment later had risen to a great height. It was guarded on either side by huge lions of gold-lacquered wood which lashed their tails on the floor and roared aloud with open mouths and moving tongues. Into this hall, attended by two eunuchs, I was brought before His Imperial Majesty. At my entrance, the lions roared and the birds sang … But after prostrating myself for the third time, when I raised my head, I beheld the Emperor, whom I had first seen seated slightly above me, elevated almost to the roof of the hall and clad in different garments. How this was managed, I do not know.

Despotism:

With respect to the system of justice, the Arabo-Persian caliphate was an absolute despotism from its inception, subject to no process of civil law. No legal defence against official oppression existed. While an elaborate system of jurisprudence had been developed under the Sharia law, the common man had no redress against the government. Civil courts were there only to adjudicate disputes between civilians. Passive obedience was expected from all. The caliph could do no wrong, although an indulgence might be sought of him. Against the authorities, nobody's life, limb, property or freedom was safe. This situation, in S.E. Finer's words, inspired "abject submission" alternating with "religion-inspired revolt". The caliph's absolute power did not exist simply because that was what he desired, but Sharia Law, as practised, stressed that the Prophet's command was to obey the caliph at all times, without exception, no matter what. Islam was headed by absolute, infallible, unchallengeable rulers.

In about 1092, a Persian Shafi'i theologian of towering intellect, Abu Hamid al-Ghazali (1058-1111) influenced by Sufi beliefs and the *Rasa'il* of the Brethren of Purity, but nevertheless an apologist for unlimited caliphal power wrote:

> An evil-doing and barbarous sultan, so long as he is supported by military force, so that he could only with difficulty be deposed and that (any) attempt to depose him would cause unendurable strife, must of necessity be left in possession, and obedience must be rendered to him, exactly as unquestioning obedience must be rendered to caliphs. Government in these days is a consequence solely of military power, and whoever he may be to whom the holder of military power gives his allegiance, that person has the rights of Caliph.

Thus, military power alone could confer legitimacy. Al-Ghazali could write this despite the Prophet's widely reported words: "Better justice without religion than tyranny under a devout ruler."

Addressing the problem of constant social unrest, caliphs and sultans found it necessary to keep military forces stationed on the edges of many urban areas. The purpose of these forces was to hold the populace in fear. Al-Ghazali was persuaded by the circumstances of the times to recognize the harsh realities. His insistence upon obedience among Muslims even under despotic rule was confirmed in a formal judgment on the same issue by the chief religious magistrate of Egypt, Ibn Jemaa, in the early 14th century, at a time when Egypt had become the leader of the Sunni Muslim world. Even if the caliphate was not totalitarian, it was despotic, arbitrary and absolute.

The Treatment of Women:
During the Abbasid age and later, while maintaining respectful recognition of women's legal rights and protections with regard to property, Arab scholars interpreted the intent of the Prophet regarding the treatment of women so as to place them in unmistakable subjection to men, revealing, it has been asserted, deep-rooted Arab unease with womankind.

Consistent with the differences in financial responsibilities of man and woman, the daughters' shares of their father's estate were set at one-half of their brothers'. In lawsuits a man's word was worth more than a woman's. Male-dominated urban Arab society believed that women had to be isolated from all men except family members. The reputation of the family in the community and certainty in men's minds regarding the paternity of their wives' children required the seclusion of women of high social rank in harems and the wearing of veils by most women. Infibulation was practised in the upper ranks of society (a procedure exported to Europe).

Other than in the harems of the powerful where it was likely that adultery (by Christian definition) occurred most days, a poor woman who had sex outside of marriage could be stoned to death. For a man to be condemned it required that there be four adult male Muslim witnesses to the crime.

In her 1987 book, *Beyond the Veil*, the Moroccan writer Fatima Mernissi wrote: "The Islamic view of women as active sexual beings resulted in strict regulation and control of women's sexuality, which Muslim theorists classically regarded as a threat to civilized society." The Iranian writer, Reza Afshari, stated in his *Egalitarian Islam and Misogynist Islamic Tradition*, of 2005, that "historical Islam has deeply ingrained the fear of female sexuality in the male consciousness … sexual equality violates Islam's premise that heterosexual love is dangerous to Allah's order … the desegregation of the sexes violates Islam's ideology of women's position in the social order." In January 2006, it was widely reported that Salman Rushdie – famously the subject of a *Fatwah* calling for his execution, proclaimed by Ayatollah Rahollah

Khomeini in 1989, following the publication of Rushdie's novel, *The Satanic Verses* – said, "The West has failed to grasp the extent to which Islamic extremism is rooted in men's fear of women's sexuality ... Much of the anger towards the West ... is because Western societies do not veil their women." In a speech in Cambridge in March 2000 on "Women and Religious Oppression", Dr Azam Kamguian pointed out that, "In Islam women should not be allowed to have any authority in society other than in their roles as wives and mothers; they are merely extensions of men ... The appearance of unveiled women in public is viewed as an attack on the very pillars of Islamic morality ... Women's rights are universal and women's liberation can only be achieved under an egalitarian, progressive and secularist form of government."

From the time of the Umayyads most of the caliphs and the Arab aristocracy fathered children by slavegirls. Indeed, from the time of Marwan II many of the caliphs (some historians say most) were the sons of slavegirls, and all the later Commanders of the Faithful had slavegirls in their ancestry. It was argued that since slaves were simply material property, "God's spoils of war", no rape, adultery or fornication in the Koranic sense could take place.

Slavery persisted in Arabia into the 20th century; it remains in the 21st century in some African members of the Arab League, while slave-trading – women and boys – persists today in the Gulf States. Such an attitude towards women among the Arabs arose in pre-Islamic times and was deepened by the conflicting interpretations of the teachings of Mohammed with regard to modesty, as to whether or not he had prescribed equal rights for women, and what equal might mean.

The treatment of women in medieval China was certainly not much better, and it was not until the late 19th century that, under the Married Women's Property Act, British women obtained similar legal rights to their property that Muslim women had had since the caliphate. Although, in Byzantium as in Rome, if mistreated in other ways, daughters still had equal inheritance rights to sons and were often educated. Thought-provokingly, women in Muslim Turkey under Mustafa Kemal Atatürk got the vote years before their sisters did in Christian France or Switzerland.

In Europe, empire or kingdom-building, and territorial aggrandisement of all kinds, was brought about historically partly by warfare, partly by purchase, but by far the commonest method was by marriage, where women carried inherited sovereign right and title to territory in their own names. Under Christianity a woman could and can hold sovereign title; in Arab Islam she could not and cannot. In ancient times, on the other hand, some of the nomadic tribes of Arabia were matriarchal, headed by "queens", and there is traditional evidence that Balkis (Bilqis), Queen of Sheba, ruled Yemen in the 900s BC. The beautiful Queen Zenobia ruled central Syria (Palmyra) in the 3rd century AD, and conquered much of Egypt before being overthrown by the Romans.

There is no example of an Arab state (except perhaps in the ethnic Berber-Moorish Maghreb) built or extended by marriage after the beginning of patriarchal urban living in the 6th century Middle East. Apart from the widow (a foreign-born, one-time slavegirl) of an Egyptian sultan recognized in Egypt for about eighty days in the 13th century as Sultana, there is no example of a Muslim Arab polity ruled formally by a woman. In the 900 years from the birth of Islam to the defeat of the (ethnic Caucasian) Mamluk régime of Egypt by the (Turkic) Ottomans in the 16th century, all Middle Eastern and North African countries were created by wars of conquest. Except for exercising behind-the-scenes, haremic influence, women were never involved as principals. It must be added, though, that daughters of leaders were frequently if not always offered in marriage to appease powerful rivals or to strengthen political alliances, as indeed they were everywhere in the world. And it is beyond question that mothers and aunts of juvenile sovereigns sometimes wielded much power, including formally becoming regent during the minority of a sovereign. Moreover, the mothers of caliphs and of caliphs' sons sometimes exercised great influence, and were often instrumental in the choice of a new sovereign. In this regard then the Arab was no different from the Christian world.

It is only in the Arabo-Persian world and Afghanistan that Muslim women have been so legally and customarily restricted. In the Muslim-majority countries of 20–21st century South-East Asia – Pakistan, Bangladesh, Indonesia and Malaysia – women, although still disadvantaged, have become heads of state, heads of government, cabinet ministers, side by side with women in the Hindu and Buddhist countries of the region. The prohibition on women occupying high political or judicial rank is Arab, not Muslim, custom. Arab culture maintains that women are too emotional to act impartially and consequently should not occupy high public positions.

In 2006 however Turkey's official religious commission, the *Diyanet*, announced that it would remove from the Hadith – the reported teachings of the Prophet, second only in authority to the Koran – the misogynist traditions condoning the oppression of women, a first step in the right direction.

Mediterranean Commerce:
Despite social disruption and political fragmentation, the 9th century was a period of thriving trade for Arab merchants who on the whole ignored political boundaries and maintained the common market from the Atlantic to Persia and beyond. While political disintegration took hold in the empire, Arabs from northern Africa and Spain, many of them operating in independent alliances and pirate bands, "corsairs", took over many of the large islands of the Mediterranean – Cyprus, Crete, Malta, Sicily, Majorca – and established raiding-trading bases in others. Only some Byzantine islands of the Aegean escaped. Fortified trading bases were also planted on the European shore. The hills behind St Tropez in the south of France are called *Les Maures* in recognition of a powerful Moorish base located near there for many decades until late in the 10th century. At the same time, Arab pirates from Tunisia installed bases on the Italian Adriatic mainland at Bari and Taranto and attacked the west coast, sacking the Vatican in 846. These activities enabled Arabs – "Saracens" – to take command of much of the trade in the Mediterranean from the 8th until the 11th century. By the beginning of the 10th century, while the caliphs were beginning to lose their fabled private fortunes, some Arab corsair dynasties were increasing theirs.

The arrival of large-scale trading gave rise during the 9th century to the development of Arab banking. Banking facilities were set up across the empire and sophisticated systems were installed permitting funds available in one country to be used profitably and securely in others. Owing to the Muslim ban on usury most of the bankers were Jews or Christians. Although the ban was widely evaded its mere existence still hindered the expansion of Arab trade and industry.

A venturesome Muslim trading class operating an extensive commercial network in the Middle East and Mediterranean had come into existence in Umayyad times and was assigned high social status because Mohammed himself was believed to have been a merchant. Even so, Arab merchants were seldom able to parlay their wealth into political power, first because of caliphal monopoly, and then from the mid-9th century and for the following three hundred years because

Middle Eastern political power lay almost exclusively in the hands of Turkic mercenary soldiers.

Reasons for the Collapse of the Empire:
The reasons for the political disintegration of the early Arab empire, as we have seen, were manifold. The first was the empire-wide disagreement over the legitimacy of the caliphs and as to who was Mohammed's rightful successor. The second was the geographical remoteness of many of the conquered lands from the administrative centre with consequent poor communications, excessive spending on defence and the need for local mercenary troops who quickly acquired independent power (Paul Kennedy's "strategical overextension.") The third was the unavoidable delegation of powers to provincial authorities, a consequence of that overextension. Another was the continued impoverishment of the common peoples of the empire by the unscrupulousness and extravagance of its rulers and by the ruinous taxation and tribute that the people were made to pay. Moreover, there existed across the empire a pervasive culture of envy, rivalry and mistrust among the ruling elites.

The economic underpinning of much of the empire was poor. The pressures of an expanding population on little-changing natural resources once the empire reached its maximum extent were a key drawback, unrelieved by any extension or improvement of irrigation. Given a population as large as it was and growing, outside of the fertile zones of Mesopotamia – the Nile, the Atlas slopes and Mediterranean littoral of the Maghreb – the vast area of barren land with its scant hydrological, mineral, or arboreal resources provided little reserve to underpin the empire in times of economic difficulty. Finally, there was the "barbarian problem". The Arab rulers were compelled to incorporate the fearsome barbarian nomads who were either threatening or were needed to defend the empire into the imperial armies or settle them on the empire's lands, or both. They could undermine the empire from within. (The Romans had had the same problem.) With such a set of difficulties there was no way of ensuring the political integrity or durability of the early Arab empire.

This materialist view of the reasons for the collapse of the empire and for the loss of power and wealth is a Western analysis. In sectors of the Islamic world, the fall is blamed more upon the Faithful straying spiritually from the path of virtue after the seizure of power by foreign Turkic troops, the "mercenaries" hired by successive caliphs after Harun al-Rashid to defend the empire. For some of those who hold this view, the 9th-century Koranic code of Mohammed Hanbal is the true path. This path, refined in 1290-1320 by the "puritan" Ahmed bin Taymiyya, and elaborated in the 18th century by another radical, Mohammed bin Abdul Wahhab (1703-92), was adopted in 1744 by Abdul Wahhab's brother-in-law, the ruler of the small Nejd market town of Diriyah (Ad-Diriyah), near Riyadh, Mohammed bin Saud, ancestor of today's Saudi royal family. Ibn Saud and Abdul Wahhab swore an oath of mutual allegiance and together created a fundamentalist Sunni emirate. (The chronicle of the Saud dynasty and Arabia continues on page 158.)

The Nejd is a plateau – sometimes inaccurately described as mountainous, although there are some hilly areas – dipping gently towards the Persian Gulf, from about 4,000 ft elevation bordering the Hejaz to 1,500 ft in the east, barren volcanic lava-fields and dry scrubland in the west with few oases, sand dunes alternating with strings of oases along *wadis* in the mid-peninsula, approaching the Gulf.

While politically the Abbasid empire fell apart, the religion of Islam continued to spread in Africa south of the Sahara and in Asia. Arabo-Islamic culture also remained full of vitality until the 12th century, but a number of economic and philosophical pressures caused the secular elements of the culture to waste away in the 13th century. Scholarship and scientific investigation virtually disappeared; only poetry, carpet-weaving, ceramics, damascene precious metal artwork and the highest expression of Islamic art, calligraphy, survived. Yet in India, Islam strengthened.

In c.1370, Firoz Shah Tughlug, Sultan of Delhi, wrote: "I encouraged my infidel subjects to embrace the religion of the Prophet, and I announced that all who repeated the declaration of faith thereby becoming Muslim would be exempt of the poll tax. Word of my decision came to the people, and many of them, Hindus, came to us, and were taken into the honour of Islam."

The Caliphate, Conclusion:

The early Arabo-Persian empire which had been built entirely by force of arms was, to quote S.E. Finer, "intellectually, artistically and religiously rich and sophisticated." The caliphate's accomplishments included converting many people to Islam, notably the Zoroastrian

Persians, the Christians of Egypt, Syria and Iraq, the pagan Berbers of the Maghreb and a number of tribal confederations of barbarian Turks. Islam instilled a lasting cultural character in these people and created an exceptional environment, comparable for a period of time with the finest moments of Roman and Greek civilization, in which scholars and pilgrims were welcome from the Atlantic to the Indus within a fraternity of art and learning.

But the acquisition of great wealth by the Arab leaders and the Turkic military castes had been achieved by conquest and plunder and by monopolizing trade. In this economic sphere, little new wealth was created by invention, discovery, improvements in agricultural science, or through handicrafts beyond the immediate needs of the population. And while rediscovering and preserving ancient cultures and transmitting their gems to Europe, the Arabs failed to make more than superficial use of them themselves to improve their institutions or to refine their cultural bases. Islamic civilization functioned on value absolutes and religious certainties. It rejected any suggestion that there may be no universal standard of ethics, that each culture might develop its own – which would better have suited Arab society's shifting needs before life's many and varying crises and contradictions. There could be no thought of changing the rules. Islam, as strictly articulated by the *ulema*, was the unbending, all-encompassing guide for all time.

As for any improvement in governance or in the wellbeing of the ordinary people or civil rights, the Iraqi caliphal empire was a failure. The standard of living of the common people seems to have improved little or not at all between 800 and 1900. Politically, the empire of the Umayyads and the Abbasids was a ragged patchwork of conquest which began to tear itself apart the day it stopped growing in the mid- to late 8th century, when the path of expansion through the sword could no longer be pursued and the flow of booty stopped.

Iraq 946 – 1155 AD, Egypt 969 – 1171 AD

The Buwaihids (Buyids) – The Fatimids – The Seljuks

The Buwaihids (Buyids):

The year 946 might be taken as the date when Iraq fell politically from its 200-year-old position as the most powerful state west of China to one humbled by its own failings and by a more vigorous neighbour. (It might alternatively be argued that from about 850 to 1000 Spain was in fact the most successful Muslim-governed state and that the caliphate of Baghdad had been supreme for little more than a century.)In 946, Daylami foot-soldiers, Shias of the "Fiver" Zaydi sect (followers of the grandson of the martyr Hussein bin Ali) from the Elburz Mountains and Caspian shores of Persia, led by their noble Buwaihid clan, took over what remained of Abbasid power and evicted the old military clique. These hardy mercenary fighters had little difficulty in taking Mesopotamia and part of Syria. Shias had finally overcome the Sunni Abbasids and their Turkic masters in Iraq and parts of Syria and Persia.

The 22nd Abbasid caliph, al-Mustaqfi, was seized by the invaders and blinded with burning irons. At this point there were then three sightless ex-caliphs alive in Baghdad, including the depraved al-Qahir who was seen begging in rags in the streets to survive. The Buwaihids, headquartered in Persia, reduced Baghdad to the status of a provincial capital. Iraq was already politically and economically bankrupt and the invaders showed little aptitude for reviving the economy or national self esteem.

Al-Niffari, another of the remarkable Sufi mystics, lamenting over social conditions in Iraq at this time wrote:

> I saw fear holding sway over hope
> and riches turn to dust;
> I saw poverty as the enemy;
> I saw this world to be a delusion
> and heaven to be a deception;
> I saw every created thing
> and it fled from me and
> I was left here alone.

Rivalry between the younger Buwaihid princes and feuds in the army soon aggravated the general disorder even if the Buwaihids managed to restore discipline and prosperity sporadically. But in 972 they lost control of Syria and Palestine to the new Ismaili force surging out of Egypt, the Fatimids. As the Buwaihids were seldom able to get the better of the revolutionary Ismaili Qarmatians, seized as the latter were of their particularly fanatical brand of Shiism, at times the Buwaihids had to resort to power-sharing or short-term alliances with them. Towards the end of the century the Buwaihids nevertheless succeeded in putting an end to the bedouin-led Hamdanid emirate in northern Iraq and Syria.

World trade patterns were changing at this time for a number of reasons. Iraqi trade with China, once very profitable, declined for internal Chinese reasons (the strife-torn transfer of power from the T'ang to Sung dynasties, during which central government broke down.) From the early 11th century, trade with Russia seems also to have languished, while a dearth of useful and precious metals caused by exhaustion of some of the mines, inter-community conflict and climate change brought further deterioration to the commercial situation of the Arab world. Territorial gains by the Christians in Spain and Sicily and Arab loss of bases on the Mediterranean islands as well as on the north shore of the Sea also played havoc with trade. The always-modest "home-grown" generation of wealth in the Arab world was in decline.

The Buwaihids ruled Iraq in the name of the Abbasids for 110 years, occasionally parading the caliph for ceremonial purposes. In spite of being deprived of all symbols of authority caliphs were still paid a modest pension for their household needs. The wastefulness of the days of Caliph al-Muqtadir was gone, but given the polygamy of the Buwaihids, their hordes of offspring and Muslim inheritance rules, they soon fought among themselves and once again the state broke up. This allowed another group of Turkic nomads to seize power – the Seljuks (Selçuks) – in 1055.

The Fatimids:

Following the Qarmation uprising that had finally splintered Iraq, Syria and Arabia, the Ismaili mission, based in Yemen after the beginning of the 10th century, sent out missionaries to north Africa promoting Caliph Ali's mid-7[th]century line of descent from the Prophet's daughter, Fatima, revering her as the Virgin Mary was revered in Christendom. These propagandists had quickly won a broad following among the Shias of Tunisia, exalting the local ruler, Ubaydallah (an immigrant zealot from Syria), as the first Fatimid "caliph".

Eyeing the riches of Egypt and the Nile to the east, and its cowed population, the Fatimids made several unsuccessful attempts to conquer their neighbour. Twice, Abbasid Caliph al-Muqtadir of Baghdad, while still in his twenties, was able to send troops under his general Mu'nis to Egypt to support his viceroy and drive the Tunisian invaders out. Nevertheless, with Baghdad fallen under Buwaihid rule (and with the powerless Caliph al-Muti as the figurehead) the Fatimids, led by their 4th Caliph, al-Mu'izz, the "Giver of Honour", finally succeeded, making him first Egyptian Ismaili "Caliph".

For decades the devout Ismailis had openly preached their version of Shiism in Egypt, finding a receptive audience in a people impoverished by the rapacity and incompetence of the ruling Ikhshids. A Baghdadi Jewish convert to Islam, Jacob ben Killis, a financial wizard who had been in the service of the Ikhshid governor but who had been mistreated by him, had fled to Tunisia where he had convinced al-Mu'izz of the weakness of Egypt and that the Buwaihids, with their own problems aplenty in Iraq and Persia, would not be able to aid the Ikhshids if the Fatimids launched an attack. In the event, in 969 and after careful preparations, al-Mu'izz's General Jawhar (Goghar), a Greek mercenary born in Sicily, and his 100,000-man army had little difficulty in beating the feeble Ikhshid army and in extending his conquest into Syria. The Ikhshid régime had held power in Egypt for just thirty-four years.

Once arrived in the Nile Delta, Jawhar began to build a base to house his army within sight of the ancient Pharaonic capital of Memphis and the pyramids of Giza. This became the City of Mars, *al-Qahirah* (Cairo), which he founded under the guidance of his astrologers when planet Mars was rising towards the zenith. In the new city he began building a palace for the Caliph, his master, and laid the foundations of the mosque-university, al-Azhar. Al-Azhar graces Cairo today and is arguably the oldest surviving university in the world. Soon after this construction work began however, Egypt was invaded by Qarmations who had become established in parts of Syria. These revolutionaries were aided by the Buwaihids, their quasi-brethren, determined to recover the lands in Syria that had so recently been lost to General Jawhar. Shiite Qarmations supported by Shiite Buwaihids were attacking Shiite Fatimids while the Sunni Caliph, al-Muti, kept his head below the parapet in Baghdad.

With little thought for sound military tactics, one of Jawhar's subordinate generals, Ja'far, took it upon himself to halt the Qarmation advance. He blundered into a trap and was killed, thus exposing the newly won Egypt once more to the Qarmation threat. General Jawhar was besieged in his new garrison town. However, by a cunning combination of superior military tactics on his part and sums of gold placed in the hands of the right Qarmation officers, Jawhar managed to inflict a severe defeat upon his enemies, driving them out of Egypt and taking more of Syria. Thus began the Fatimid caliphate in Egypt.

His newly built palace ready for him, and following a trip to review conditions in his base in Sardinia and his dependency of Sicily, "Caliph" al-Mu'izz arrived in Cairo from Tunisia in 973 with all his possessions and the coffins of his ancestors. General Jawar was retired with honour and wealth. Yaqub ben Killis was made vizier, and the sermonizing Mu'izz proceeded to instruct his new subjects, who were largely Sunni, on the Shiism he represented, which, apart from a special reverence for the Prophet's daughter, was just the same as far as they could tell as that of the fanatical enemy who had just been driven out the country.

There is an apocryphal story that the pious al-Mu'izz, when asked about his assertion of descent from Fatima, confirmed the authenticity of his pedigree by brandishing his sword and announcing "Here is my blood-line."

In the following year the Qarmations returned and besieged the caliph in his new capital. Once more they were driven out enabling the Fatimids to expand in Syria, to the Hejaz province of western

Arabia, and to establish an eastern border facing the Buwaihids in Mesopotamia. At this point the Fatimid empire reached from Tangiers to Mecca. With the rise of the Fatimids and the continued weakening of the Buwaihids in the last quarter of the 10th century the centre of influence of the Muslim world moved from Iraq to Egypt. It was never to return.

The early decades of rule by the Fatimids were marked by memorable artistic and cultural achievement, notably in architecture. The leaders amassed immense personal wealth and surrounded themselves with luxury and elaborate formal ceremony. But they also established a school system that was wide in its enrolment. As with the early Abbasids, during their acme the Fatimids had little better to do with their riches once the needs of state and of their families had been satisfied, than to invest it in scholarship, art and architecture, monuments to their enterprise and joyous celebration of their Faith.

One of the Fatimids' important early moves was to shift the main lines of trade with the Orient from Arabia and the Persian Gulf, whither it had moved under the Abbasids, to Egypt and the Red Sea. Alexandria strengthened its position as the transit point for luxury goods transshipped from the East to the Arab world, and also to new markets in the West beginning to show signs of prosperity. Fatimid fleets controlled the eastern Mediterranean and much of the Indian Ocean. They expanded foreign trade and the export of Egyptian product. Revenues not only enriched the rulers but the people also enjoyed times of plenty. Population quickly increased, triggering problems. While the Viking, Erik "the Red" and his son, Leif, were colonizing Greenland in mild weather in 980-1000 and exploring the American coast, and wine grapes and olives were being harvested in England, drought and famine appeared in Mesopotamia and north Africa.

In the early 11th century, as al-Qadir, the only *Hanbali* caliph, was striving to exercise authority in Iraq, and Umayyad Spain was overwhelmed by civil conflict, although nominally under the apparently insane command of the 3rd Egyptian caliph (titled al-Hakim), the Fatimid nation rose to become the most powerful polity in the Muslim world. Despite being ravaged by exceptional temperatures and consequent famine in the years 1000-1007, Cairo became Islam's pre-eminent spiritual and intellectual centre.

The Egyptian Caliph al-Hakim is worshipped as divine by the heretical Druze sect of the Ismailis now living mainly in Syria and Lebanon. In today's Lebanon, the Druzes are a significant element in the political

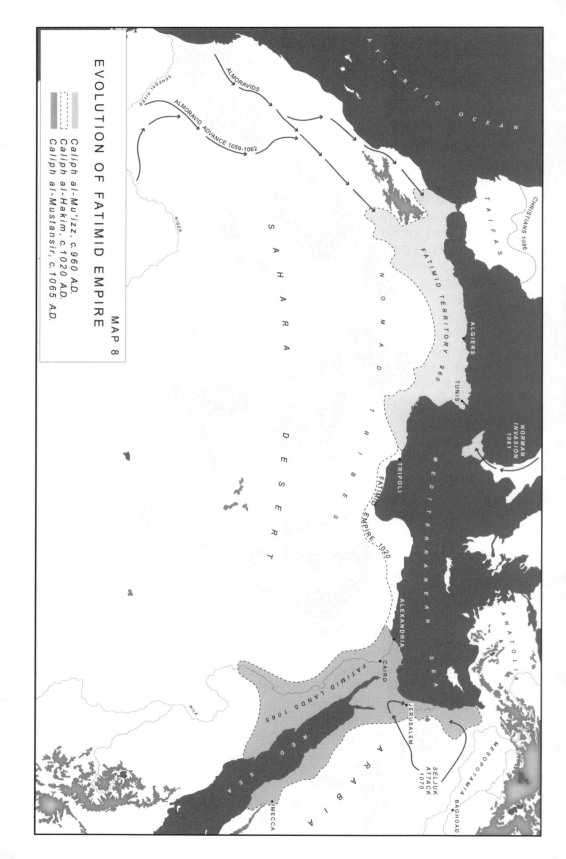

MAP 8

EVOLUTION OF FATIMID EMPIRE

Caliph al-Mu'izz, c.960 A.D.
Caliph al-Hakim, c.1020 A.D.
Caliph al-Mustansir, c.1065 A.D.

ALMORAVIDS

ALMORAVID ADVANCE 1059-1062

SENEGAL RIVER

NIGER

S A H A R A   D E S E R T

N O M A D   T R I B E S

ATLANTIC OCEAN

CHRISTIANS 1086

T A I F A S

FATIMID TERRITORY 960

ALGIERS

TUNIS

NORMAN INVASION 1061

FATIMID EMPIRE 1020

TRIPOLI

M E D I T E R R A N E A N   S E A

ALEXANDRIA

CAIRO

NILE

FATIMID LANDS 1065

R E D   S E A

A N A T O L I A

MESOPOTAMIA

BAGHDAD

JERUSALEM

SELJUK ATTACK 1070

A R A B I A

MECCA

mosaic. The blue-eyed al-Hakim, enthroned at the age of eleven, was the son of a Russian Christian slave mother. Jealous of his rights and suspicious of those around him, at the age of fifteen he is said to have murdered his tutor, Barjuwan, and imposed a reign of terror on Cairo. As the "Caligula of the East", guilty of bizarre conduct, executing and mutilating many of his closest, he announced that he was divine, an incarnation of Allah. He disappeared in 1021 at the age of thirty-six, likely assassinated, rather than ensconced in occultation, another Hidden Imam, as the Druzes would have us believe, reappearing, they hold, as the true *Mahdi* when the tribulations of Mankind become intolerable. Most sects and sub-sects of Shiism have their own *Mahdi-in-Hiding*.

Under the guidance of his talented vizier, al-Jarjar, both of whose hands had been cut off by al-Hakim, the 5th Egyptian Caliph, the mulatto al-Mustansir, enthroned at the age of seven, was able to maintain much of the power and prestige of his caliphate until he began to falter with the death of the vizier in 1045. A decade later, following another devastating two-year famine, al-Mustansir, still in his spirited twenties but lacking the wise counsels of al-Jawar, let loose on the unruly people of Libya and Tunisia the wild tribes of the Beni Hilal and Beni Sulaim, who had migrated into Egypt from Arabia in the 8th century conquest. (It was they who are said to have introduced the Arabian horse to Africa.) These tribesmen, given their head, swept "like an army of locusts" along the already desertifying north African coast, sacking the Tunisian capital and accelerating the deterioration of the region.

In 1057, however, Caliph al-Mustansir supported a Buwaihid general, Turkic soldier of fortune Arslan al-Basasiri, in holding Iraq as a vassal Egyptian province while the Seljuks, who had overthrown the Buwaihid régime two years before, were occupied dealing with a rebellion in their ranks in Khorasan, 900 miles to the east. Until the Seljuk leader, Toghril Beg "the Falcon", was able to return to Baghdad a year later, General Basasiri held Iraq for the Egyptian Fatimids. At Caliph al-Mustansir's behest the General proclaimed Shiism from the halls of power of Sunni Baghdad, prevailing upon Abbasid Caliph al-Qa'im to swear allegiance to his rival in Cairo.

Egyptian Caliph al-Mustansir faced violent rivalry between Turkic, Berber and negro elements of his army. As he aged he began to lose control, losing power to the military, just as the Abbasids in Baghdad had lost it to the army two centuries before. The economy suffered further and structural decay made its appearance in Egypt proper. With the great famine of 1065-72 national order and discipline evaporated. Some of the Fatimid leaders converted to Sunni Islam. In the middle of the famine the military commander, Nasir ud-Daula, brought his army into Cairo, ransacked the Caliph's palace and reduced him and his family to poverty. General ud-Daula negotiated with Baghdad to return Egypt to the Sunni faith, but was assassinated before achieving his aim. Ud-Daula's assassin became vizier and, with the country beyond redemption, the following decades were times of unremitting violence and anarchy, worsened by more famine and pestilence. In the later part of the century the caliphs of impoverished Cairo were kept as little more than puppets by the viziers and generals; *plus ça change!*

The Fatimid golden age of wealth, power and confidence had lasted only as long as the Abbasid, some sixty years. And then in 1070, Jerusalem was lost to Alp Arslan "the Lion", the new leader of the Seljuks who at the age of thirty-eight succeeded his uncle, the childless Falcon.

Soon after Caliph al-Mustansir's death in 1094 the first Crusaders, mainly Franks, arrived in Palestine, taking the holy territory from the Fatimids. Turmoil continued in Egypt, including the crucifixion in 1125 of a vizier and his five brothers after losing battles against the Franks. The caliph who ordered this, al-Amir, who had become the seventh Fatimid Caliph at the age of five, was killed by the Assassins when he was in his early thirties. Of the last four Fatimid caliphs, last of a line of child caliphs fought over by scheming viziers, one was murdered by his vizier at the age of twenty-two, one died of anguish (or perhaps during an epileptic seizure, as suggested by a different account) at the age of ten, and the last one, the eleventh Egyptian caliph, was, questionably, executed in 1171 at the age of twenty by Salah al-Din Yusuf, "Saladin", the Kurd who would shine brightly in the Arab firmament. The Fatimids had ruled Egypt for 202 years.

When Caliph al-Mustansir died in 1094, in his sixties, the established religion of the Ismaili Fatimid empire, still under pressure from members of the ruling caste to convert to Sunni Islam, as the majority of the population was still Sunni, divided into an Egyptian Ismaili branch and a Syrian-Persian branch. The latter in turn divided into other branches, the Khoja – with 15 million followers today in Iran, Syria, India, Pakistan and East Africa – becoming the most prominent.

The Seljuks:
The dominant tribe of the twenty-four comprising the Turkic Oghuz confederation living along the eastern side of the Caspian Sea (now Turkmenistan) had been converted by Sufi missionaries to Sunni Islam. In 1031 they crossed the Oxus River in search of better lands and booty, and were quickly incorporated into the frontier force of an eastern Persian prince. The Seljuks soon took command of their host's lands – the barbarian problem again. Joining with other eastern Sunni princes over the next fifteen years, with the zeal typical of converts, the Seljuks campaigned resolutely against the Shiite Buwaihids. Under Toghril Beg, the Seljuks took Azerbaijan and Armenia and, following an appeal from Abbasid Caliph al-Qa'im in 1055, they entered Baghdad without a fight, freeing Iraq from the loose hold of its politically divided Buwaihid masters. General Basasiri fled. The Buwaihid chief Malik al-Rahim was taken prisoner. With the restoration of Sunni dominance over Iraq, al-Qa'im welcomed the Falcon as his deliverer from the heretics, granting him the title "King of the East and the West". The Caliph though was not too surprised when the seventy-year-old Falcon added Mesopotamia to Persia under his own rule while indulging himself in the victor's right of taking the Caliph's daughter to wife.

As the Seljuk capital remained in Ray (near Tehran) on the plain at the foot of the Elburz Mountains, al-Qa'im was allowed to remain on his throne in Baghdad. And as Sunnis, the Seljuks would pay more respect to the Caliph than the Buwaihids had, adding the cloak of legitimacy to their conquest. The Seljuk leaders, as supreme secular authorities, assumed the title of Sultan, commanding government and the armed forces. They left spiritual matters to al-Qa'im who once again had his own vizier as a symbol of the restoration at least of his religious authority.

Like the caliphal court in Golden Age Abbasid times, two and a half centuries before, the courts of the Seljuk sultans (but not those of the caliphs) were comprised of Persian viziers, Christian geographers, poets, scribes, jesters, storytellers, mathematicians, Jewish doctors and Hindu astrologers. One of these was the Persian Omar Khayyam (1048-1131) whose *Rubáiyát* in translation by Edward FitzGerald so enchanted the English-speaking world in the late 19th and 20th centuries. Famously, but possibly erroneously attributed to Omar Khayyam is the quatrain:

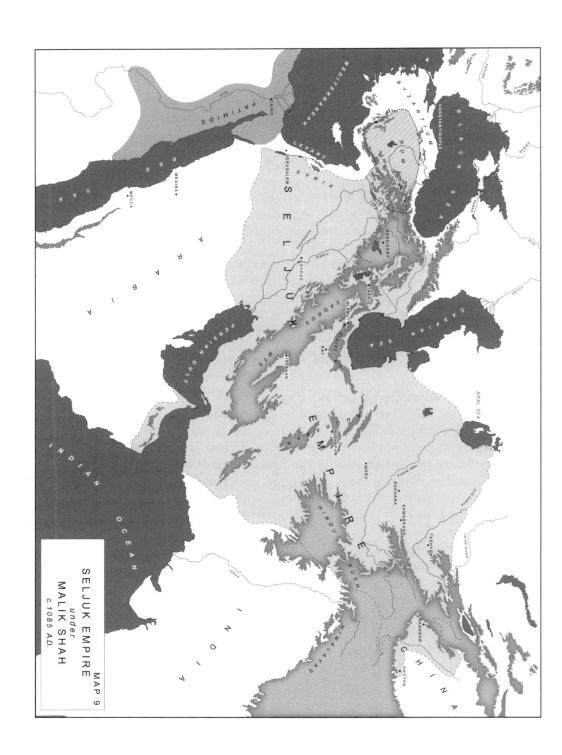

SELJUK EMPIRE
under
MALIK SHAH
c. 1085 A.D.

MAP 9

Here with a Loaf of Bread beneath the Bough
A Flask of Wine, a Book of Verse – and Thou
Beside me singing in the Wilderness –
And Wilderness is Paradise enow.

Omar Khayyam, son of a tent-maker, was born in the ancient city of Nishapur (Neyshabur) in Khorasan on the Silk Route to Samarkand and China. In 1038, ten years before Omar Khayyam was born, Toghril Beg had taken Nishapur on his line of attack towards Baghdad. It appears however that from the beginning this warring Seljuk chieftain encouraged scholarship and the arts, providing fertile ground for the gifted. The eloquent Omar Khayyam was a man of encyclopedic learning. Philosophy, law, history and medicine were among the subjects he mastered. As a phenomenal young scholar he served as astronomer, mathematician and poet to Alp Arslan's son, Malik Shah, when barely twenty-four years old, Malik Shah being six years his junior. Alp Arslan and Malik Shah were fortunate though to enjoy the tutelage of the legendary Persian vizier Nizam al-Mulk, author of the *Siyasset-Nameh, The Book of Government* (preceding Niccolo Machiavelli's *Prince* by four centuries, and Adam Smith's *Wealth of Nations* by seven). It was under Nizam's guidance that the network of religious schools called *madrassas* was established through much of the Islamic world. In about 1067 the Lion also established a major seat of adult learning in Baghdad, the Nizamayeh Academy, named after his vizier. The great theologian al-Ghazali taught at this Academy in the period 1091-96, and it was during that time that he was driven to characterize the caliphate and Islamic leadership as necessarily autocratic so as to maintain solidarity among the Faithful.

In 1070, Alp Arslan drove into Palestine, expelling the Fatimid government from Jerusalem. He extended his reach into Anatolia where in 1071 at Manzikert (today's Malazgirt, on the upper reaches of a source of the Euphrates) he defeated the Byzantine army, capturing the Emperor, Romanus IV Diogenes. Alp Arslan treated his imperial captive respectfully and freed him after agreeing ransom terms. Emperor Romanus was treated less respectfully when he arrived home, where he was overthrown and had his eyes gouged out by his stepson, Michael VII Ducas, thereby voiding the agreement with Alp Arslan. This defeat at Manzikert marked the beginning of the end of the Byzantine empire.

The Seljuks however were at the limit of their capacity, over-extended, and the Egyptians were soon able to take Jerusalem back. Just after this, while campaigning on the Oxus River, in a moment of disdainful indiscretion, the Lion was fatally stabbed by a captive chieftain named Yusuf Khurezmi while the Sultan was preparing to have the chieftain staked out and cut into pieces.

Malik Shah acceded to the throne, but the empire soon began to divide under the rivalries of the many branches of the imperial family. The most powerful division, founded by a cousin in Anatolia in 1077, was the Sultanate of Rum which lasted until 1243.

In 1086 Malik Shah recaptured Jerusalem and held it until he died of poisoning six years later, at the age of thirty-eight. The instability resulting from Malik Shah's death was intensified by competition between the mothers of his several sons. As with their predecessors, the Seljuks' Muslim custom of dividing their empire between the sons and brothers of the deceased leader led to civil war and the Seljuk empire's disintegration The united Seljuks under Malik Shah and his father had been the most powerful Muslim state for forty years. One of the results of the break-up was that the Fatimids of Egypt were again able to occupy Jerusalem. Then, in 1099, the crusaders arrived in the Levant and Jerusalem changed hands once more.

During their ascendancy over the caliphate the Seljuks, militarily strong though governmentally weak, failed to prevent the arrival from Egypt and the spreading to Syria and Persia of a Fatimid-related Ismaili sect, the Nizaris, the infamous Assassins (from the Arabic *hashishin*, hashish-eaters – Assassins, infamous in the West but revered in much of the Ismaili world as sincere believers in the teachings of the *Rasa'il* of the Brethren). For 250 years in the 11th–13th centuries these suicide martyrs were sent out in their scores (but often singly and with only a knife) by the Old Man of the Mountain, as the successive Grand Masters of the sect were called, to kill Abbasid and Fatimid princes and Christians (though at times, allied with Sunnis or Christians). They murdered Nizam al-Mulk, at the instance of Sultan Malik Shah it was rumoured, just before the Sultan's own death, assassinated it was also rumoured by Nizam's servants in revenge for the murder of their master. In their youth, interestingly, Omar Khayyam had been a friend of the Persian founder of the Assassins, Hassan i-Sabbah. The Assassins were not ousted from their Elburz Mountains "Eagles' Nest" fortress of Alamut and eliminated in Persia until the Mongol invasion of the mid-13th century. Marco Polo was the first to bring word of the Assassins to Europe, having passed through the Alamut area c. 1271-72, fifteen years after their removal.

The term Nizari derives from Prince Nizar, eldest son of Fatimid Caliph al-Mustansir, who was passed over by the autocratic vizier of the time, an Armenian named Badr al-Jamali, for the Egyptian throne upon the death of the Caliph, in favour of a younger son, Ahmed. Ahmed became the sixth Egyptian Caliph, entitled al-Mustali (r.1094-1101). His elder half-brother Prince Nizar and Nizar's son were murdered in prison in Egypt. Vizier al-Jamali died soon after the caliph whose will he had frustrated. According to Assassin tradition an infant grandson of Prince Nizar was smuggled out to Persia and was brought up by Hassan i-Sabbah to found a new line of leaders of the sect. The 4th Grand Master of the Assassins, Hasan ala Dhikrihi, claimed to be the son of the infant smuggled out of Egypt and founded a new branch of the sect, the Khoja. The present-day philanthropic Aga Khans, heads of this branch of the Ismailis, are his spiritual, if not biological, descendants.

Malik Shah's 20-year term as Sultan of Iraq (1072-92) coincided with al-Muqtadi's reign (1075-94) as 27th Abbasid Caliph. As the Seljuk empire reached its summit of influence, the Sultan allowed the Caliph to be recognized in Muslim Asia as head of the church and nominal head of state. In reality the Caliph had no more power than his predecessors even though he was married to a daughter of the Sultan's.

In the same year (1094) that both Fatimid Caliph al-Mustansir and his vizier al-Jamali died in Egypt, Abbasid Caliph al-Muqtadi died in Iraq and was succeeded by his son, al-Mustazhir. This Abbasid caliph, having no stake in the ensuing fratricidal conflict, remained a passive onlooker while Malik Shah's teenaged sons and their supporters fought it out for power after their father's death. Iraq ended up in the hands of one of the branches of the Seljuks, led after 1105 – following another period of disorder – by Sultan Mohammed who kept his capital in Khorasan, leaving Iraq again as a distant province controlled by governors. After him, Seljuk power in Iraq faded to a point that encouraged local governors, warlords and bedouin tribal chiefs to seize provincial power for themselves. In later years, as responsibility for Baghdad's defence against rebellion rested upon the caliph, one entitled al-Muqtafi II, the 31st Abbasid leader, was able to form a defence force of his own. By about 1155 this force had been able to impose order on the greater part of Iraq. The caliph's militia eventually became strong enough to challenge his Seljuk masters and drive them from much of the country, while leaving many of the immigrant Seljuk pastoralist nomads – Turkmens – in place. At the time of their fall the Seljuks had governed most of Iraq and much of Persia for 100 years.

8

Resurgent Europe

Norman Sicily – The Reconquest of Spain

Norman Sicily:

Following raids by Syrian Arabs that had begun in the mid-600s, in the 820s, Tunisians, allied at times with fighters from Spain sent by Abd ar-Rahman II, made a base for themselves at Palermo on the island of Sicily. It took seventy years however to complete the conquest of the island. A century later the Fatimids of Egypt replaced their Tunisian cousins in command. But, in what might be described as the first nail in the coffin of Arab commercial hegemony over the Mediterranean, starting as early as 871– while in Baghdad the Abbasids were occupied with the Zanj slave revolt – corsair bases on the northern shore of the Mediterranean in France and Italy began to be dislodged by Christian forces. Crete and Cyprus were retaken by the Greeks between 961 and 965.

In 1061, Norman adventurers led by Count Roger de Hauteville (with the connivance of the Pontiff), crossed from Italy into Arab Sicily, landing at Messina no great distance from the Arab capital of Palermo. A decade later the Normans led by Roger and his elder brother Robert, then Duke of Apulia and Calabria, took Palermo and over the following twenty years drove the rest of Egyptian Caliph al-Mustansir's vassal forces out of the island, creating a homeland for themselves.

In 1087, while anarchy and famine were taking hold of Egypt during the Fatimids' failing years the last of the Arab bases and pirate lairs on

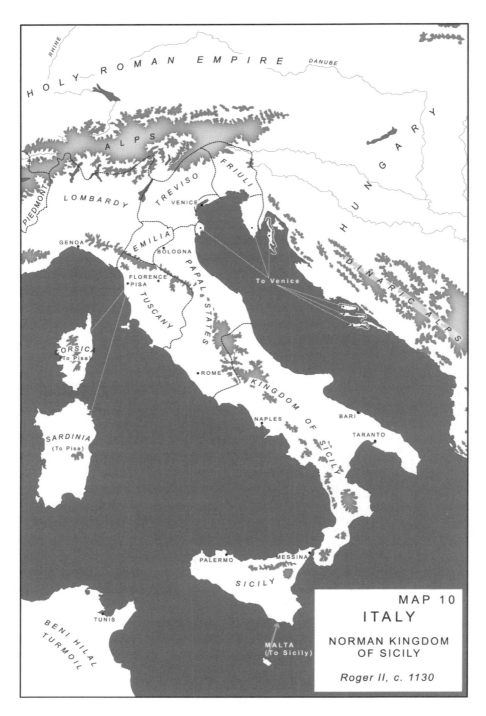

RHINE

HOLY ROMAN EMPIRE

DANUBE

ALPS

H U N G A R Y

PIEDMONT

LOMBARDY

TREVISO

FRIULI

VENICE

GENOA

EMILIA

BOLOGNA

D I N A R I C   A L P S

FLORENCE
PISA

TUSCANY

PAPAL STATES

To Venice

CORSICA
(To Pisa)

ROME

KINGDOM

NAPLES

BARI

OF

TARANTO

SARDINIA
(To Pisa)

SICILY

PALERMO

MESSINA

SICILY

BENI HILAL
TURMOIL

TUNIS

MALTA
(To Sicily)

MAP 10

ITALY

NORMAN KINGDOM
OF SICILY

Roger II, c. 1130

the mainland Italian coast were driven out by men from Genoa and Pisa. Then the Normans sailed to Malta, fifty miles off the south coast of Sicily, and expelled the Tunisian Arabs from this stepping-stone to the north African shore. At the same time the men of Pisa expelled the Saracens from their old strategic bases in Corsica and Sardinia.

At the time of the conquest of England in 1066 by William "the Bastard", Duke of Normandy (who also had the blessing of the Pope Alexander II for that attack), the Norman invaders of Sicily found a civilian population of Goths, Arabs, Romans, Jews and Greeks. With the arrival of the Normans many of the cultured civilian population of Sicily, mostly Arabs and Jews, fled to Tunis and Cairo. Others were driven out. (They did though leave behind their secrets of how to distil alcohol – *al-kohl*.) From those who remained, the formidable French-speaking invaders – many of them little removed from their Viking ancestors, although some of their leaders were men of refinement – oversaw a remarkable mixed culture. They sheltered and financed artists, teachers and scientists, many of them Muslims, and added to the transfer of knowledge and sophistication from the Islamic to the Christian world. In the intellectual, artistic and commercial spheres it was the Arabs and Jews who provided the infrastructure of this society, guided as circumstances dictated by Norman nobles. The Arabs had greatly increased farm production in the island by encouraging irrigation of the farmlands. As in Umayyad Spain, they had introduced many worthwhile agricultural products – oranges, mulberries, sugarcane, date-palms and cotton – in the then warm climatic conditions.

Count Roger of Sicily's (fifth) son, also named Roger, obtained papal agreement to be raised to the rank of king. He was duly enthroned in Palermo Cathedral in 1130 as Roger II, King of Sicily and southern Italy. The king employed Arab soldiers and military planners in his expansionist wars in the south of Italy, and Arab engineers for his construction work. He enriched the cultural character of his court by adopting the Arab practice of appointing poets to his entourage. Roger II's grandson, William II, spoke Arabic, and his subjects in Palermo looked and dressed like Arabs. Thousands wept when he died, his death being in the presence of his Arab astrologer and his Arab doctor. (In the *Divine Comedy*, Dante placed this King William "the Good" in Paradise.)

The Normans ruled Sicily until the end of the 12th century when they were ousted by Germans, the Holy Roman Emperors. Even so, official records continued for a time to be kept in Arabic as well as Latin and

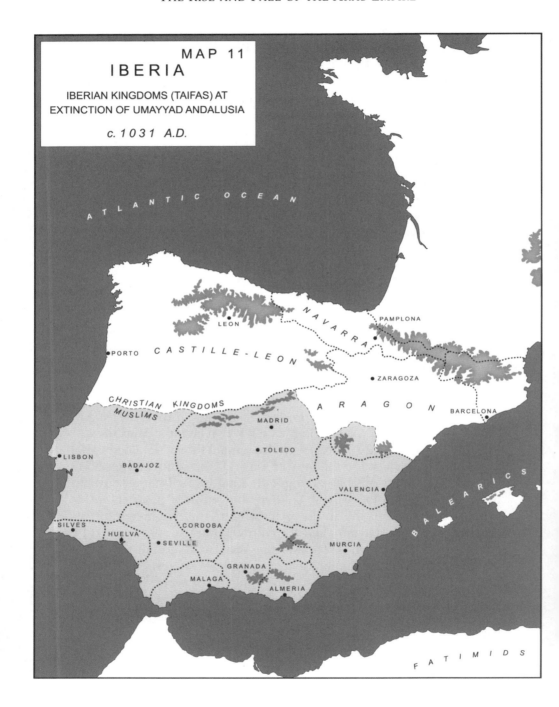

MAP 11
IBERIA

IBERIAN KINGDOMS (TAIFAS) AT
EXTINCTION OF UMAYYAD ANDALUSIA

c. 1031 A.D.

ATLANTIC OCEAN

LEON

NAVARRA

PAMPLONA

PORTO

CASTILLE-LEON

ZARAGOZA

CHRISTIAN KINGDOMS
MUSLIMS

ARAGON

BARCELONA

MADRID

LISBON

BADAJOZ

TOLEDO

VALENCIA

BALEARICS

SILVES

HUELVA

CORDOBA

SEVILLE

MURCIA

GRANADA

MALAGA

ALMERIA

FATIMIDS

Greek. The German rulers were replaced by French in 1268. Fourteen years later a rampaging populace in Palermo massacred 4,000 of their French persecutors in the "Sicilian Vespers" revolt, launched at vespers prayer time on Easter Monday, and financed secretly by Emperor Michael VIII Paleologus – in a rare example of truly Byzantine diplomacy, executed just before the Emperor's own unexpected death. After this, Sicily and southern Italy became part of the empire of Spain's kingdom of Aragon. This rebellion drew the battle-lines for a long-term Franco-Hispanic confrontation, reverberations of which would continue to the 19th century. (Some people claim fancifully that the secret societies that fomented the Sicilian Vespers revolt were the ancestors of the 19th-century Mafia.)

In the absence of Arab rule and of records being kept in that language, Arabic died out in Sicily, and the Muslim religion faded away through emigration and recantation. With changes of ruling family and governing power – Norman, German, French, Spanish and others – the Kingdom of Sicily (alternately, the Kingdom of the Two Sicilies and the Kingdom of Naples) lasted as a political entity with borders ebbing and flowing until it was overcome by Garibaldi's Thousand in 1860, eight hundred years after this earlier Norman conquest.

The Reconquest of Spain:

While Arabs were governing Sicily, the Umayyad emirate of Andalusia, self-styled "caliphate" since Abd ar-Rahman III's assumption of a caliphal title, was rapidly approaching its end. Municipal records show that in about 970, Córdoba was still the largest city in the West with 113,000 houses, 70 libraries and bookshops, and 21 outlying suburbs. (A different source says 213,000 houses and 60,300 noble mansions.) By the turn of the century however, the bindings of the ruling dynasty had undone. Civil war broke out reflecting complex inter-communal rivalries and the usual inheritance disputes. After the death in 1002 of the vizier Almanzor, as repeatedly happened in the Arab world following the death of a powerful leader, the state broke up. All the larger cities of Spain such as Granada, Valencia, Toledo and Seville then reconstituted themselves as mini-states, known in Arabic as *taifas*, party-kingdoms. After four decades as an independent "republic" Córdoba was absorbed in 1070 by its ally, Seville.

In the mountainous northern regions of Spain several small areas were never conquered by the Moors: Asturias, Navarra and Aragon.

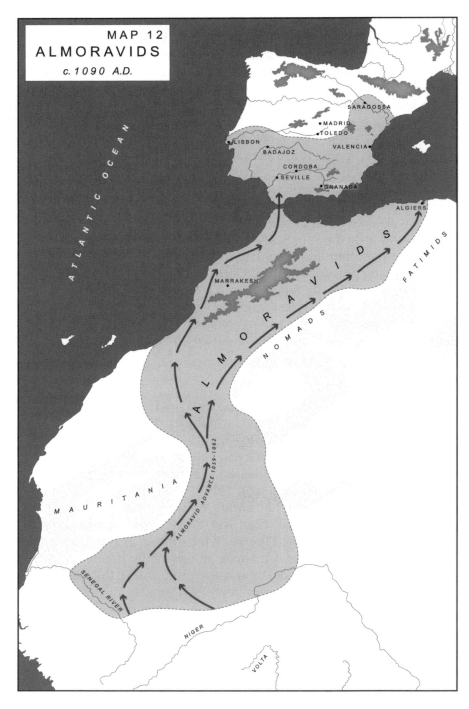

MAP 12
ALMORAVIDS
c. 1090 A.D.

ATLANTIC OCEAN

SARAGOSSA

MADRID
TOLEDO
LISBON
VALENCIA
BADAJOZ
CORDOBA
SEVILLE
GRANADA

ALGIERS

A L M O R A V I D S

MARRAKESH

FATIMIDS

NOMADS

MAURITANIA

ALMORAVID ADVANCE 1059-1062

SENEGAL RIVER

NIGER

VOLTA

All of these eventually became Christian kingdoms. The kingdom of Navarra was founded in the Pyrenees area c. 900. Later in that century the kingdom of Asturias was founded with its capital in León and when, with wilting Umayyad power, Asturias expanded southwards, it gave birth to the Kingdom of Castile in 1031. In 1037, Castile extending south and eastwards to the Mediterranean coast gave rise in turn to the Kingdom of Aragon. By 1031 when the last Umayyad caliph, Hisham III, was assassinated, more than two dozen *taifas* – some of them not much more than armed villages – had replaced the once great nation of *Al-Andalus*. Into these statelets Castile-León and Navarra then expanded, taking by force what had been taken from the Visigoths by force 300 years before.

In 1085 (when the Domesday Book was being completed in England for William the Conqueror, and the 230-foot embroidered Tapestry had just been brought to Bayeux) Alfonso VI of Castile, flushed with success in expelling the Arabs from the little town of Madrid two years before, took the key city of Toledo, freeing many European slaves and for the first time leaving great numbers of Muslims under Christian rule. Alfonso's free-lance general Rodrigo Dìaz de Vivar, who sold his military services equally to Muslim princes, was to the Christians that paragon of noble chivalry, to the Moors that unprincipled adventurer, El Cid.

Toledo, at the geographical central point of Spain, had for centuries been the home of the largest Jewish community in the country, some 12,000 people. With this capture, Judeo-Muslim learning became available to Christendom, adding to the stream of enlightenment out of the Middle East. The cathedral schools of the West, some of which would become universities, became the particular beneficiaries. Alfonso's victory at Toledo was not only the first telling political move in the Christian reconquest of Iberia; it was also, together with the Norman conquest of England, a key move in the reawakening of Europe. These military successes foreshadowed the rise of the West.

It was at this time that a Norman poet – perhaps Turold – wrote the earliest *chanson de geste,* the masterpiece *Chanson de Roland* inspired by the Christian advance and a fabled battle between (in fact) the Franks and the Basques, not the Moors. Nevertheless, the range and quality of medieval Muslim poetry was still unsurpassed.

In c. 1060, the Almoravids, a *confrérie* of camel-mounted militants, veiled like their womenfolk and speaking dialects of the Berber language, had ridden out of the Senegal river valley and Mauritania to bring the fractious Muslims of north-east Africa back to the path of righteousness. They had founded Marrakesh in Morocco as their capital. Called by the *taifa* kings of Spain to help stem the Christian advance, the Almoravids led by Yusuf bin Tashfin had crossed the Straits of Gibraltar in 1083. Moving north they quickly absorbed the *taifas* of southern Spain and in 1086 at Badagoz on the (present day) Portuguese border they defeated Alphonso VI's forces, sending cart-loads of Christian heads to the cities of Spain to drive home their mes-sage – we have come for your land and your women.

The Christians were slow to regroup, but in 1094 the doughty El Cid won back the Mediterranean port of Valencia. He offered it to King Alfonso who made him Duke of the city. Soon after El Cid's death however in 1099 the Moors recaptured Valencia and, while failing to retake Toledo, they reached into northeast Spain, into the king-dom of Aragon, taking Saragossa its capital. The tide of battle finally turned against the Almoravids in 1118 when the Christians regained Saragossa. During the next thirty years divisions arose among the Muslims and the disunited emirate broke up into another set of mini-kingdoms, again greatly weakening Islam in Spain.

In 1147, a fleet of Christian knights, Germans and French with a sprinkling of English, on their way to crusade in Anatolia, landed at and captured Lisbon, on the Atlantic Ocean. Many of the men then decided to remain in the attractive lands around that city, and founded what would become the Kingdom of Portugal.

Later that same year, the Almohads, another wave of puritani-cal, Tamazight-speaking Berbers arrived from Morocco under Abd al-Mumin, and displaced the Almoravids. They failed though to recapture Lisbon, ending Islam's centuries-long occupation of much of Atlantic coastal Iberia. The Almohads made Seville their capital, a rich agricultural town with access to the Ocean, fifty miles down the Guadalquivir and entry to the Mediterranean by the Straits of Gibraltar. Córdoba, a dependency of the powerful Seville ninety miles downstream, remained the cultural heart of Spain.

The Almohads battled many times with the Christians, winning a resounding victory over them at Alarcos in 1195 under the command of Yaqub al-Mansur, defeating Alphonso VIII of Castile. Seventeen years later the Almohads, led by "Caliph" al-Nasir, were beaten by the same Alphonso VIII at Navas de Tolosa. Alphonso had united his forces with those of his rivals Aragon and Navarra, and this victory marked the beginning of the end of the Almohad emirate and of five hundred years of Muslim domination of Spain (712-1212).

The two Berber régimes had each been master of Moorish Spain for about sixty years – a familiar term. Zealous warriors seize the land and its resources, their sons savour it, their wastrel grandsons and great-grandsons lose it.

Both Berber régimes mellowed from zealotry to principled government and patronage of scholarship and the arts, although in the early days the Almohads persecuted and hounded out Jews of talent. One of these, the Córdoban Maimonides, the most celebrated Jewish philosopher of the age, became physician to Saladin, when in residence, and to Saladin's vizier in Cairo. Maimonides' philosophical writings would inspire his co-religionist, Baruch Spinoza, living in Amsterdam centuries later.

After about 1220, few of the Moorish *taifas* which had reappeared with the collapse of the Almohads were any match for militant Christianity. Córdoba fell in 1236, Valencia again in 1238, and Seville in 1248 with the ethnic cleansing of all its Muslims. At the same time, the Muslim population of Minorca in the Balearic Islands was taken by the Christians and enslaved. (The Spanish were more partial to slavery than most other Western Europeans.)

By mid-century, the remaining Moors had been driven to the extreme south of the country, around the Sierra Nevada mountains. Here, the 30,000-sq km Nasrid emirate was founded by Mohammed al-Ahmar in 1238. Its capital, Granada, became a centre of refinement, learning and riches, of artists, scientists and physicians. With rugged, stony hills separating broad areas of fertile and wooded countryside, eucalyptus forests fringing the shoreline, Mediterranean ports fostering Atlantic coastal trade and fishing, seventy walled towns and a population reaching 400,000, the emirate flourished despite adversities for two-and-a-half centuries.

Remarkably, even though political decline of Muslim Spain through the rivalry of its leaders was well under way by the late 11th century, intellectual life was little diminished. With the Almohads in power, "Averroës", Abu al-Walid bin Rushd (1126-98), scientist, Maliki scholar, philosopher and physician of genius, mentor of Maimonides – and sponsored at times by Yaqub al-Mansur – profoundly influenced Christian theological thinking through his writings in Córdoba. Averroës believed that religion contained "truth", even though such truth was often veiled in allegory. He sided with the Brethren of Purity in the view that religion represented the route to truth and salvation for the simpler mind, for the unlettered multitude. He also said, in paraphrase, "that the relegation of women to the sole task of procreation is probably one of the causes of poverty and the decline of (Muslim) civilization."

Averroës who over a period of three decades of study introduced Europe to the great works of Aristotle, a mainspring of medieval European "natural philosophy", the study of nature and the physical universe, and a major factor in the evolution of Christian doctrine. His comments on Aristotle, written despite the objections of many of the *ulema,* were translated into Hebrew by the Jewish physician Ibn Tibbon of Marseille, who corresponded also with Maimonides.

Averroës' writings were translated as well into Latin by the Holy Roman Emperor Frederick II's Scottish savant and astrologer, Michael Scot, in c. 1220-30. The work of these men and of the prolific but shadowy Gerard of Cremona working in Toledo in Alfonso VII's time (1126-57) spread Arabic, Greek and Hispano-Hebrew scholarship throughout Europe. It has been related that Averroës also introduced Euclid's *Elements* to Europe; but a copy of this commanding work may well have been translated into Latin and spirited out of Spain half a century earlier by Adelard of Bath, in about 1120. But this story may be mythical.

The laying of the foundation stones for the first great Gothic cathedrals at this time indicates the growing wealth of western Europe. Foundations were laid in the mid-12th century, with several consecrations by the mid-13th. Also, the best-known western European poem of the late medieval period, Guillaume de Loris' *Roman de la Rose,* was written at the same time, about 1230. *La Rose* is important as the first allegorical narrative to be written in the first person, a dream vision about love. The second part, by Jean de Meun and completed in about 1280, is radically different, often satirical and containing an encyclopedic mass of information drawn from other works. This poem, which Geoffrey Chaucer translated into English, is said to have been the single most important literary influence in his writings.

Muslim philosophical endeavours in Spain ended with Averroës' death in 1198, and his views on the nature of "truth" were largely set aside with the death the next year of Yaqub al-Mansur. With their deaths, liberal culture was eclipsed in Spain and radical fundamentalism, ossified a century later by the pronouncement of Ahmed bin Taymiyya that "caliphal tyranny was better than free-thinking anarchy", put an end to the ungodly speculations of philosophy in the Muslim world.

The 20th-century British philosopher Bertrand Russell, however, argued that Arabic philosophy was never like non-Islamic thinking because Muslim "philosophers" were actually only "commentators". Because the faithful Muslim must allow reason to give way to revelation, there could be no such thing as an Islamic philosopher, philosophy depending on reason without restrictions on the intellect. He considered that Islamic revelation had burdened Muslim thinkers with an insuperable philosophical handicap. Muslim "philosophy" had been solely the quest for confirmation of the truths that had been revealed to mankind through the Prophet Mohammed.

The idea of the communication of enlightenment and information by divine agency was rooted in all three Abrahamic religions and it took a long time for it to loosen its grip on Christian thought. Yet even before the time of Charlemagne there had been Christian thinkers who believed that philosophy must be separated from the study of religion and religious ideas and beliefs.

Revelation to more outspoken Western thinkers was "the great blight of intellect". In 1260, the Italian, Thomas Aquinas, who had read in translation some of the writings of the sage, al-Ghazali, argued that reason alone was a source of truth. It was legitimate in its own terms without qualification. He maintained that reason and faith were naturally in harmony as they belonged to quite different intellectual realms. But much earlier than this, in the 1120s, the Frenchman Pierre Abélard had written in his *Sic et Non* that "By doubting we come to enquiry, and by enquiry we grasp truth".

Medieval Spain had no equal. During the time of the early Almohad Moors there were six kingdoms in the country and all three Abrahamic religions. A dozen or more languages were spoken – Arabic, Tamazight, Castilian, Portuguese, Galician, Asturian, Aragonese, Catalan, Basque, Hebrew, and Ladino, a mix of Hebrew and Castilian akin to the Hebrew-German-Slavonic Yiddish, together with several provincial Judaic languages, notably Shuadit in southern France. (The last known native speaker of Shuadit, the French librettist Armand Lunel, died in Avignon in 1977.)

It was through the tolerance of the Muslims that talented Jews were able to play a prominent role in government, science, business and the arts. Moorish and Sephardic culture and scholarship were inseparable and intellectually cross-fertilizing. Some modern writers claim nonetheless that this widely accepted view of harmonious relations between Spanish Muslims and Jews is a romantic myth broadcast in the 19th

95

century by Jews in their political struggle with Christians, and that the Jews were treated little better in Spain than they were in Christian Europe. Still, the magnificent buildings of many of the renowned cities of Spain are a testimony to the wealth, art and tastefulness of this society. In comparison, throughout the Middle Ages Jews played little or no part in the culture of Christian countries. Jews, as Bertrand Russell pointed out, were too persecuted by Christian society to be able to make any contribution to Western civilization beyond "supplying money for the building of cathedrals and such enterprises."

With the final military thrust by the Christians in 1492 and the surrender of Moorish Granada after ten years of armed confrontation, the Jews were faced with a decree issued by the sovereign Queen Isabella (admittedly under pressure from her confessor, the Spanish Inquisition's fearful Thomas Torquemada, who is estimated to have had 2,000 people burned at the stake for heresy) enforcing conversion to Christianity or expulsion from the country. This was in spite of promises she had earlier made of religious toleration.

Of something between 100,000 and 300,000 (the real numbers are simply not known) Sephardic Jews, half chose exile in Europe and, ironically, in Muslim north Africa and Turkey whence the Sultan Bayazit II sent ships to transport them to Smyrna and Istanbul. (Jews of Spanish heritage continued to speak their Ladino language in Turkey into the 20th century.) Jewish converts to Catholicism became known as Marranos.

Following an unsuccessful rebellion, by royal decree in 1502, the Muslims of Spain were given the same choice of conversion to Christianity or exile. Those who converted were called Moriscos. In Christian Spain, the taking of Granada was seen as revenge for the loss of Constantinople to the Ottomans in 1453.

A witness to the fall of Granada in 1492 had been an adventurous forty-one-year-old Genoese sailor, son of a weaver, one Cristoforo Colombo (Cristobal Colón), in Spain negotiating with the authorities to finance an expedition westward across the Atlantic in search of India and an alternative route for the spice trade. Some months before Columbus set sail, accompanied by his no-nonsense mother, Aisha al-Hurra, on their way to exile in Africa, the last Arab king of Granada, Abu Abdullah Mohammed XII, surnamed "the Unfortunate", "Boabdil" as he was known to the Spanish, paused on the hilltop vantage point now called the Moor's Last Sigh overlooking the brightly sun-lit towers and battlements of the Alhambra, and sobbed, "When did misfortune ever equal mine?" History records that she rounded on him mockingly: "You weep like a woman for what you could not hold as a man!"

Some time after his arrival in Morocco, Boabdil, then in his sixties, is said to have thrown his life away recklessly fighting for his cousin, the ruler of Fes.

9

The Crusades

Early Success – The Zangids, Saladin, the Ayyubids, Frederick II –
Western Benefits from the Crusades

Early Success:
Eleventh century military successes of Christians in Spain prompted
Pope Urban II to call for similar action in the Holy Land where, after
seizing Jerusalem from the Seljuks in 1092, Fatimid zealots had been
restricting access for Christian pilgrims to the Holy Places. To recover
unimpeded access to the Holy City of Jerusalem and to place it under
Christian protectorship, another military expedition was mounted.
The object of this action was not initially imperialistic, as believed by
the Arabs – some of whom thought the Nile delta was also an objective
– but to recover by war what had been lost by war – Jerusalem and the
Holy Land which had been mainly Christian, the home of Christian
Arabs, for two hundred and fifty years before the Islamic conquest of
638. It was argued that notwithstanding voluntary conversion of some
Christians to Islam, the motivations, the rights and wrongs of military
action, were no different from what they would have been if roles had
been reversed and Christians had been in possession of Mecca.

As an incentive to fight the good fight, Urban II offered the armed
pilgrims (later to be called "crusaders") spiritual privileges, foremost
among which was reduced time spent in Purgatory for the atonement
of sin. This was widely interpreted as a guarantee of early entry to

Heaven if the holy warrior were to lose his life fighting for the Faith – no different to Islamic martyrdom. There was a difference though. The Christian martyr would be greeted at the Pearly Gates by Saint Peter and brought into Paradise. On the other hand, the Muslim martyr on arriving in Paradise would be offered seventy-two virgins, *houris*, with each one of whom he would be allowed to sleep once for each day he had fasted during his life in Ramadan and once for each good deed he had performed. (Questions have been raised by linguistic scholars regarding this reading of ancient Islamic writings.)

The first campaign was called by the Pontiff in 1095 following a direct appeal from the Byzantine emperor, Alexius I Comnenus, for help to fight the Seljuks and free Jerusalem. The Pope had seen this as an opportunity to settle some of the differences between the Roman and Orthodox churches. As a tactical matter also, the call coincided with the breaking apart of Malik Shah's Seljuk empire when military opposition to a Christian invasion would be less effective.

As in Spain, among the driving forces behind the Crusades were the intense dynastic rivalry and sectarian disunity of the Muslim world, and the cessation of barbarian conquest in Europe. At last, all the races and tribes of Europe (except for the numerically negligible Jews) had converted to Christianity.

Under the primogeniture inheritance practices that were being adopted in many parts of Germanic tribal society, upon the death of a nobleman his eldest son usually inherited the title, castle, lands and villeins. Among the peasantry the eldest boy got the farm. Younger sons often had to make their own way in the world. Although it is debatable how important and widespread this was as a motivation, the "Crusades", as they would be called, did offer a means for the younger sons of the 11th-century feudal European nobility to win status, booty and land. The Crusades moreover presented commercial opportunities for entrepreneurial Italian traders. While the Middle East had to endure the havoc wrought by pillaging Turks from the mid-9th century, from the early 11th century Christendom was galvanized into action. Bertrand Russell pinpoints the moment: "The year 1000 may conveniently be taken as marking the end of the lowest depth to which the civilization of Western Europe sank. From this point onwards the upward movement began and continued until 1914."

Of the five crusader legions that assembled in western Europe, the first, the Peasants Crusade, comprising a ragtag army of 20,000 men, most of them unskilled in war, set out from France in 1096 in

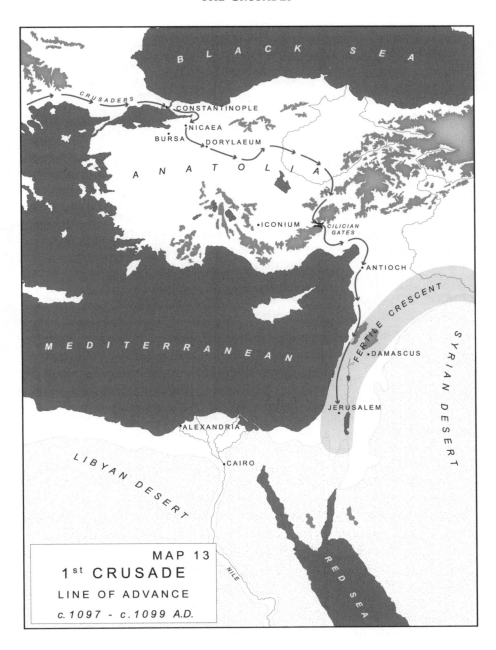

MAP 13
1st CRUSADE
LINE OF ADVANCE
c.1097 - c.1099 A.D.

columns led by Peter "the Hermit" and Walter "the Penniless". Marching through the Rhineland and along the Danube, in passing, they killed 8,000 Jews, to sharpen their skills, perhaps. Travelling through the Balkans, urged on by the then wary agents of the Byzantine empire, they crossed the Bosporus into Anatolia where at Nicaea (now Iznik) Walter's contingent, lacking support from the Greeks, was quickly overcome by waiting Seljuks.

The main force on the other hand, coming along behind, stiffened by militarily experienced French and Norman knights under Godefroi de Bouillon (the *Da Vinci Code's* founder of the *"Priory of Sion"*), Bohemond de Taranto and Baldwin de Boulogne, with effective intelligence, won an early victory at Dorylaeum (now Eskişehir) in northern Anatolia. Guided then by Armenian Christians across Anatolia, along Alexander the Great's 334-333 BC route, they passed through the Cilician Gates mountain pass into the Levant. In July 1099, filled with virtuous loathing of him whom they termed the "false prophet", the crusaders took Jerusalem, massacring both the Muslim and Jewish populations – 70,000 people according to one account – in a frenzy of religious ecstasy, self-righteousness, and plunder. This was not unprecedented conduct when surrender and slavery, or ransom had not been negotiated. Fortunately for them, the Christian community had earlier been expelled from the city by the Fatimid governor.

This First Crusade, unsurprisingly, awakened deep animosities between Christianity and Islam; and the Byzantines who witnessed some of the atrocities committed by the Frankish Christians were reinforced in their determination to oppose the reunification of the Roman and Orthodox branches of Christianity.

The crusaders succeeded in the Holy Land – to the extent that they did succeed – mainly because of dynastic and political divisions among their opponents. The Seljuks and Fatimids were busy fighting each other as well as the invaders, allowing the crusaders to play off the Muslim powers against each other. The crusaders divided their new territories into a belt of counties and a kingdom along the Levant coast from southern Turkey to Gaza, interrupted by a stronghold of the recently founded sect of Assassins at Masyaf in Syria. Castles were built and garrisoned by the devotees of the military monastic orders of the Knights Templar and Knights Hospitaller. However, attempts to attract more than a few settlers as reinforcements failed and crusader numbers shrank. Though the religious fervour of these Christian holy

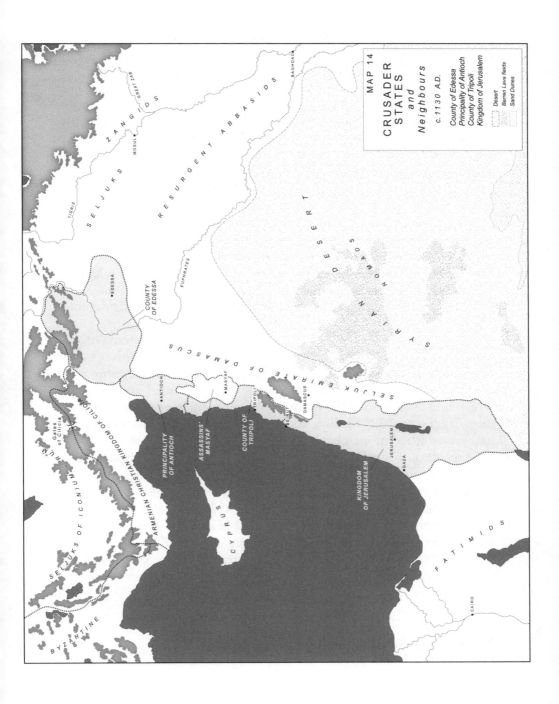

MAP 14

CRUSADER
STATES
and
Neighbours

c. 1130 A.D.

County of Edessa
Principality of Antioch
County of Tripoli
Kingdom of Jerusalem

Desert
Barren Lava fields
Sand Dunes

ZANGIDS

SELJUKS

MOSUL

TIGRIS

GREAT ZAB

RESURGENT ABBASIDS

BAGHDAD

EDESSA

COUNTY
OF EDESSA

EUPHRATES

SYRIAN DESERT

NOMADS

SELJUK EMIRATE OF DAMASCUS

ANTIOCH

MASYAF

TRIPOLI

BEIRUT

DAMASCUS

KINGDOM OF CILICIA

Gates
of Cilicia

R.U.M.

ARMENIAN CHRISTIAN KINGDOM

SELJUKS OF ICONIUM

BYZANTINE

PRINCIPALITY
OF ANTIOCH

ASSASSINS'
MASYAF

COUNTY OF
TRIPOLI

CYPRUS

JERUSALEM

GAZA

KINGDOM
OF JERUSALEM

FATIMIDS

CAIRO

warriors was intense, as their numbers were so few, their supply lines so stretched and their communications with European homelands so fraught with uncertainty, there was little chance of their ever being able to maintain permanent control even of Jerusalem.

The most important state, the Latin Kingdom of Jerusalem, lasted eighty-eight years. Major losses of territory began in 1144, attacks coming from reorganized, strengthened Seljuks. Still, in alliances with other Sunni Arabs, the French crusader King Amalric (Amaury) I of Jerusalem invaded the Nile Delta several times between 1164 and 1168 in expansionist campaigns, but was never able to hold Egyptian Fatimid territory for long. The Christian invaders, too, fought among themselves as much as they fought the Muslims.

What the crusaders did which was of lasting value however was to reopen the eastern Mediterranean to trade and travel by Europeans, building upon what Jewish traders had begun in the 9th century. Before the Crusades, Middle Eastern Jews in business partnership with the Fatimids had controlled most of the trade with Europe. After the early Crusades, Italian and French traders fastened upon a considerable portion of the Jewish part of this business.

During the 12th century, while the people of much of Christian Europe lived little above subsistence level, the Italians created wealth beyond their immediate needs by industry and commerce, craftsmanship and fruitful business cooperation, in contrast to the plunder and taxation which had been among the more important mainstays of Arab economies. By the mid-12th century, Italian merchants in the Mediterranean had joined Muslim merchants in dominating trade with the Far East. As a result of this expansion of commerce, Italian cities – notably the maritime republics of Venice, Genoa and Pisa – flourished, enriching a wider section of the community, creating a bourgeoisie and laying the foundations of a broader middle class. By the late 12th century, hundreds of skyscraper towers, *torri*, had been built in Italy, the rich vying with each other to build the tallest. And by the beginning of the 14th century, twenty-three cities in northern and central Italy had populations over 20,000. In these cities poverty was alleviated. France, the early driving force of the Crusades, was quick to follow.

The Zangids, Saladin, the Ayyubids, Frederick II:

In 1127, while Seljuk power over Iraq was waning, a Turkmen notable, Imad al-Din Zangi, gained control of the important northern city of

Mosul. At this time in the Levant the crusaders were absorbing local culture, adopting local customs and marrying local Christian women. Some were even converting to Islam. Zangi set about reuniting the Seljuk statelets of northern Iraq, Syria and Anatolia by recovering territory from the crusaders. First, he rode out from Mosul and took Aleppo, the leading city of northern Syria, 400 miles to the west, just as the Hamdanids had done two centuries before. Aleppo lay adjacent to the crusader kingdoms of Antioch (Antakya in today's Turkey) on the Mediterranean coast and the ancient Roman garrison town of Edessa (today's Urfa or Şanliurfa) in Anatolia. Zangi installed himself in Aleppo as governor, putting pressure on the crusaders. In 1144, he attacked and overwhelmed Edessa, for centuries an Armenian Christian town. He killed all the men and sold all the women into slavery. This loss triggered the Second Crusade (1147-49) manned by the Germans and French who, on their way to the Crusade, although successful in taking Lisbon from the Almoravids, were ambushed and demoralized crossing Anatolia and failed in their objective.

When Zangi died in 1146, his twenty-six-year-old son, Nur al-Din Mahmud, took up his work. Damascus and southern Syria were at this time in the hands of a Seljuk prince who had allied himself with Baldwin III, King of Jerusalem – and brother and predecessor of the Amalric I – in order better to stand up to his northern rival the Seljuk Zangi. Baldwin betrayed his ally and although failing in his siege of Damascus, weakened the ruler of the city enough to enable Nur al-Din quickly to incorporate it and the rest of Syria into his territories. Nur al-Din's success created a Muslim state throughout the whole of Syria, for the first time confronting the crusaders with a unified enemy. Nur al-Din then appointed Saladin, a son of his father's general Ayyub, to act on his behalf in Egypt where, although a Sunni, the statesman-like Saladin served for a year as vizier to the Shiite Fatimid caliph.

Meanwhile, central and southern Iraq, south of Mosul, was under the rule of Abbasid Caliph al-Mustaqfi II whose militia had defeated a Seljuk force in 1155. The caliph had thenceforth been able to enjoy a time of revived influence because his personal qualities and his acknowledged spiritual authority enabled him to arbitrate disputes between Middle Eastern princes. The 450-year Muslim domination of Spain was dissolving, the country having been overrun by the Almohads since 1158 while fighting the Christians much of the time. And the Fatimid caliphate of Egypt was in its death throes with internal chaos and repeated crusader attack. But in the Norman Christian kingdom of Sicily, Arab culture

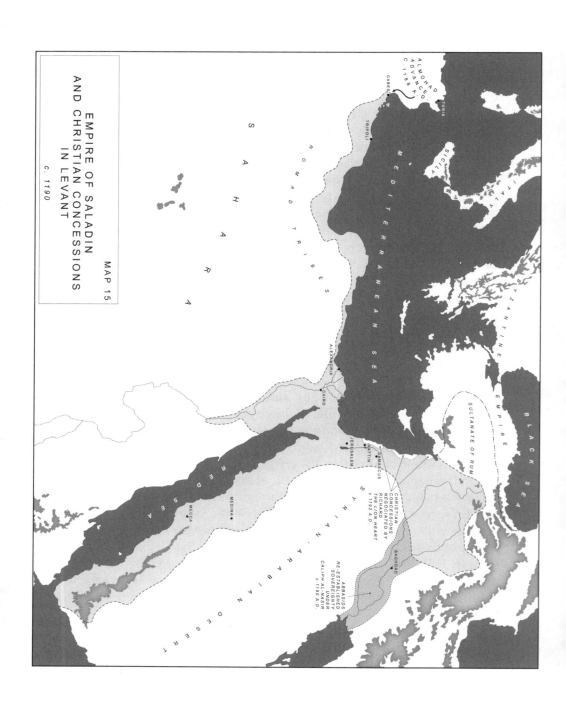

EMPIRE OF SALADIN
AND CHRISTIAN CONCESSIONS
IN LEVANT

c. 1190

MAP 15

ALMOHAD
ADVANCED
C. 1188

GABES

TUNIS

SICILY

ITALY

TRIPOLI

M E D I T E R R A N E A N   S E A

B Y Z A N T I N E   E M P I R E

S A H A R A

N O M A D   T R I B E S

BLACK SEA

ALEXANDRIA

SULTANATE OF RUM

CAIRO

JERUSALEM

HATTIN

DAMASCUS

S Y R I A N - A R A B I A N   D E S E R T

R E D   S E A

MECCA

MEDINA

CHRISTIAN
CONCESSIONS
NEGOTIATED BY
RICHARD
THE LION HEART
C. 1192 A.D.

BAGHDAD

ABBASIDS
RE-ESTABLISHED
SOVEREIGNTY
UNDER
CALIPH AL-NASIR
C. 1190 A.D.

continued to enrich society; the Arabic language was spoken together with French and Latin; and Arab agricultural practices had transformed the countryside to the benefit of the people.

Nur al-Din and Saladin reinforced the Zangid dynasty's grip on its extensive territories and in 1169-71, employing a strong force of mercenary "Mamluk" troops, Saladin put an end to the Fatimids, in their final stage of decrepitude, executing the last Fatimid caliph, al-Adid (other accounts say he died of natural causes). The caliph was not quite twenty-one years old at the time of his death. Nur al-Din raised Saladin to the rank of viceroy of Egypt. As a foretaste of his rule, Saladin confirmed the appointment of the notable exiled Sephardic philosopher, Maimonides, as court physician and later also, some accounts maintain, as Cairo city mayor.

Recognizing the theological dominion of the Abbasid caliphs – even though Shias and infidels were together more numerous than Sunnis – Saladin returned Egypt to the orthodox fold after two centuries of Shiite theocracy. One should note however that while the overthrow of the Fatimids and Saladin's recognition of Abbasid religious authority might give the impression of restoring the Abbasids to exclusive right to the caliphate, their restoration to power in Iraq actually had the effect of underlining their status as rulers of only one of many small Muslim kingdoms in the lands between the Indus and the Atlantic seaboard.

When Nur al-Din died in 1174, thirty-six-year-old Saladin overthrew the Prince's young heir, as-Salih Ismail, a boy in the hands of court eunuchs, expelling him to Aleppo, and made himself Emir of Damascus. To reinforce his legitimacy Saladin resorted to the time-honoured stratagem of taking Nur al-Din's widow to bed. Her son as-Salih continued nevertheless to resist from Aleppo until he was murdered in 1181. Saladin was then acknowledged formally as sovereign Sultan.

Saladin's Kurdish dynasty, the Ayyubids, was named after his father. As ruler of an empire with joint capitals in Damascus and Cairo, Saladin revived the economy of Egypt after the failings of the past decades and revitalized industry in Syria. As a memorial to himself he built the Citadel, Cairo's Kremlin.

The Assassins made two abortive attempts on Saladin's life yet, intriguingly, he came to an accommodation with them over the common enemy, the crusaders. It was not until 1187 however that he was able to muster enough strength, including forces sent from Spain by the Almohad Yaqub al-Mansur, to recover Jerusalem and other crusader lands. In an historic battle at the "Horns of Hattin", near the

Sea of Galilee, Saladin defeated the Christians and had all the captive Knights Templar and Hospitaller beheaded. Several Levantine ports were recovered four years later by Richard "the Lionheart", but not Jerusalem. Through diplomacy and the personal respect of Saladin, Richard was able however to maintain a truce between the two sides and a foothold in the Holy Land until Saladin's death in 1193.

Saladin is revered in the East as the paragon of princely virtue who reversed the current of Christian conquest. He is admired for his chivalry towards the weak, for his abiding modesty, his invariable equanimity, his piety and courage. An admirable and heroic figure certainly; but as a military commander he was less than supreme, being twice defeated by Richard in (less-than-crucial) battles. Nor, by many measures, was Saladin a statesman, and he left no constitution or code other than the exemplary lessons of his personal conduct. (Dante placed him in Limbo among the "virtuous infidels", and Sir Walter Scott treated him sympathetically in *The Talisman* of 1825.) Upon his death at the age of fifty-five, seemingly from malaria, his possessions and lands were shared out by his heirs. They quickly found reason to quarrel, and the imperial unity of the Ayyubids crumbled. They had been united and imperial for barely twenty years. While clashing with his brothers, one of Saladin's sons, Malik al-Aziz, was able to keep hold of Egypt, supported by Mamluk troops – until these mercenary fighters decided to have one of their own leaders seated on the throne.

At the time of Saladin's death and the subsequent disruption of his realm, Caliph al-Nasir, the longest reigning of all the Abbasid caliphs of Baghdad, newly rearmed and heartened, put a complete end to Seljuk power in Iraq. At the time of their politico-military demise, the one-time nomadic Turks had exercised significant if volatile political power in Iraq for 350 years.

Seven Ayyubid sultans, relatives and descendants of Saladin, successively occupied the throne of Egypt, ruling what at first was a much diminished empire. As the Medieval Warm Period approached a scorching climax, the early part of the reign of the third successor, Malik al-Adil I (a half-brother of Saladin's), was marked by famine severe enough to lead to cannibalism in Egypt.

During the famine of 1201-1204 that so troubled the reign of Malik al-Adil, in an account the authenticity of which has been questioned, it had been written that: "A vast multitude sought refuge in Cairo where they were to meet appalling circumstances; for when the sun entered the sign of Aries, the air became corrupt, and pestilence and a deadly contagion began to take its toll and the poor under the pressure of ever-growing want, ate carrion, corpses, dogs and animal parts. They went further, and reached the stage of eating little children. It was not unusual to find people selling children, roasted or boiled. The commandant of the city guard ordered that those who committed this crime should be burned alive, as should those who ate such meats. I myself saw a little roast child in a basket. It was brought to the commandant, and led in at the same time were a man and woman who were the child's father and mother. The commandant condemned them to be burned alive. When the poor first began to eat human flesh, the horror and astonishment that such extraordinary meals aroused were such that these crimes formed the topic of every conversation. No one could stop talking about them. But eventually people grew accustomed, and some conceived such a taste for these detestable meats that they made them their ordinary provender, eating them for enjoyment and even laying in supplies. When some unfortunate who had been convicted of eating human flesh was burned alive, the corpse was usually found to have been devoured by the following morning. The flesh being fully roasted did not need further cooking." Accounts exist of similar cannibalism in the great famine of 1065-72.

During the famine of 1201- 04 Ibn al-Farid, Sufism's most venerated young mystical poet, began to write his love poetry in his retreat outside Cairo. And famine or not, war with the crusaders continued. Saladin's empire was partly reconstituted, and Malik al-Adil's son Malik al-Kamil succeeded in driving the few remaining crusaders out of Egypt in 1221. Malik the younger was remembered as a capable and just ruler.

In the turmoil following Saladin's death, Syria had broken up again, allowing the crusaders to recover more Levantine ports. They failed however to regain Jerusalem until 1229. The retaking of Jerusalem was achieved, astonishingly, without fighting. The Holy Roman Emperor, the inimitable Frederick II of the German Hohenstauffen dynasty, was also King of Naples and Sicily. It was his father who had defeated the Normans of Sicily and taken their southern Italian kingdom. His queen, Isabella (Isabeau), was the daughter of Jean de Brienne, the throneless heir to the Latin kingdom of Jerusalem, lost to Saladin forty years before. Upon the deaths of Isabella and her father, Frederick claimed the throne and in 1228-29 went to Palestine to negotiate with Sultan Malik al-Kamil. Frederick explained to him the part that Jerusalem played in Christian culture, promised free access for Muslims and convinced him that the city had no strategic value. By way of encouragement, Frederick provided military assistance to the Sultan in a dispute he was having with a nephew and was rewarded with the throne of Jerusalem – but without the important Papal rites of assent. As this had become a Christian kingdom subject to Papal fiat, it was contested for years by rival French claimants. The city was lost in 1239 to Malik al-Kamil's son, Malik al-Adil II.

Frederick II is fabulous. Not only was he the crusader who talked the Muslims into giving him the throne of Jerusalem, he was also fluent in six languages; and roguish he could be in all of them. He was a philosopher and an authority on falconry. He was a poet, patron of the arts and, famously, a keeper of a harem of early Abbasid abandon, manned by eunuchs of course. His Muslim bodyguard was an outrage to Christendom. No wonder he was known as the Christian Sultan. In his court, poetry flowered through his eulogists with the creation of the sonnet verse form, and under him advances were made in mathematics with his sponsorship of the numbers man, Fibonacci, who among other achievements brought the place-valued decimal system to Europe.

Frederick was cruel, blinding and mutilating prisoners, and he put down Muslim insurgency most savagely. He governed his Empire well from Palermo although he was criticized for his grandiose military ambitions. He was twice excommunicated by the Pope, Gregory IX, who called him a "rake, a heretic and an anti-Christ." The first time followed a widespread rumour that Frederick had declared that, "The three great imposters are Moses, Christ and Mohammed!" And at the time he went to Jerusalem and negotiated its throne for himself, he was under excommunication for having refused Gregory's demand to retake Jerusalem by force! This coup of Frederick's is said to have enraged the Pope even more. Until he died in 1250, Frederick reigned over a magnificent court embracing Christian, Muslim and Jewish traditions, art and erudition. While he was Holy Roman Emperor, Palermo was the centre of Western civilization replacing the past glories of Muslim Córdoba. For the cultured of Europe, Frederick was simply the *stupor mundi*, the wonder of the world.

After 1239 when Frederick lost Jerusalem the crusaders made no more headway in the Holy Land. Bit by bit they lost territory. The last crusader stronghold on the mainland, Acre (today's Akko, in Israel), fell to the Egyptians under the Mamluk al-Ashraf in 1291, after the ruling Ayyubid House had fallen to the swords of the mercenaries. The final crusader toe-hold, a minute island off the coast of Syria, was taken by Mamluks under the seventeen-year-old Malik al-Nasir in 1302.

More important than crusader efforts to hold parts of Palestine in the 12th and 13th centuries were Mongol attacks on the Muslim world. Contemporary Arab commentators seem to have considered the few remaining crusaders as no more than tiresome leftovers from the failed attempt at empire-building. That was why Frederick II was able to talk his way onto the throne of Jerusalem in 1229. The Arabs saw the formidable horsemen from central Asia as far greater a menace to Islamic civilization, as indeed they were.

Western Benefits from the Crusades:
Most agree that that the Crusades showed the West as both barbarous and inept, discrediting the Christian faith. It has been said that "the only fruit of the Crusades kept by the Christians was the apricot". This is not entirely true. The Crusades had an important positive effect on the Western participants: they were exposed to Islamic civilization. The First Crusaders found much to envy in the living conditions of the Arabs compared with their own circumstances in Europe. After the final defeat of the Crusades in the Middle East, merchants from the Occident, many of them from Italy, France and Aragon, were encouraged by several of the Muslim rulers to return to or remain in their cities. Remarkably, it was the losers, not the victors, who obtained trading bases and privileges in the others' lands. These bases were to become a crucial element in the strengthening of the Western economies and the weakening of the Arab hold on trade. The European merchants became transferors of more Muslim technology, science and culture to the West, adding to the stream of practical information that earlier had flowed out of Umayyad Spain and Norman Sicily. Even before Saladin defeated the crusaders, the Arab authorities were mistaken in their belief that the presence of Western-owned entrepôts in the Levant and Egypt was to Muslim advantage. Saladin had written to Caliph al-Nasir in Baghdad: "The Venetians, the Genoese and the Pisans bring into Egypt choice products of the West, especially arms and war materials. This provides an advantage for Islam and an injury for Christianity." On hearing of this through his spies, the Pope had come to the same conclusion and had condemned the trade, holding the threat of excommunication over the heads of the Christian merchants. Not much notice of this threat was taken by Jewish traders.

Mediterranean maritime trade came to be dominated by Venice and Genoa by the mid-13th century. Both city-states had taken advantage of the Crusades to build up trade links with Asia, the source of luxury products – silks, spices and gems. The term "spices" in fact covered dozens of true tropical spices for the kitchens of the moneyed classes, together with dyestuffs, cosmetics, medicinal products, tropical fruits, silkworm cocoons and supposed aphrodisiacs. In about 1330 the Florentine Francesco Pegolotti published a list of 300 spices. Five kinds of ginger were offered.

By the 1250s – when the early Gothic cathedrals were being consecrated in western Europe – Italian and French traders had taken on the additional crucial role of financing and underwriting craft production and trade. International banking houses based on interest payment emerged. But so also did banking failures, among the earliest being the House of Buonsignori of Siena, "the Rothschilds of the Middle Ages", in 1298. Usury was regarded as a sin just as much in Christendom as in the Muslim world in the late Middle Ages. Jewish practice, on the other hand, while forbidding usury between Jews, permitted charging interest to non-Jews, giving Jews an important advantage in the money-lending business. All the same, many Christian bankers concealed interest payment by not recording the sums loaned, only those to be recovered.

With conflict constantly raging in Europe, opportunities for profit arose. Italian bankers refined financial and accounting practice. From the late 13th century, instruments such as letters of credit, third-party guarantees, double entry book-keeping and bills of exchange improved the performance of business. The first marine premium insurance contract was signed in Genoa in about 1350.

Italian commerce was severely damaged again in 1343-46 by the bankruptcy of the then leading Florentine banking houses of Bardi, Peruzzi and later, Acciaiuoli, called "the Pillars of Christendom", the three ruined in the final analysis by defaulted loans to King Edward III of England for his (second) abortive attack on France during the Hundred Years' War. Then, the Black Death arrived in 1347. Beginning in the 1350s, despite all these setbacks, Florence struggled back to solvency. The banks revised their financial practices and modern capitalism was born.

The historic record does not show to what extent, if any, the Franco-Italian business customs, institutions and financial techniques were borrowed from the Arabs. Still, it seems reasonable to suppose that just as the Arabs had learned about Greek, Persian and Hindu science and mathematics and had built upon them, the Italian and French traders of the 13th and 14th centuries had adopted and refined existing Arab business practices.

10

The Mamluks Seize Power, 1250 AD

Establishment of the Mamluk Sultanate – Sultans of Egypt, 1171 - 1517

Estsablishment of the Mamluk Sultanate:
From the Arabic word for slaves, the Mamluks were the slave-troops of Seljuk and Arab Syria and Egypt. They were purchased as young boys of pagan background from one or other of several nomadic Turkic tribes, the Kipchaks, occupying the steppes north of the Caspian Sea, the lower Volga basin and what is now Kazakhstan. After the Black Death decimated the Kipchak steppes in the mid-late 14th century, many of these teenagers were obtained from the less ravaged Circassian tribes, some of them Christian, transhumant nomads from the foothills and plains of the north flank of the Caucasus mountains, as far west as the shores of the Black Sea, and south of the Kuban River. Among the Mamluks there were Mongols, Greeks and Kurds and even some adult Western adventurers, mercenaries, fighters for spoils. The Kipchaks spoke Turkic languages. The Circassians spoke Kabardian and some of the many other Caucasian languages, giving rise no doubt to communication difficulties with their Kipchak counterparts.

In 1171, many of the Kipchak soldiery were relocated by Saladin to Egypt from Syria for his invasion. Fifty-seven years after his death, the Mamluks became the ruling caste of Egypt, an aristocracy of white slaves, just as their precursors had been in 9th-century Iraq. As in Iraq, these slaves were emancipated when their military training was

complete but, unlike in early Abbasid times, this ten or twelve thou-
sand-man professional army not only seized political control of Egypt,
they made the country their own. The seizure took place in 1250, just
after the Mamluks had defeated the Seventh Crusade led by King Louis
IX of France, at Damietta in the Nile delta. This Seventh became the last
Crusade the Christians would aim directly at the Arab heartlands.

The Mamluk victory at Damietta was won following the death,
apparently from natural causes, of the Ayyubid Sultan, al-Salih, and
just before his successor, Turanshah, a great-grandnephew of Saladin's,
was enthroned. Within months Turanshah, who had not been on the
Damietta battlefield, was murdered by his Mamluk bodyguards who,
they say, felt threatened by his intimidating manner. Turanshah was
the last Ayyubid sultan. After Saladin, the Ayyubids had survived a
typical dynastic term, fifty-seven years. (The Ayyubid family itself
nevertheless survives in today's Lebanon and claims to have Saladin's
sword. One wonders what that might fetch at auction.)

Turanshah's step-mother a former slavegirl Shagarat al-Durr ("Spray
of Pearls"), widow of Sultan al-Salih and one of the most outstanding
women in Arab history, took the title of Sultana and for some weeks
seems to have been accepted in Egypt as the legitimate sovereign. But
neither the princes of Syria nor the Caliph of Baghdad, final arbiter of
Islamic protocol, would countenance such an affront to Arab sensibili-
ties as having a woman on the throne.

Aybak, a Mamluk officer who likely had a part in the murder of
Turanshah, then married Shagarat and began 267 years of Mamluk
sultanship in Egypt. For appearances, Aybak seated on the throne at
his side a member of the Ayyubid House, who in fact he kept locked
up for the rest of the wretch's life. Accounts suggest that Shagarat
remained for a time the power behind the throne.

In 1257, in a fit of insecurity over Aybak's planning to take another
wife, Shagarat lured him into her bath and had her eunuchs stab him
to death. Following this, on the orders of Aybak's first wife, mother
of the infant heir to the throne, her slaves kicked Shagarat to death
with their wooden bath clogs and threw her body over the wall of the
Citadel to the dogs below.

After displacing Aybak's heir, another Kipchak officer, Qutuz, for-
merly a slave of Aybak's, succeeded to the throne of Egypt. Beginning
with Sultan Aybak, these freed slaves, the mainly Turkic Kipchaks
(some of whom were said to have been red haired and fair skinned)
occupied the Egyptian throne from 1250 until 1381. As a consequence

of the Black Death and of weak government the Circassian Mamluks were then able to seize power and hold it until they in turn were over-come by the Ottomans in 1517.

Under the Kipchaks, the succession of Mamluk sultans was more or less hereditary. Under the Circassians, it was the strongest and most unscrupulous who was seated on the throne. Of a total of fifty-three Mamluk sultans only ten died in office of natural causes; nineteen were executed or assassinated; and twenty-four were deposed.

Until the Mongol horsemen appeared over the horizon in the mid-1200s the Mamluk empire reached from Cyrenaica (eastern Libya) to Mesopotamia. After 1260, the Egyptian empire was generally limited in the east by the Syrian Desert. Despite the arid conditions, the period of more than a hundred years beginning with Saladin's conquest of Egypt in 1171 and continuing through much of the Kipchak era was a time of some prosperity for Egypt because of the Nile valley's resources, its textile industry and its importance as a trade route. Of prime importance, Egypt remained the principal entrepôt for goods moving through the Red Sea to the developing European cities. This trade was vital to Egypt's economy both for the goods themselves and for the customs revenues they brought in. But Italians were gaining the upper hand in the Mediterranean, and Arab share of the business was falling. In contrast to the reigning oligopolies of the Arab states, the Italians gained further ground because competition among their mercantile cities and merchant families led to their greater efficiency in business matters.

Once again, with their surplus wealth the early, successful Mamluk régime lavished money on architecture, mosques, the arts and letters. They sponsored the writing of history and the compilation of encyclo-paedias. Yet, for all their support of scholarship, the rulers were still military men living a separate existence from the civilian community, speaking alien tongues, a violent clique terrorizing the Egyptian popu-lace. Murderous internal struggles between rival Mamluk groups par-alleled resolute solidarity in the face of external foes. Though deadly rivalry for the throne was the order of the day among the Mamluk princes, within the Mamluk sphere no power arose to overturn the established, rock-solid system.

The Mamluk leaders became the landed aristocrats of Egypt. Aristocracy with a difference: the children of a land-holding officer usually had no right to his land after his death, thus forestalling the emergence of an entrenched hereditary aristocracy and averting a problem that plagued Arab dynasties for centuries. Except for ruling Kipchak families, Mamluk officers generally received their land for their lifetimes only and their children became commoners.

As with the Ayyubids, while corruption and extravagance persisted, when external foes grew stronger, and as the commercial dynamic of the Mediterranean evolved in the 14th century to the advantage of Europe, Western merchants with the trading privileges they had been granted in Muslim lands strengthened their hold on commerce, and Mamluk power and prosperity waned.

After being driven out of their corsair bases on the mainland coasts of France and Italy in the late 9th and 10th centuries the Saracens seem to have failed to make any particular attempt, when the possibility arose in the 13th century, to negotiate peaceful trading facilities for themselves on the European shore, comparable to the "factories", trading bases, conceded to Christians in Arab lands. Misunderstanding of the commercial value of such concessions and lordly Arab disdain for Europeans, their lifestyles and lands, were important factors in this failure.

The deterioration of the Arab economies was running its course at the same time that Europeans were profiting from their greater areas of arable land, the helpful climatic conditions of the 11th and 12th centuries, and greater abundance and variety of raw materials – mineral ores and wood for smelting, fuel, construction and boat building. The rich forests of Europe fuelled at low cost the iron, copper, tin, zinc and lead smelting industries on which much depended. Europeans had better supplies of cheaper metal tools, implements, equipment, and weapons for all manner of wealth-producing activity and defence. Europeans were blessed with huge supplies of fish in accessible fishing grounds in the adjacent seas and ocean. Manufacturing centres expanded, their numbers increasing markedly. Geographical variety of Europe – great rivers, mountain ranges, plains, rich soils, forests – climate and natural resources led to differentiated products and widening trade networks.

Simple technological and practical improvements in the West finally boosted farm output above the levels achieved in Roman times – the three-field crop-rotation system, the three-piece wheeled-plough, windmills (this last, of probable Persian origin about the time of the Arab conquest). All were in use already from England to Poland-Lithuania by the mid- to late 12th century. The padded horse collar appeared in about 1100, perhaps earlier. The introduction of the three-field rotation system alone (as opposed to the Roman two-field system) improved peasant productivity beyond their dreams. Water-powered sawmills, technologically a giant step forward, came into wide use around 1240. In the mid-1200s, the first ships' rudders in the Occident replacing the oar for steering and the bowsprit for sailing closer to the wind came into use, greatly improving Western ships' manoeuvrability and speed.

With later marriage than in Muslim lands, monogamy and smaller families, wealth was more easily pooled in Christendom for productive purposes. European indivisible inheritance customs (that spread wide in the 11th century to support militaristic feudalism), European treatment of women, together with women's wider employment in the workforce and the widespread avoidance of the Roman Church's ban on interest payments for loans provided the people of the West with additional advantages over those of Muslim cultures. Already, as early as 1200 the scene for Western pre-eminence was set: for the supplanting of the Arab-Byzantine-Jewish commercial hegemony over the Mediterranean that had been eroded so insidiously by a confluence of debilitating forces.

Sultans of Egypt, 1171-1517

Sultan	Ruled	Notes
The Ayyubids		
Saladin	1171-93	Inflicted first major defeat on Crusaders.
al-Aziz	1193-98	Fought brothers for power after Saladin's death.
al-Mansur	1198-1200	Infant, deposed by uncle.
al-Adil	1200-1218	Extended empire. Disasters. Civil war.
al-Kamil	1218-38	Dominions divided with brothers.
al-Adil II	1238-40	Supplanted by brother.
al-Salih	1240-50	Recovered Syria and Jerusalem from Crusaders.
Turanshah	1250	Assassinated.

The Mainly Kipchak Mamluks		
Aybek	1250-57	Murdered by Shagarat.
Nureddin Kotuz	1257-59 1257-60	Son of Aybek. Once Aybek's slave. Defeated Mongols. Assassinated by Baybars.
Baybars (al-Zahir)	1260-77	Raised Mamluk empire to its apogee.
al-Said Nasir	1277 1277-79	Quickly supplanted. Son of Baybars.
Qala'un	1277-90	Successful sultan. Shrewd diplomat and militarily successful.
al-Ashraf	1290-93	Beat Crusaders at Acre. Assassinated by deputy.
Baidara	1293	Assassinated.
al-Nasir	1293-94	9 years old. Dethroned.
Kitboga	1294-96	Mongol usurper. Assassinated.
Husam ud-Din	1296-99	Assassinated.
al-Nasir	1299-1309	2nd reign, starting age 14.
al-Mozaffar	1309-10	Circassian. Executed.
al-Nasir	1310-41	3rd reign. Married Mongol princess.
(thirteen short-term sultans)	1341-81	Chaotic years. Black Death.
The Mainly Circassian Mamluks		
al-Zahir	1381-99	Established relations with Ottomans.
Faraj	1399-1405	Mongol incursions, abdicated.
al-Mansur II	1405	Deposed in two months.
Faraj	1405-12	2nd reign. Quelled Syrian revolts, deposed.
Musta'in	1412	Abbasid, deposed in months.
al-Mu'ayyad	1412-21	Invaded Anatolia.
(three short-term sultans)	1421-22	Chaos.
Barsbay	1422-38	Conquered Cyprus.
al-Aziz	1438	Infant. Deposed.

al-Zahir II	1438-53	Raided Aegean.
al-Mansur III	1453	Dethroned after six weeks.
al-Ashraf II	1453-61	Friendly relations with Ottomans.
al-Mu'ayyad II	1461	Deposed in four months.
Khoshkadam	1461-67	Greek Mamluk. Violent rivalry with Ottomans begins.
al-Zahir III	1467	Deposed in two months.
al-Zahir IV	1467	Deposed in a month.
Kait Bey	1467-96	Relations deteriorate with Ottomans.
(four short-term sultans)	1496-1501	Chaos.
Kansuh al-Ghuri	1501-16	Died fighting Ottomans, at age 68.
Tuman Bey	1516-17	Last Mamluk Sultan. Hanged by Ottomans.

11

The Mongols and the Re-emergence
of Persia

*The Mongols, Genghis Khan – Hulagu Khan and the Razing of Baghdad
– The Ilkhanate – The Safavids*

The Mongols, Genghis Khan:
While Saladin was putting an end to crusader kingdoms in the 1180s,
a far more terrible enemy for the Arabs was forming on the steppes
of Asia, a belt of grassy, mainly treeless plains 5,000 miles long and
100 to 300 miles wide, from the Ukraine to China. From the Urals to
the Great Wall of China the land was peopled by two ethno-linguistic
tribal groups of warlike mounted pastoral nomads, the Turkic peoples
and the Mongols. Both were expert horsemen from childhood. They
herded cattle, goats and sheep while spending much of their energy
feuding with each other and raiding settled communities on the margins of their lands. They had no towns or permanent settlements of
their own. Violence was endemic. Perpetual shortage of resources gave
rise to waves of migration and constant armed conflict.

The chief of a relatively minor tribe, a Mongol of striking authority,
born ominously with a blood clot in his fist and who had succeeded
his father to the leadership of his tribe at the age of thirteen, came
to believe that the Supreme Being had charged him with the task of
bringing prosperity to the peoples of the steppes by unifying them. He
believed he was appointed to rule the Earth. His name was Temujin
(Temuchin). Geoffrey Hosking relates how it was that in order to

121

discharge this responsibility Temujin made the young men of his tribe the best trained cavalry on the steppes. Unlike any other army of the time, military command under Temujin was based on leadership quality and martial skill. His entourage were technical experts, including Chinese engineers and trusted political and military lieutenants with delegated powers. There were no servile flatterers. Leadership of Arab armies at the time was based (as it was in European forces) on social rank, family and clan. Temuchin was a born motivator able to bring together many of the larger Mongol tribes of the steppes. So successful was he at defusing intertribal disputes that Turkic tribes, former rivals, joined his Mongol alliance. Together, in the Year of the Tiger, 1206, the leaders of the alliance elected the thirty-nine-year-old Temujin their Supreme Leader, the "Genghis Khan".

In their religious beliefs the Mongols were shamanists – like the American plains Indians whose life-styles and beliefs seem to have had many similarities. Many Mongols worshipped the Sky God Tengri and revered natural phenomena such as trees and springs. In the main, they were tolerant of other religions, and priests of all faiths in the lands they conquered were often relieved of the burdens of taxes, military service and the corvée. For all that, while practising religious toleration the Mongols systematically perpetrated fiendish barbarities on their opponents, boiling people alive, among other horrors. They created terror to intimidate their enemies and undermine their resolve to fight. They looked like monkeys, barked like dogs, ate raw flesh, drank their horses' urine, knew no laws and showed no mercy. Among the many Turkic tribes that joined the alliance were the Uighurs, masters of a lengthy section of the Silk Road in the Sinkiang province of China. The Mongols had no script, so Temujin adopted the Uighurs' for keeping records.

The brilliant Mongol cavalry were the "first army in history to wage total war", according to the British military historian Liddell Hart. When taking Herat (in today's Afghanistan) in 1221 they killed the entire population, for no reason it seems other than blood-lust.

The expansion of Mongol power that followed Genghis Khan's election was probably the most important political event in the 13th century. It changed the history and shape of Asia. The internal motive forces of his army were such that without serious work to do it would soon have broken up again into feuding clans. The Great Khan therefore adopted a policy of all-round aggression through which he quickly gained a reputation for appalling ferocity. "My greatest joy," he is reported to

1. At the height of early Islamic expansion, the Arabs enter Latakia in Syria on the Ras-Ziyara Peninsula in 636. The Crusaders captured the city in 1097 and Saladin retook the port in 1188.

2. The al Aqsa Mosque in Jerusalem was finished in 691, making it one of the earliest Islamic monuments.

3. The tombs of the Caliphs in Cairo, photographed about 1860. Most of them date from the second, or Circassian, Mamluk dynasty (1381-1517).

Opposite page: **4.** Diagrams of the astrolabe, published in 1597. The astrolable and other aids to navigation were reintroduced to Europe by the Arabs.through Islamic Spain in the 11th century. Most historians consider Hipparchus (2nd century BC) to have invented it.The 8th-century Persian mathematician Fazari was probably the first astrolabe maker in the Islamic world. The astrolabe would remain the most important navigational instrument for an extraordinarily long time, until the sextant of the 18th century.

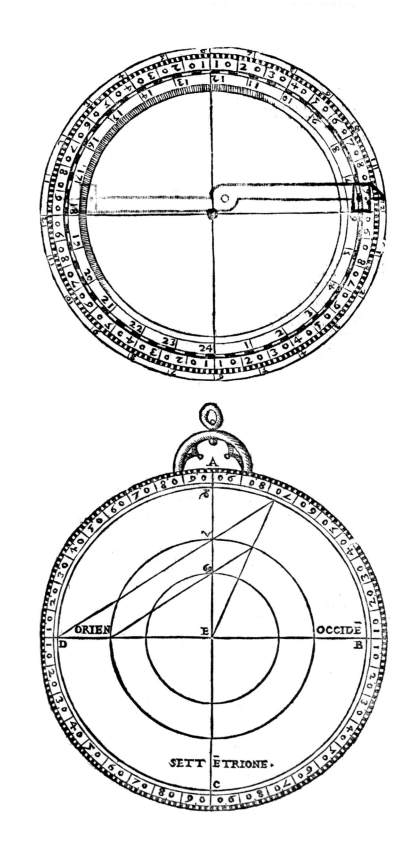

Above: **5.** The tomb at Samarkand of the Holy Kassim ibn Abass (Shakh Zinde). The Koran was donated by Emir Nassula of Bukhara. An even larger copy of the Koran was produced in Indonesia in 2006 (seven feet long). The Koran is not merely a repository of religious knowledge; it is an object of veneration in itself, far more so than the Bible.

Above and opposite below: **6 & 7.** Some of the tiles decorating the cupola and exterior of the tomb.

8. Interior detail in the mausoleum of Abu Tengi, Samarkand. The Islamic ban on figurative imagery was certainly upheld in religious contexts – there are no human or animal figures in mosques, or illustrated Korans. But figures can be found in some of the artworks produced for courts of Islamic rulers. The ban released the innate Arabic love of, and skill in, abstract design that can found in the early decoration of weaponry and in textiles.

9. Egyptian children learning the Koran by rote, 1899; just as children had done for centuries before and still do today.

Above and below: **10 & 11.** The western expansion of Islam did not of course stop at Spain, but Portugal, and examples of Moorish influence abound, as here at the Palacio Nacional de Sintra. (The westernmost point of Europe, Cabo da Roca, is 18

km away.) After the *Reconquista* the Palace became a royal residence and would eventually, through expansion, include elements of Gothic, Mudéjar, Manueline and Renaissance architecture. Not only in these beautiful tiles but also the later, famous *azujelos,* coloured tiles of the 15th and 16th centuries, symbolic of Portugal, Islam resides.The word 'Mudéjar', which came to refer to the Moors who remained and by extension the vernacular Moorish-inspired Iberian architecture that came *after* the *Reconquista* is a corruption of the Arab *Mudajjan,* meaning "those who accept submission" – both submission to Islam and to the temporal power of the Christian kings.

12. Charlemagne is crowned *Imperator Romanorum* on Christmas Day, 800, by Pope Leo III in Rome. This fanciful Victorian interpretation is far from the truth. Charlemagne had little desire for such an honour and the Pope's attempt to revive the Roman imperial title in the West was part of a desperate effort to shore up the authority of the papacy. The Byzantine imperial throne at Constantinople was at that time occupied by a woman, Irene, her sex enough reason in itself for the Pope to desire a new, Western powerbase.

13. Abbasid Caliph Harun al-Rashid receives a delegation from Charlemagne in Baghdad, probably in 801. Charlemagne received an Asian elephant and an ingenious kind of cuckoo clock for his good manners.

14. Genghis Khan (c.1162-1227); portrait at the National Palace Museum, Tapei, Taiwan. The 13th-century chronicler Minhaj al-Siraj Juzjani described the conqueror of much of Eurasia as "awe-inspiring, a butcher, just, resolute, an overthrower of enemies, intrepid, sanguinary and cruel." There was never an example in all the blood-letting of "the butcher" and the Mongol hordes engaging in religious war.

15. Tomb of Tamerlane's relatives in the Shah-i Zandeh complex, Samarkand. Timur bin Taraghay Barlas (1336-1405), sacker of Baghdad, Damascus and Delhi, founded the Timurid dynasty that would last in some form until 1857. As a patron of the arts, much of the architecture he commissioned still stands in Samarkand (present-day Uzbekistan).

16. Niccoló Machiavelli (1469-1527) on the right with his mentor the statesman, general and churchman Cesare Borgia, model in part for Machiavelli's description of the *principe nuovo*, the ruler who maintains the health and stability of the state, in *Il Principe*. His rational, secular approach to statecraft led to his book being indexed by Rome. But perhaps his other great work, *Discourses on Livy*, is more relevant to the modern world. It emphasises the superiority of a republic over a monarchy and includes the concept of checks and balances.

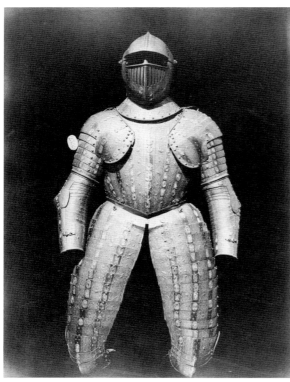

Above and left: **17 & 18.**
Portrait of Christopher
Columbus (1451-1506)
attributed to Bartholomeo de
Suardo; and a reminder of
what the great explorer was
above all else – his armour
in the Madrid Armoury – a
soldier and a conqueror. The
natives of Cicao on Haiti
were obliged to find a quota
of gold, signified by a token
around their necks. Those
who failed would have
their hands chopped off. No
contemporary portrait of
Columbus actually exists.

1600

ABDVLGVAHID ·

ÆTATIS:42 ·

LEGATVS REGIS BARBARIÆ
IN ANGLIAM ·

19. Secretary to Sultan Ahmad al-Mansour of Morocco, Abd al-Wahid bin Ma'ood bin Mohammed 'Annouri, from Fes. In 1600 he led an extraordinary and secret mission to England and the Court of Elizabeth, to suggest an alliance to attack and defeat Spain both in Europe and in the Spanish colonies of the West Indies. What an extraordinary alliance that would have been. The Queen was genuinely tempted: as one of her advisers later noted, "Her Majesty in using the King of Fes, doth not arm a barbarian against a Christian, but a barbarian against a heretic." Had the English ships and the Barbary horses been employed in common cause, the history of the Americas (and therefore of Europe) might have been entirely rewritten.

20. Mathematician and philosopher René Descartes (1596-1650). Arguably the leading intellect of the Scientific Revolution, his greatest contribution to enlightenment (to simplify laughably the work of a man whose writings have provided a framework for Western philosophical enquiry to the present day), was doubt.

21. The greatest scientist, Sir Isaac Newton (1643-1727) actually expended more words on religion than on natural philosophy, astronomy, mathematics and classical mechanics.

22. "Arabs from the 'Garden of Allah', NY." Even in the city that has seen it all, this group of Arabs stimulated some interest at the beginning of the last century. Though as for almost all ethnic minorities, assimilation has been easier for the 1.2 million (variable according to definition) of Arabic ancestry in the US, than it is in Europe. There have been no US-born or second-generation Islamic terrorists who have acted on home soil, unlike the pattern in the UK and elsewhere in Europe.

23. Two sons of King Ibn Saud of Saudi Arabia, Amir Khalid and Amir Faisal, photographed in 1940 (or 1941) at the Mayflower Hotel, Washington DC. They had just completed an extensive tour of the US studying irrigation projects. Four years earlier, Standard Oil of California had found promising amounts of oil and gas at its first Saudi Arabian test well, Damman No. 1. Twenty years later, OPEC was formed; 22 years later, slavery was abolished in the Kingdom; 25 years later, women's education was introduced.

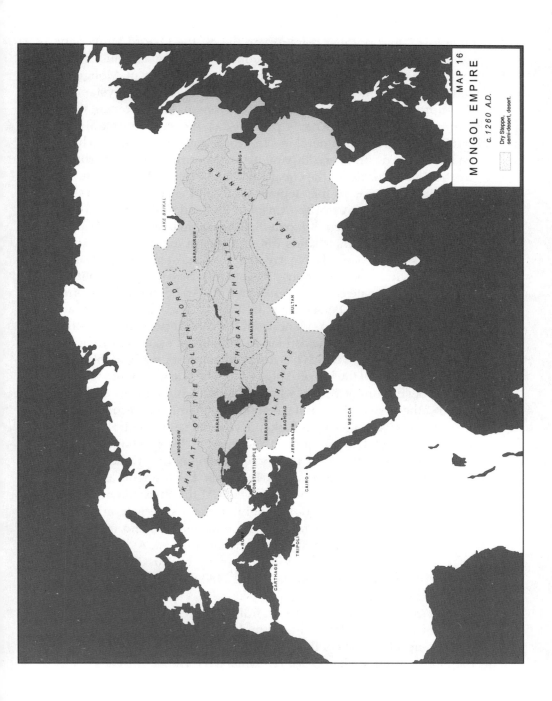

MAP 16

MONGOL EMPIRE

c. 1260 A.D.

Dry Steppe,
semi-desert, desert.

have said, "is to shed my enemies' blood and wring tears from their womenfolk," and not just tears. Bryan Sykes, the Oxford University geneticist, says that 16 million of today's central Asian men carry Genghis Khan's Y chromosome as he, the alpha male of Mongolia, killed the leading men in the territories he conquered and systematically impregnated all the most attractive women. With women, then, the number of Genghis Khan's present-day descendants would be about 32 million. At his funeral in 1227, forty maidens are said to have been burned to death to accompany his virile spirit into the afterlife.

By the time of his death the Great Khan had extended his dominions from their heartlands in the steppes south and east of Lake Baykal, westwards to the shores of the Caspian Sea and eastwards through northern China to the Sea of Japan. Following this, his four acknowledged sons extended their lands through Russia into eastern Europe, parts of Persia, China and Korea, creating the largest land empire of all time. They divided this enormous area into four *khanates*, principalities, of which the Ilkhanate covered Persia and the Arab lands with its first capital in Maragha, in Persia (later, in Tabriz). The Kipchak Khanate of the Golden Horde covered land from the central point of Asia – the Altai Mountains – to the Carpathian Mountains of eastern Europe. Its capital, Sarai (the site of which has not been unquestionably identified), was likely located on the Lower Volga river. The Great Khanate with its capital at Beijing under Kublai Khan, included China, Korea and East Asia. And the Chagatai Khanate, named after Temujin's second legitimate son, with its capital at Samarkand, covered south-central Asia.

In the winter of 1236-37, sinister mounted archers, Mongols, were found scouting the broadleaf forests of Russia, an occurrence deeply scarring the historical memory of the Russians. The Mongols as always were preparing their attack. No one ever beat the Russians in winter war, except the Mongols under Genghis Khan's successor, his third son Ogedai who in the year following the reconnoitre and using rivers as pathways for attack and supply, defeated them. As a result the Mongols were able to exact rich tribute from the Russians for more than two hundred years. It was not until 1480 that the Russians were able to throw off this burden.

In the 1230s, Ogedai completed building the first Mongolian capital of Karakorum that his father had founded on his favourite campsite, late in his life. (The ruins of the city, two hundred miles west of today's Mongolian capital of Ulan Bator (Ulaanbaatar), were discovered only in 1889 by a Russian explorer.)

Having overrun Persia in the 1220s and '30s (while the Christians were overrunning the Muslim *taifas* in Spain) leaving a trail of burnt cities and depopulated countryside, the Mongols invaded Anatolia in 1243. The Seljuk Sultanate of Rum with its capital in Iconium (Konya), independent for 172 years and ruled at the time by Kaikhosru II, was reduced to vassal status, placed under Mongol viceroys and made to pay tribute. The Seljuks' successively united empire and disunited clan-based emirates had been important political players in the Middle East for 200 years when their independence fell to the swords, spears and arrows of the Mongols.

Hulagu Khan and the Razing of Baghdad:
Eight years after the Mamluk leader, Aybak, seized power in Egypt the Mongols and their Uzbek allies under one of Genghis Khan's grandsons, Hulagu Khan (Hulago) who was born in Persia, stormed into Iraq. Hulagu had already wiped out the eastern branch of the Assassins in their mountain fastness and had hanged the Grand Master of the sect, Rukn ad-Din Khurshah. By refusing Mongol demands to ally his inviolable person with them against the Assassins, in 1258 the 37th Abbasid Caliph, al-Mustasim, had provided a pretext for Hulagu (whose wife was a Christian) to summon this the Prince of Believers to appear before him, commanding him to surrender his city of Baghdad and seals of office in the caliphate. Upon al-Mustasim's fearful refusal, Hulagu, descending as did Byron's "Assyrian coming down like the wolf on the fold," razed the city and put 200,000 of its inhabitants to the sword. The Christians and their churches were spared. (Other implausible accounts give numbers of deaths up to a million.) The job though is said to have taken forty days. To show his contempt for the Caliph, the Mongol chieftain had him kicked to death by his troops (the authenticity of this has not been demonstrated), the ultimate ignominy in the Arab world where the foot is "unclean". Except perhaps for one son, all of the Caliph's family members were executed. The imposing buildings, the still efficient public works of the city and the dilapidated but still functioning irrigation system of central Mesopotamia were destroyed. The libraries were burned, books thrown into the Tigris. The caliphate of Baghdad was abolished. Little in the history of civilization compares with the swift extinction of the Iraqi caliphate, even in its shabby, impotent later years, still a centre of culture.

Michael Wood quotes the words of the Persian poet Saadi of Shiraz, who was in Abadan when he heard the news of the destruction of the "first city of the world". Looking out from his lodgings over the Shatt al-Arab, in his mind's eye he saw the river running with blood. "You ask me", he wrote, "about the sack of Baghdad? It was so horrible there are no words to describe it. I wish I had died earlier and had not seen how the fools destroyed these treasures of knowledge and learning. I thought I understood the world, but this holocaust is so strange and pointless that I am struck dumb. The revolutions of time and its decisions have defeated all reason and knowledge."

Bernard Lewis argues that the destruction wrought by the Mongols in Iraq was exaggerated by the chroniclers, as everything was in those times. Most of it, he maintains, was tactical not wilful, and destruction ceased after the campaigns of conquest were complete. Mongol history, at least in Persia, seems in part to confirm this view. Whatever Hulagu Khan's motives, whatever devastation, the conquest was in practice unprecedentedly ruinous for Iraq. With the destruction of the irrigation canals, the canal heads, the locks, extensive areas of central and southern Iraq were turned into swamp or dry steppe. The labour of thousands of African slaves over centuries in draining the marshes of southern Iraq was wasted. And the surviving farmers, consumed by malaria and malnutrition, were too weak to rebuild the canal system or prevent rapacious bedouins, long since disaffected, from raiding and terrorizing the countryside.

In the year following the destruction of Baghdad, the Mongols reached northern Mesopotamia and put an end to several Seljuk minikingdoms. They sacked Damascus and destroyed most of the remaining Seljuk and Ayyubid statelets in Syria and Anatolia, laying siege to Palestine and the Egyptian homeland. Hulagu Khan's Christian military commander, Kitbugha, aimed at Egypt the same threatening demands that his master had made of Baghdad twenty months before. But the Mongol army travelled with and depended on thousands of horses for the conduct of its operations, two to four horses and mules per man. Such numbers needed extensive grazing lands. Not enough existed in northern Iraq and Syria. Shortage of fodder imposed a major restraint on the Mongols. The tactics of their army were designed for, and the army was certainly at its most effective in, open grassland. The long supply lines added to quarrelling among Genghis Khan's grandsons, limited the army's determination to continue the expansion. The unity forged half a century before by the Great Khan had been lost, and with it had gone his unequalled authority.

The defence of Islam against the menace of the Mongols had fallen to the Egyptian Mamluks, and in 1260 at Ain Jalut (the spring in Palestine where legend had it that David had slain Goliath, *Jalut*) the new sultan, Qutuz, defeated Hulagu Khan's army, capturing General Kitbugha and beating him to death, the first defeat for the Mongols since Genghis Khan's rise. With Hulagu Khan's absence from the field, quarrelling with his cousins, and the paucity of grazing land, the over-confident Mongol army had been at no more than division strength.

Qutuz' victory put an end to Mongol expansion in the Middle East, enabling him to regain land east of the River Jordan. And, barely a gen-eration after Ain Jalut, troubles in Persia drew the Mongols away from Syria and from parts of Anatolia, causing them to reduce the forces along their western marches, to withdraw their boundaries to the line of the Euphrates, and into the Kurdish highlands of eastern Anatolia. As a result, local leaders were then able to revive some of their princi-palities in Syria and plateau Anatolia and to find a balance of power with the Mamluks in the Levant. Although defeated in Palestine, the Mongols still remained the dominant power east of the Euphrates for some 75 years, until about 1335.

The Ilkhanate:
Hulagu Khan's lands from the Euphrates across Iraq and Iran to Herat and the Kirthar mountain range skirting the plain of the Indus, comprised the Ilkhanate. With the Mongols headquartered in Persia, Iraq was again subordinated as a vassal province and ahead lay 500 years of poverty and neglect. In Persia with its ancient civilization and its more temperate plateau climate a new period of economic and cultural development began. Hulagu located his capital in Maragha, his birthplace. The town, at an elevation of 5,300 ft, quickly became the intellectual capital of the western Mongol world. Its library is said to have contained 400,000 books (or 40,000, according to other sources). Maragha's astronomic observatory, under the guidance in the 1260s of Nasr ed-Din Tusi, the Persian, Khorasani, former chief scholar and scientist of the Assassins' Alamut lair (where in fact he may have been held against his will), drew the learned from afar, replacing the devastated Baghdad. Using astrolabes, quadrants and armillaries – the telescope was not invented until 1607-08 – they mapped the heavens.

The Ilkhanate protected its native religions, including Christianity. Hulagu Khan's wife Dokuz Khan, and his general Kitbugha, killed at

Ain Jalut, had been Nestorian Christians. Hulagu's son Abaqa was a Buddhist. The third Ilkhan Ahmed Takudar adopted Islam despite outspoken opposition. As a result he was dethroned by a cabal of Buddhist and shamanist subordinate princes and replaced by his nephew Arghun (r.1284-91). Arghun unwisely appointed a Jewish doctor, Sa'd ad-Dawla, as finance minister. Ad-Dawla imposed high taxes on a growing Muslim population, leading to his undoing and execution.

Like conquerors before them, nonetheless, the Mongols were finally civilized by success. Arghun's son Ghazan Mahmud succeeded in 1295. He moved his capital from Maragha to Tabriz and readopted Islam as the state religion. The Ilkhanate then evolved a high measure of culture, and Ghazan's patronage of scholarship and the arts atoned for much of the depravity of his ancestors. Even so, some years later Ghazan made a final but failed assault on Mamluk-governed Syria.

Works of art from the times of several Mongol Ilkhans fetch enormous prices on the art market today. The gold- and silver-inlaid brass inkwell and pen case of Sultan Ahmed Takudar's vizier, Shams a-Din Joveyni, sold at auction at Sotherby's in London in 2003 for £1,120,000, ($1,960,000).

After Ghazan's untimely death at age thirty-two, the gains of his reign were squandered, though the political and religious results were still important. Sunni Islam had become the official religion of the state. But in 1335, upon the death without male issue of the last Ilkhan, Ghazan Mahmud's nephew Abu Said, internal stresses caused the Ilkhanate to break up into a clutter of Mongol, Turkmen and Persian territories and to perish as a distinct political force. The Ilkhanate had lasted seventy-seven years.

The economy of Persia decayed, worsened by the disruption of trade routes and disastrous plagues. (The plagues may well have been forerunners of the Black Death, localized rehearsals.) When the Ilkhanate broke up, a Mongol, Hasan Buzurg, seized Iraq, rebuilt parts of Baghdad and made it his winter capital. Then Baghdad lost much of its population again in the Black Death of 1348, like most cities of the Middle East. Still, in the 1360s Hasan Buzurg's son Uways was able to extend his realm into Azerbaijan, creating an important state.

Filipe Fernández-Armesto maintains that despite the carnage of their conquests the Mongols played an unequaled role in the socio-economic development of Eurasia. They united China for the first time and put the East in touch with the West. After overcoming their fears, people from the Ukraine to China were joined in an empire of laws and security. The steppes could for the first time be crossed safely and swiftly, clearing the way for trade and the communication of information. The technology of the blast furnace reached Europe this way. This, too, was part of the route trod by Marco Polo to Kublai Khan's Beijing in the 1270s, and by Kublai Khan's emissary the Nestorian monk Rabban Sauma, in the opposite direction to Paris. "I tell you," Marco Polo is reported to have said after sailing up the Grand Canal in China, "in all truth, the riches and resources, it's all on such a stunning scale you wouldn't believe it. If the Chinese were warlike they would conquer the rest of the world. Thank goodness they are not." In fact, the Mongols were in charge, and were warlike. The Mongol peace carried Chinese ideas to the Occident when the flow of knowledge from the Arab world had largely ceased. Persia enjoyed some of this boon, but Iraq and Arabia little or none.

Tamerlane:

By 1300, the Arabs of the Middle East were concerned almost exclusively with survival. Over the centuries, they had alternately been indulged, exploited, plundered and massacred by the Byzantines, by sects during Umayyad times, during inter-communal fighting among the Abbasids and their perfidious provincial governors, by venal Turkic mercenaries, the Buwaihids, the Seljuks, and by fiendish Mongols. Alone among the peoples of these territories, the bedouins, long since withdrawn into their deserts, had seen little change in their age-old way of life.

In 1393 (when in England, the poet, customs comptroller and bureaucrat, Geoffrey Chaucer, was writing the *Canterbury Tales*), Tamerlane (Timur), an Uzbek Turk claiming descent from Genghis Khan and already fifty-seven years old, invaded the Middle East with another Mongol-Uzbek horde. He had just completed an invasion of India where he had slaughtered the Muslim population of Delhi, ruled by Mohammed Shah III.

Tamerlane's campaigns were studded with savagery, not only in India but over all Persia. The city of Isfahan was the scene of one of his atrocities. Tens of thousands were killed and towers built with their skulls, monuments to his victory. On arriving in Syria in 1400, after killing 20,000, he carried off to his capital Samarkand all the learned men, artists and skilled craftsmen of Damascus. Samarkand thrived on war booty even more than had Damascus under Umayyad Caliphs Mu'awiya and Walid centuries before. Syrian agriculture and industry, which had expanded strongly under Saladin and the early Mamluk sultans, never recovered fully from Tamerlane's depredations. In 1401, Tamerlane turned to Iraq and massacred the people of Baghdad again, 90,000 of them it was said, and built more towers with their severed heads. (But in his blank verse play, *Tamburlaine the Great*, Shakespeare's contemporary Christopher Marlowe portrayed an unexpected complexity of character in this blood-chilling empire-builder, suggesting grandeur as well as brutality.)

The Mamluks ruling Egypt in the 1390s, confined as they were to the territories west of the Syrian desert, were able to stand up to Tamerlane and keep his forces out of Palestine. Upon Tamerlane's death in 1405, his empire which – once again – reached from the Euphrates to the Indus, reviving the Ilkhanate, had broken up due to fighting among his sons. These conditions enabled rival nomadic Turkmen confederacies known as the Black Sheep and the White Sheep alliances repeatedly to fight over and occupy Iraq. But by the middle of the century, Tamerlane descendants (Timurids) had succeeded in re-asserting control over eastern Persia and Afghanistan. They made their capital in Herat where they established a Persian-style culture that in time would support the arts and sciences.

The Safavids:
In 1501-02 (while Queen Isabella of Spain was decreeing the mandatory conversion of Muslims to Christianity) a powerful unifying movement under a Sufi-inspired Turkmen dynasty, the Safavids (known as the Red Hats), who had adopted Shiism, came to power in Persia, overthrowing White Sheep Turkmens. They were led by a fourteen-year-old princeling, Shah Ismail, whose reign awakened fury in the hearts of the radical Sunni Ottomans on his west flank, led by Bayazit II (he who would welcome Jews expelled by Isabella from Spain), and also the passions of the Sunni Uzbeks, an unstable element on his northeast flank, in the former Chagatai Khanate. Ottoman hatred of Shiism was so visceral that Sultan Bayazid II's successor, Selim "the Grim", sought out and put to death 40,000 of his own subjects whom he suspected of being Shias. Since 1501, Persia's (Iran's) national religion has been Shiism. Soon after the founding of the Safavid imamate, Iran became a theocracy venerating the boy Ismail in near-idolatry.

After the disintegration of the Abbasid empire, it was the Sufi movement of both Sunni and Shiite orientations which supplied a common basis of religious culture and a degree of social cohesion among the mass of Iraqi, Persian and immigrant Turkmen people in Iraq and Persia. While the majority of Sufi brethren were Sunni, many of them still revered Caliph Ali, the inspiration of Shiism.

The Sufi movement motivated a succession of Persian artists and literati who gave Twelver Shiite Persia, with its capital after 1501 once more in Tabriz, its finest poetry. Artwork of striking beauty was also produced in silk and woollen fabric and in metals, ceramics, ivory and jade. Under Ismail, lands from the Euphrates to the marches of India and Afghanistan were again reconstituted as a political unit. The rise of the theocratic Safavids marked the re-emergence in Iran of a powerful central authority with much the same geographical extension as had been reached long before by the ancient Iranian empires. But Iraq was lost to the Ottomans in the 16th century and remained under Turkish control for much of the time until World War 1.

The Safavids took Baghdad once more in 1623, holding it for fifteen years. Fighting between the Sunni Ottomans and the theologically hostile Shiite Safavids over Iraq continued. However, in the 18th century, Baghdad, nominally still in Ottoman hands, was strong enough for a local dynasty of Sunni pashas to exercise quasi-independence.

12

Mamluk Egypt, 1260-1517 AD

Egypt and the Mamluk Mercenaries – The Guns-and-Ships Revolution
– The Mamluk Fall

Egypt and the Mamluk Mercenaries:
In 1260, following the Mamluk victory over the Mongols at Goliath's Spring, a senior Kipchak officer in the Egyptian army named Baybars, a former slave of Mongols, killed Sultan Qutuz and seized the throne. One of Baybars' fathers-in-law was a grandson of Genghis Khan, illustrating the close bond between the Kipchaks and the Mongols. Baybars, who had been implicated in the murder of Sultan Aybak whose slave he had once been, though gifted, was quite unscrupulous. One of his more astute and historic acts of statecraft was to enthrone Abul Kasim Ahmed, a son of the thirty-fifth Abbasid caliph, al-Zahir, as figurehead "Caliph" al-Mustansir in Cairo. His aim was to combine religious leadership of the Arabs by Egypt with the nation's existing economic pre-eminence. Baybars induced al-Mustansir to confer on him the title of Sultan, furnished this cat's paw with an army, and sent him off to recapture Baghdad from the Mongols. He failed and was killed.

In the following year Baybars installed another scion of Abbasid descent, al-Hakim I, who "reigned" in Cairo for forty years. For another two hundred years the Abbasid bloodline was regularly appointed with pomp and ceremony as shadow caliphs in Cairo, mere creatures

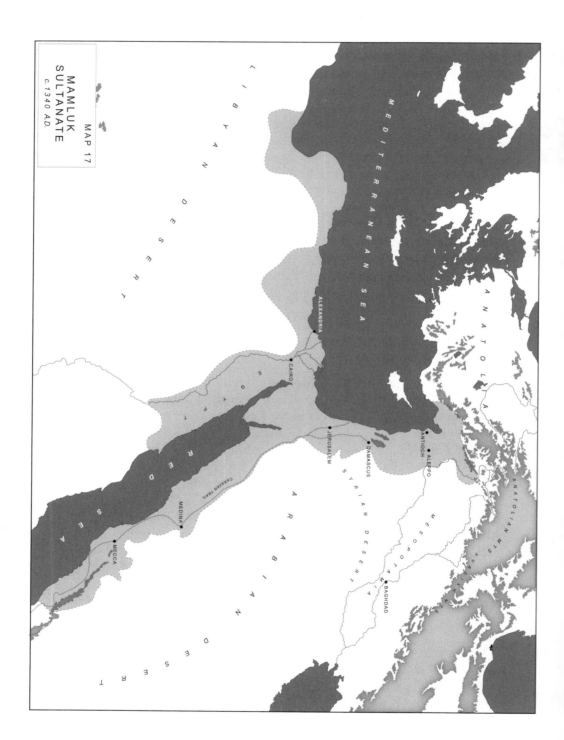

MAP 17

MAMLUK
SULTANATE
c. 1340 A.D.

MEDITERRANEAN SEA

L I B Y A N   D E S E R T

ANATOLIA

ALEXANDRIA

CAIRO

E G Y P T

R E D   S E A

CARAVAN TRAIL

JERUSALEM

DAMASCUS

ANTIOCH

ALEPPO

S Y R I A N   D E S E R T

MESOPOTAMIA

EUPHRATES

ANATOLIAN MTS

MEDINA

A R A B I A N   D E S E R T

BAGHDAD

MECCA

of the court installed by their Kipchak and Circassian masters. The caliphs' job was simply to provide the régime with an air of legitimacy. Iraq under the Buwaihids and Seljuks had been much the same. These caliphs, lodged in Cairo's Citadel, were usually allowed to leave the city only when accompanying a Mamluk sultan. However, for part of the time between 1406 and 1414 one of them, Musta'in, occupied the Egyptian throne as both Caliph and Sultan. Otherwise, rarely was it that any of them was allowed the pleasure of being recognized by a foreign ruler as an equal (to be addressed in the equivalent Muslim protocol of the day as "Sir My Brother and Good Friend"). As intended, Baybars' act of enthroning Abul Kasim as Caliph al-Mustansir in 1261 did in practice elevate Egypt to the religious leadership of the Arab world, complementing Egypt's pre-eminent commercial position first established 250 years before by the Fatimids.

Comparisons are made between the achievements of Baybars and the noble Kurd, Saladin. Baybars however did more, reuniting Egypt with western Syria and holding the Mongols at bay. He destroyed several more crusader strongholds and further reduced the Assassins in Syria. His successes were more lasting than Saladin's. In the many wars he fought, he was usually victorious. He extended the territory of Egypt into the Sudan and brought Arabia, except for Yemen, under his rule. As a tactic in the eternal political struggles within the Sultanate, instead of decreeing as national law a single choice from the four *fiqhs* of Sunni Islamic law, he declared them all to be equal under the watchful gaze of Allah. Obtaining approval from one school or other then enabled him to outmanoeuvre any *ulema* opposing his wishes. His rule was cruel, extravagant, but apparently quite popular, and one of fairly efficient government. He died in 1277, in his fifties.

Another of Baybars' fathers-in-law, Qala'un, who had fought the Mongols in the battle of Ain Jalut seventeen years before, had his men kill the two eldest of Baybars' sons and took the throne for himself. Qala'un expelled crusaders from more Levantine ports, beat back another Mongol attack, and extended Egyptian-Syrian commerce. He is noted too for having founded a hospital that was highly praised and functioned until it was replaced in the 1920s by a modern facility. Qala'un's successor, his eldest son al-Ashraf drove the crusaders out of Acre, but was murdered by his deputy and accomplices a few years later.

Qala'un's descendants ruled Egypt for ninety years, father-to-son, with periodic interruptions until the Circassian Mamluks seized power in 1381. One of Qala'un's younger sons, al-Nasir, reigned three times, being twice dethroned. He was first installed in 1293 when he was nine years old. He was not permitted to rule at that age and was forced by his deputy named Kitboga (not to be confused with Hulagu Khan's general, Kitburgha) to abdicate in the following year, and lose his throne. When he was fourteen al-Nasir was reinstated following the overthrow of the usurper and of another one, Husam ud-Din, who had managed to occupy the throne for three years.

During these troubled times Ilkhan Ghazan Mahmud took advantage of the situation to invade Syria, laying hold of Damascus and other cities, but was driven out in 1300. The final Mongol attempt to acquire more Mamluk land by storm came in 1303. This too failed. Some years later, al-Nasir was again supplanted, by one of his father's former slaves, a Circassian called al-Mozaffar. This one lasted a year and paid for his treachery with his head when his sovereign returned to power. The youthful Sultan was then able to come to terms with a distant cousin of the last Ilkhan (Abu Said), Uzbeg Khan the reigning Prince of the Golden Horde who, like the leaders of most of the Mongol khanates, had by this time converted to Islam. Al-Nasir improved relations with the Mongols by marrying one of Uzbeg Khan's daughters.

Since the time of Saladin, Egyptian sultans had on occasions chosen to employ the Assassins in pursuit of their personal objectives. The annals show that al-Nasir used a company of more than a hundred of them in Persia in an attempt to avenge himself upon one of the murderers of his brother, Sultan al-Ashraf. The Assassin contingent was however outwitted by the malefactor who was only finally killed on the orders of Ilkhan Abu Said, as a favour returned for a similar courtesy paid him earlier by the Mamluk Sultan.

Al-Nasir sent many embassies abroad, to Tsar Michael Shishman of Bulgaria; Mohammed bin Tughlug, Sultan of Delhi; most other Muslim leaders; the Monophysite King of Abyssinia; the Pope; and the kings of France and Aragon. But al-Nasir's government became recklessly wasteful at the expense of the people. He died in 1341 at fifty-seven having in all, man and boy, reigned for forty-two years. With his death ended the relatively successful period of Mamluk rule.

During the next forty years, fighting for power among al-Nasir's nine sons, turmoil, earthquake and the Black Death set the scene for the Circassian power-grab of 1381 when the ruthless al-Zahir would take the throne and even greater instability would take hold.

Having escaped the fury of the Mongol attack of 1258, Egypt continued to be the guardian of Arab civilization until the Ottoman conquest rampaging out of Anatolia a century-and-half later. Even so, most of the later Mamluks and Circassians, living off the spice trade, frittered away their wealth, governing the state with ruinous ineptitude. As the terms of international trade changed further in favour of Europeans, the Mamluks could find no solution to the sultanate's growing economic difficulties. Decay set in again as it had for the Ayyubids and the Fatimids.

In the year 1400, Tamerlane arrived, laying waste to Syria, even if the beast was kept out of Egypt and southern Palestine. These crises caused Sultan Barsbay, who ruled Egypt from 1422 to 1438 (not to be confused with the Kipchak Baybars) and his successors, to strive to extract more revenue by making sugar and spices royal monopolies, by drastically increasing taxes and levies on trade, and by debasing the currency. Such measures and those of several dissolute predecessors led to inflation, currency depreciation, increasing loss of market share and foreign reprisals. Venetian merchants exacted better trade terms for themselves from the Sultan, while the King of Aragon and the Prince of Catalonia seized Egyptian vessels in reprisal.

Even though north African climatic conditions had improved with the onset of Europe's Little Ice Age, population numbers in Egypt had already plummeted. In a census made in Barsbay's time, the number of towns and villages recorded in the country had fallen to 2,170. In the Fatimid heyday of 990-95, there had been some 10,000. Through part of Barsbay's reign, the Mamluks maintained friendly relations with the belligerent Ottomans and joined them in celebrating the capture of Constantinople in 1453. Later, rivalry set in and by 1470 they were skirmishing.

The Guns-and-Ships Revolution:

A catastrophe for the Mamluks came at the end of the 15th century. While Leonardo da Vinci was in Milan painting *The Last Supper,* a Portuguese navigator Vasco da Gama rounded the Cape of Good Hope, reached India and returned to Lisbon, his ships laden with silks, dyes, aromatics and spices. Ten years earlier, the Portuguese explorer, Pedro da Covilhã, had reached India via the Red Sea, raising the possibility of Europeans trading directly with the Orient, if they could overcome Arab determination to maintain their control of the Red Sea passage, the caravan trails and their monopoly of direct contact with the Asian suppliers.

From early in the 16th century Arab warships in the Indian Ocean tried in vain to halt the Portuguese merchantmen that had rounded the Cape. Their failure rose from two lines of technological advancement made by Westerners during the 15th century – which were to be defining accomplishments in the rise of the West. These were gunpowder, the formula for which the Arabs had long before obtained from the Chinese. The Arabs had improved the formulation and transmitted it to Europe where it arrived in the late 13th century. Westerners put gunpowder to good effect in the bronze cannon designed in the early 16th century for ship-board use (though 20th century Muslim writers maintain that Muslim alchemists first concocted military grade gunpowder.) The Ottoman Turks soon caught on. The dominant force in the Arab world, the Mamluks, let the technology slip by.

The second improvement was the redesign by Westerners of sailing ships to provide them with greater ocean-going capability. These improvements, some of which followed Chinese ideas, had been taking place slowly over a century or more. The slave-driven galley with secondary sails gave way in the West to the fully-rigged ship with stern-post rudder. The first three-masted, square-rigged, stern post-ruddered ship was built in Italy about 1435. (But by then Chinese naval architects had been designing ships with water-tight bulkheads and stern-post rudders for two hundred years.) The coupling of these technologies in the new ships, the "gunpowder revolution" or "guns and ships", by the Venetians in the late 15th century, added to expanding markets, increased availability of investment capital and the newly designed banking and insurance safeguards enabled the maritime nations of the West to profit directly from the treasures of the East while in the main cutting out Arab middlemen.

(In 1420-33, during the reign of Ming Emperor Hsan-tsung, the Chinese Muslim eunuch admiral, Zeng He [Cheng Ho], had sailed his fleet of scores of ships including giant 500-ft long stern post-ruddered vessels on voyages of commerce around the Indian Ocean from the East Indies and India to the Persian Gulf and Mozambique. It is noteworthy that there is no record of these aggressive military expeditions ever having plundered or murdered. The 1433 expedition was the last, and after this China turned in on itself, retiring from the world of navigation and maritime trade to devote its energies, it has been suggested, to extending the Great Wall and expanding the canal system. But then, disastrously, printing was brought under censorship and control and China slipped into long-term decline from which it did not emerge on the world scene until the 20th century. The claim made in 2002 by the former submarine commander Gavin Menzies that a Chinese fleet reached the American coast in 1421 seems to have little support among professional historians.)

After 1500, Arab oared-warships in the Indian Ocean found they were no match for the swifter, masted, cannon-armed Portuguese merchantmen. The days of boarding the enemy ship from galleys and fighting it out at close quarters were over, except for the Mediterranean, inshore waters and other inland seas. Seventy years after the Chinese withdrawal, the Portuguese came to dominate the Indian Ocean, systematically destroying Arab merchant shipping. The Portuguese penetrated the Persian Gulf, reaching Qatar, and the Red Sea, where they were less prevailing. They planted trading bases on the Indian shore and defeated a joint Mamluk-Indian fleet. In 1510, the Portuguese captured Goa on India's west coast, made it the capital of their eastern empire, and held on until it was annexed by India in 1961. Soon after the taking of Goa, the conquistador Alfonso de Albuquerque secured the port of Malacca on the Malay peninsula from where for decades the Portuguese were able to corner much of the spice trade. It was the contemporaneous advent of practical and powerful gunpowder, the new ships, and the invention of the printing press – all technological developments – which propelled the West from the feudal-agrarian society to the modern age.

Of the several factors in play, it was the opening of the Cape route to India which in the end turned the eastern Mediterranean Arab lands into an economic backwater and seriously weakened Italy. The fading of Italy was seen in the shift of economic power to the nations of northwest Europe – Spain and Portugal, France, England, Holland – adding to the pressures that Italy was subjected to by the Ottomans, and its dynastic and religious wars. The two hundred years from 1550 to 1750 were politically the forgotten centuries of Italy, even if in art it reached its zenith early in this period (1480-1610) when Leonardo, Michelangelo, Raphael, Correggio, Titian, Tintoretto, Veronese and Caravaggio revolutionized the world of painting and sculpture.

For 350 years following the time of the Ayyubids, the Mamluk military machine had seldom been beaten in war, losing rarely even against the Mongols. Although the economy of Egypt was in ruinous condition by 1500, it was the military machine which failed the country in the end. The Mamluks were soundly defeated by the Ottomans, not because the Ottomans could bring to the field a bigger or better trained army, but because of the Turks' close geographical proximity to, and technological contact with, Europe, where the cannon and the new harquebus infantry weapon – the musket – were being perfected. European and Ottoman weapons and battlefield tactics had been adapted to the new realities of warfare. In the Mamluk empire few units were armed with the costly new weapons. Vanity, historical success, over-confidence, had led the Mamluk élite haughtily to reject the new machines and to continue fighting from horseback with bow and arrow, sword and lance, with the predictable outcome. And the year 1500 may therefore fittingly be taken as marking the end of the thousand-year domination of the Asian battlefield by mounted archers – the bedouins, the Mongols, the Mamluks. For the first time in history military technology enabled "civilized" man to overcome the "barbarian". (It is not surprising that Leonardo's notes at this time included sketches for a machine gun, a sort of battlefield tank, a steam-powered cannon, and something like a helicopter.)

The Mamluk Fall:
After a long period of political chaos in Circassian Mamluk Egypt and a succession of ephemeral sultans, a new leader was seated on the throne in April 1501: "The enthronement of Kansuh al-Ghuri as Sultan was to be legalized by the Caliph once the faqihs (religious judges) had arrived. They brought the new Sultan the emblems of sovereignty, the black cloak and turban in which they now arrayed him …The whole of Cairo was lit up like a halo…The new Sultan was at this time about sixty years of age (in fact fifty-three). His beard showed not a white hair. This was an auspicious omen." When however Kansuh al-Ghuri allied himself with the Ottomans' mortal enemies, the Safavids of Persia, he sealed the fate of Egypt for the next 300 years.

In 1516, the Ottomans, led by Selim I and well equipped with the harquebus, smashed the Mamluks and their Persian allies in the battle of Marj Dabiq, near Aleppo, killing the then sixty-eight-year-old Sultan Kansuh. The next year they defeated the Mamluks again at Al-Raydaniyah, near Cairo, where they caught Kansuh's successor, Tuman Bey, led him unsuspecting to the Bab al-Zuwaila city gate of Cairo, and hanged him.

The last Abbasid "caliph" al-Mutawakkil III was deposed and taken in bondage to Istanbul. He was later released though and returned to Cairo to live out his days, the record suggests, in drunken dissolution.

After this, the title of Caliph was held exclusively by the Ottoman sultans, even though little evidence exists of any formal assignment of al-Mutawakkil's nominally sovereign powers to Sultan Selim. (Other, questionable records suggest that assignment was indeed made, with the handing over of sword and regalia.) At this moment not only were the successors of the Abbasid Arab empire gone, but the triumphant Turks were striving to assume the dignity and leadership of their religion, Islam, no orthodox principle or practice of which would they seek to change.

At its defeat in 1517, notwithstanding the country's many ups and downs, Egypt had been the economic-commercial leader of the Arab world for 500 years – since the early years of the Fatimids – and its religious leader for 250 years – since the extinction of the Baghdad caliphate. Later that same year, 1517, a German monk Martin Luther fired his own revolutionary shots at that other ancient institution, Rome, opening the way for the reform of Christianity, introducing new principles and practices in spiritual matters, and taking an emphatic step towards restructuring society in Europe.

The ascendant Ottomans incorporated Egypt into their empire and left Janissaries, their own slave troops, many of Balkan Christian origin, under a pasha in control of the country. Otherwise they made few changes in the administration. In taking Egypt however the Ottomans had obtained a possession which was a mere shadow of its once imperial self. Egypt had never completely lost command of transit trade with the Far East but had always needed a near-monopoly of this trade to complement its output of foodstuffs and manufactured goods and slow its rate of economic decline.

The Mamluks remained as an Ottoman auxiliary unit and were permitted to continue importing slave boys from the steppes of Asia to be trained as cavalrymen. But as the Ottoman central government itself weakened in the 17th century, Mamluks replaced Ottoman officials and in due course made themselves rulers of Egypt once more. The Mamluks continued administering the country until 1798 when their colourful medieval army was devastated by the massed ranks and massive fire-power of *Nabulione Buonaparte's* French expeditionary force. As fate would have it, however, within weeks Napoleon's victory on land was turned into defeat at sea by Horatio Nelson's sinking of the French fleet at Aboukir, close to Alexandria, in the Battle of the Nile – thereby calling a brief halt to Napoleon's life-long mission of orchestrating his own legend.

The Mamluks survived in power until the Ottomans, once again administering Egypt, sent the Balkan Muslim Mohammed Ali to Cairo as governor in 1805 following the withdrawal of the French land forces. Mohammed Ali, born in today's Greece, is variously described as being of Macedonian, Greek or Albanian origin. He had entered Egypt as leader of the Albanian and Bosnian contingent of the Ottoman army. It was he who disposed finally of the Mamluks by the expedient of inviting their 500 leading members to a banquet in the Citadel (a landmark of today's Cairo) and having them massacred to the last man, to the last but one, it is said.

This Turkish-speaking ethnic Slav, Mohammed Ali, was the modernizer and revitalizer of Egypt, although the European powers obstructed the country's additional progress after about 1840. Mohammed Ali was the great-great grandfather of that other Mutawakkil III, the notorious pornography collector, Farouk, the last king of Egypt who at the age of thirty-two was forced into abdication and exile in Rome in 1952 by Gamal Abdul Nasser. Nasser could claim reasonably that Farouk was not of pure Egyptian blood.

13

The Ottoman Empire

*The Ottomans – Byzantine Emperors, 610 - 1453 – Empire Extinguished
– Ottoman Sultans, 14ᵗʰ-16ᵗʰ Centuries – The Rise of the House of Saud
– Enter the al-Rashids*

The Ottomans:

After Hulagu Khan's 1258 conquest of Mesopotamia, the principal
Seljuk dominion in Anatolia, the Sultanate of Rum, which had been
reduced to vassal status by the Mongols fifteen years earlier, broke
up into rival emirates. The neighbouring Byzantines led by the newly
enthroned Michael VIII were too weak to take advantage of the political mess, and so the situation allowed for the rise of a minor mercenary
Turkmen clan led by a chieftain named Osman Ghazi. The clan was
related through the Oghuz tribal confederation to the Seljuks. Osman's
father, Ertugrul, who had ridden out of Khorasan decades before with
400 mounted warriors and their families, had for a time been retained
by his distant cousins, the Sultans of Rum – already then vassals of the
Mongols – to provide a *cordon sanitaire* along the Byzantine marches.

   In 1281, the twenty-three-year-old Osman succeeded his ninety-
three-year-old father and began building a state from the political
débris of Anatolia. Progress was slow, but in 1299 Osman cut out part
of what had been the Sultanate of Rum for himself, based on the city of
Sögüt. This act was the founding move, and Osman was the founding
master of the Ottoman Empire.

When a political dispute broke out in the adjacent Balkans, the Greek Emperor Andronicus II recruited Osman's forces to secure his south flank, and Osman maintained this improbable alliance until his death in 1326. Osman's successor, his forty-five-year-old son Orhan, then moved into the rest of north-western Anatolia putting an end to the disordered ranks of Mongol-Seljuk mini-states, and moving his capital seventy miles to the rich old city of Bursa. In 1345, at the behest of (usurper)-Emperor John Cantacuzene, Orhan crossed the narrow waters of the Dardanelles on to European soil to assist his ally in a local Balkan conflict. But after the affair was settled the Ottomans announced that they intended remaining on the Christian shore. This to Edward Gibbon was the "last and fatal stroke in the long fall of the Roman Empire." Pandora's box had been opened. The Muslims had again arrived on European soil – by invitation!

Orhan entrenched his army on the European shore and at the age of sixty-four demanded the hand of a Cantacuzene daughter in marriage. Within months, however, all were laid low by the Black Death, and it was not until 1354 that Orhan, a survivor in his seventies, was able to move along the coast and take the port of Gallipoli commanding the Dardanelles. Constantinople, under John V Paleologus, the last bastion of the Roman Empire, the last stronghold of classical European learning, was denied free maritime access to the Mediterranean.

Seven years on, Orhan's grandson, Murad, advanced his army 100 miles north of Gallipoli, making a new capital for himself in ancient Adrianople which he renamed Edirne (now a border town between Turkey and Greece), threatening the Balkans. Even so, little help for the Byzantines came from the rest of the Christian world.

The disunity of their Christian foes had been crucial in paving the way for the Ottoman advance. A legacy of icy, centuries-old mistrust separated the Orthodox Byzantines from the Catholic West. The 1054 schism of Christianity had "left an implacable dispute over minor matters of ritual – the less fundamental they were, the greater the rancour," as Barbara Tuchman put it.

In 1389, the sixty-three-year-old Murad I reached Serbia and won the historic battle of Kosovo on the Field of Blackbirds (close to today's Pristina), the grave of Serbian independence for the next five centuries. This defeat is deeply ingrained in Serbian national consciousness and was the principal historical event inciting the ethnic cleansing of Muslims in the Balkan wars of the 1990's. Murad was knavishly killed on the battlefield, leaning over it is thought to catch a whispered word from a dying Serb who had the strength left to thrust a knife into his enemy's bowels. (A different account maintains that Murad was killed by a valiant Serb officer posing as a traitor.)

Murad was succeeded by his twenty-nine-year-old son Bayazit "the Thunderbolt" who, after killing his Serb prisoners, carried on the conquest north to the River Danube. There, in 1396, in a history-making battle at Nicopolis (now, Nicopol in Bulgaria), the Thunderbolt reinforced by turncoat Serbs smashed the less-than-united alliance of Christian knights led by French noblemen, and secured southeast Christendom for Islam and his destiny. The immediate aftermath of the Ottoman victory was another bloody massacre of prisoners ordered by Bayazit enraged at the great losses his forces had suffered, prisoners being tied in bundles and chopped to bits. It is not clear how many men died this way. Accounts range from 300 to 3000. Some Western noblemen were able to negotiate ransom arrangements for themselves and ultimately got their freedom.

The Ottoman advance was halted in 1400 by Tamerlane's incursion into the Middle East. Overrunning Anatolia, leaving another trail of ruined cities and pyramids of skulls, Tamerlane met and bested the Ottoman army at Ankara in central Anatolia in 1402. Bayazit the Thunderbolt was captured. According to legend, he was kept alive in an open cage on a wagon, fed through the bars and dragged along on the Mongol campaign until he died a miserable shameful death the next year, at age forty-three. Triumphantly displaying a captive chieftain in this way designed for humiliation was the theatre of the times.

The Mongol campaign subsided, having over-extended itself, but Bayazit's four sons understanding little beyond violence began immediately struggling for their father's vacant throne. Eleven years of fratricidal civil war then followed, during which time Tamerlane died as he was setting out on an expedition to China. His death laid to rest the threat to the Ottomans. Behind him, though, the mysteriously-driven but reputedly highly intelligent Tamerlane left only ruin and death.

When in the 1410s, Mehmet I, the youngest of the Bayazit sons, defeated his brothers, killing them one after another, he turned to extending the Ottoman state deeper into the Balkans. His son, Murad II, advanced further. In 1453, Murad's 20-year-old son by a slavegirl, Mehmet II, later dubbed "the Conqueror", with 80,000 men (against 7,000-8,000 defenders), a 26-foot bronze cannon cast by his Hungarian gunsmith, hurling 600-kg stone balls, and obsessed with matching the imperial record of Alexander the Great, took Constantinople, filled with the treasures and tribute of centuries. The last Emperor, Constantine XI, disappeared in a welter of carnage and rapine.

At the time of the Emperor's death, Constantinople – which Mehmet renamed Istanbul, meaning in classical Greek "In the City"– was the leading city of the East, more civilized, more populated than Alexandria, Cairo, Damascus, Baghdad or Samarkand. The majestic Orthodox cathedral of St. Sophia, the finest example of Byzantine architecture, built forty years before the birth of Mohammed, was turned into a mosque (it is now a museum), and the construction of the Topkapi Palace for Mehmet (now also a museum) began the next year. The Roman Empire had at last ceased to exist.

For reasons of state the Conqueror did a deal with the Greek theologian Gennadios, an Aristotelian scholar of high repute and moral reputation, investing him as Orthodox Patriarch, and allowing the Greek Church to continue ministering to its flock in Istanbul in return for the civil loyalty of the Christians. One of the results of this was that until the 20th century the Istanbul population remained about 40% Christian and Jewish. The year of conquest, 1453, is a useful date to take as closing the medieval era and beginning the modern.

Byzantine Emperors, 610-1453

Ruled	Emperor	Ruled	Emperor
610-41	Heraclius I	1034-41	Michael IV, the Paphlagonian
641	Constantine III Heraclius	1041-42	Michael V Calaphates
641	Heracleonas Constantine	1042	Zoe and Theodora
641-48	Constans II Heraclius, the Bearded	1042-55	Constantine IX Monomachus
668-85	Constantine IV Pogonatus	1055-56	Theodora Porphirogenita
685-95	Justinian II, the Slit-nosed	1056-57	Michael VI Stratioticus
695-98	Leontius II	1057-59	Isaac I Comnenus
698-705	Tiberius III Apsimar	1059-67	Constantine X Ducas
705-11	Justinian II, 2nd rule	1067-68	Michael VII Ducas
711-13	Philippicus Bardane	1068-71	Romanus IV Diogenes,

713-15	Anastasius II	1071-78	Michael VII Parapinakes
716-17	Theodosius III, the Tax-collector	1078-81	Nicephorus III Botaniates
717-41	Leo III the Isaurian	1081-1118	Alexius I Comnenus
741	Constantine V, the Dung-named	1118-43	John II Comnenus
741-43	Artabasdus, rival emperor	1143-80	Manuel I Comnenus
741-75	Constantine V, 2nd rule	1180-83	Alexius II Comnenus
775-80	Leo IV, the Khazar	1183-85	Andronicus I Comnenus
780-97	Constantine VI, the Blinded	1185-95	Isaac II Angelus
797-802	Irene, the Athenian	1195-1203	Alexius III Angelus
802-11	Nicephorus I, the Accountant	1203-04	Alexius IV and Isaac II Angel.
811	Stauracius	1204	Alexius V Ducas Murzuphlus
811-13	Michael I Rhangabe	1204-22	Theodore I Lascaris
813-20	Leo V, the Armenian	1222-54	John III Ducas Vatatzes
820-29	Michael II, the Stammerer	1254-58	Theodore II Lascaris
829-42	Theophilus	1258	John IV Lascaris
842-67	Mic Michael III, the Drunkard	1258-82	Michael VIII Paleologus
867-86	Basil I, the Macedonian	1282-1328	Andronicus II Paleologus
886-12	Leo VI, the Wise	1328-41	Andronicus III Paleologus
912-13	Alexander III	1341-91	John V Paleologus
913-59	Constantine VII Porphyrogenitus	1345	John VI Cantacuzenus, usurper
919-44	Romanus I Lecapenus (co-emp.)	1376-79	Andronicus IV Paleologus
944-45	Stephen & Constantine	1379-91	John V Paleologus
959-63	Romanus II Porphyrogenitus	1390-1408	John VII Paleologus
963-69	Nicephorus II Phocas	1391-1425	Manuel II Paleologus
969-76	John I Tzimisces	1399-1402	John VII Paleologus (co-emp.)
976-1025	Basil II, the Bulgar-slayer	1425-48	John VIII Paleologus
1025-28	Constantine VIII Porphyrogenitus	1449-53	Constantine XI Paleologus
1028-34	Romanus III Argyrus		

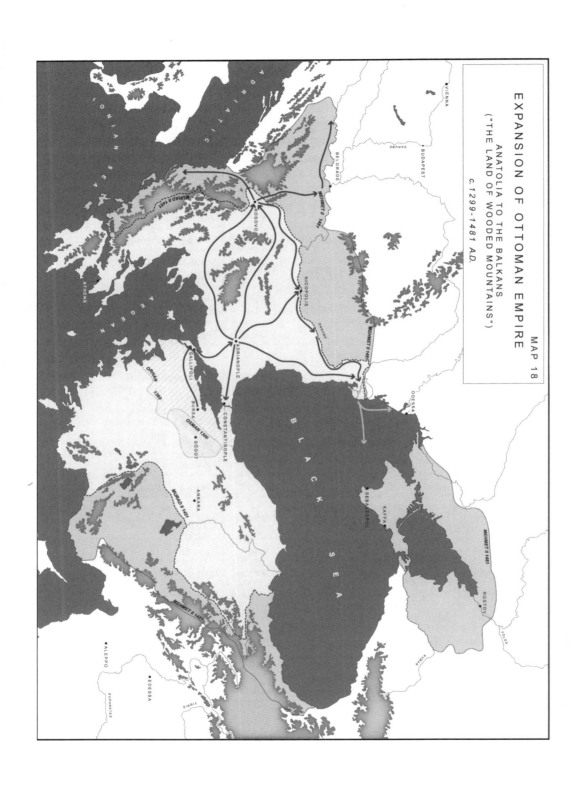

MAP 18

EXPANSION OF OTTOMAN EMPIRE

ANATOLIA TO THE BALKANS
("THE LAND OF WOODED MOUNTAINS")

c. 1299-1481 A.D.

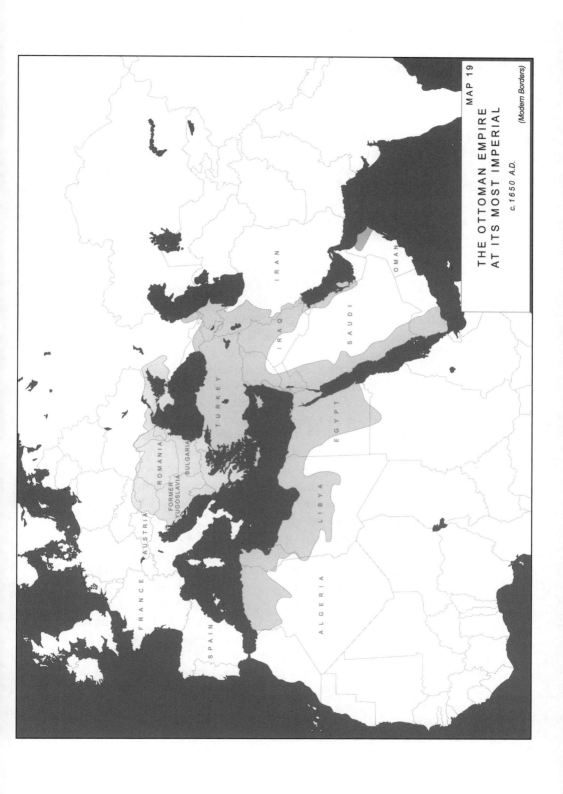

THE OTTOMAN EMPIRE
AT ITS MOST IMPERIAL

MAP 19

c. 1650 A.D.

(Modern Borders)

FRANCE · AUSTRIA · SPAIN · ROMANIA · FORMER YUGOSLAVIA · BULGARIA · TURKEY · IRAN · IRAQ · SAUDI · OMAN · EGYPT · LIBYA · ALGERIA

Empire extinguished:

Following his victories over the Persians and Mamluks in Syria and Egypt in 1516-17, Selim the Grim drove the Persians out of Kurdistan. In the 1520s, his son the Magnificent Suleiman crossed the Danube and reduced Hungary to vassal status. Renewed expansion in the Mediterranean began in 1522 with an attack on Rhodes and the surrender of the Knights Hospitallers. Algiers fell to Ottoman forces early in 1529. Suleiman's siege of Vienna, the Habsburg capital, in September-October of that same year was broken more by heavy rains making the approach roads unusable, the early freezing snowfall of the Little Ice Age, and overstretched supply lines than by any Habsburg action. In the final analysis of this campaign it was this overextension, the weather, and the Sunni Ottomans' abiding determination to destroy the Shiites of Persia that saved central Europe.

In the 1530s, Suleiman expelled the Safavids from Mesopotamia, pushing them back into the Zagros mountains and to plateau Persia. In 1538, he extended his control over Yemen to most of the country, as far south as Aden, and took Qatar from its Portuguese pearl trading adventurers who had arrived a decade or more before. Westward along the African coast, taking Tripoli in 1551, the Ottoman Empire reached the borders of Morocco. All this gave them a network of caravan routes extending from the western Mediterranean to the gates of Beijing.

Under Suleiman, renowned soldier, statesman and patron of the arts, the Ottoman Empire approached its peak. Suleiman's empire was now a significant part of the European political scene and entered into a series of alliances with France (Francis I) in 1536-44 against the Habsburgs in Spain and Germany under Holy Roman Emperor Charles V. And Suleiman's admiral-of-the- fleet Khair ad-Din, "Barbarossa", evacuated Muslim and Jewish refugees from Spain under the continuously threatening cloud of the Inquisition, as his grandfather, Bayazit II, fifty years before, had landed them safely in Moorish Algiers and Greek Salonica.

An epitaph to Suleiman the Magnificent reads in his own words: "I am God's slave and Sultan of this World. By the Grace of God, I am head of Mohammed's community. God's might and Mohammed's miracles are my companions. I am Caliph in Mecca and Medina. In Baghdad, I am Shah; in Egypt, Sultan; (I am he) who sends his fleets to the seas of Europe, North Africa and India. I am the Sultan who took the crown and throne of Hungary and granted it to a humble slave."

The first ten Ottoman leaders were without exception formidable and mightily successful in their purposes. Their dozens of successors, with few exceptions after Suleiman, were grotesque failures – several of them certifiably insane, one would surmise. Bernard Lewis called them "incompetents, degenerates and misfits"; S.E.Finer said that "war was the operative principle" of the Ottoman empire; Edward Gibbon said that the Turks "were on a perpetual search for new enemies and new subjects". In the 393 years between 1399 and 1792 the Ottomans were at war for 333 years. (Another count defining war differently gives 274 years.)

Under Suleiman and his father – between them reigning for fifty-four years – the Ottoman Empire had been invincible, with disciplined armies and an effective bureaucratic structure. The Ottomans had also become the dominant naval force, controlling the eastern Mediterranean and much of its commerce, depriving the maritime republics of Venice, Genoa and Pisa of part of the revenues that they had enjoyed, had depended upon for centuries. These benefits had already begun to be diminished by Portugal's opening up of the Cape route to the Far East during Sultan Selim I's time. The north Italian republics lived by trade and would suffer if much of it were lost.

Suleiman was succeeded in 1566 by his son, Selim II, devoted more to wine and women than to affairs of state. He never commanded his armies in the field or at sea, the first Ottoman not to do so. But with, according to a mischievous folk tale, his fondness for Cypriot wine, Selim II ordered the taking of Cyprus from Venetian control. Preparations for this attack caused the Catholic states, supporters of the Habsburgs – Venice, Genoa, Pisa / Tuscany, Spain, Savoy, Malta and the Papal States – to assemble a "Holy League" fleet of fighting ships under the command of Don John (Juan) of Austria.

In August 1571 the Ottomans launch their attack on Cyprus and easily take the lightly defended island. Cyprus was to remain Turkish for the next 300 years – until the British took it over in 1876 – and until he died a few years after taking the island, Selim was kept well supplied with his favourite wine from it.

A few weeks later, in October 1571, two great fleets of about equal numbers of men and *matériel* meet at Lepanto (Nafpaktos) in the narrow Gulf of Corinth in what would be the last major naval battle in world history fought solely between oar-driven, rowed vessels. The fighting ships were predominantly the common 37-42-metre long, Mediterranean galley, flat, low in the water, usually with 18-24 oars on each side, 144-192 oarsmen, 4 men per oar; a complement of mariners; a single, fixed, forward-firing main cannon and several small-caliber ancillary guns mounted in the bow; and crowded with 100 fighting troops armed with crossbow, harquebus/matchlock musket and close quarter weapons. Many of the men on the Christian side were the elite Spanish infantry, many thousands of them, the best in Europe, and the Italian *condottieri*, highly experienced mercenaries. The Ottoman fleet of about 280 vessels included some 50-60 galliots, small, light galleys. The Ottoman force seems not to have had more than 2,000-4,000 Janissaries, in esprit and training the equal of the Spanish elite. The two commanding admirals were both men of talent and experience.

The 220-ship Christian fleet had two advantages that were not immediately apparent. It had six Venetian galleasses, converted merchantmen, much larger vessels equipped at the last moment with five times the cannon fire-power of galleys, many more troops and the advantage of height above the enemy decks. And whereas the Turkish ships were rowed almost exclusively by galley-slaves, many of them European Christians, only the Spanish vessels of the Holy League, about 80 ships, had significant numbers of slaves and convicts. The rest of the fleet was driven by salaried, bounty-hunting professional oarsmen who knew what they were about.

Don John (Juan) of Austria reputedly ordered his captains not to fire until "close enough to be splattered with Muslim blood". The first shots are fired, and five hours later the Ottoman fleet is destroyed, 15-25 ships sunk, and astonishingly, 170-200 captured; many are seriously damaged however and have to be scuttled. Only 30-50 Muslim boats escape. Tens of thousands of Turks are dead, wounded or captured. The Turkish admiral is captured half way through the battle, beheaded on the spot. His head is held high for all to see, and to demoralize his men.

The Holy League loses 17 ships sunk, none taken by the enemy, about 20,000 men killed or wounded, and 12,000-15,000 Christian galley-slaves are liberated. As always, none of these numbers can be confirmed, but victory for the Christians was certain, the first victory against the Ottomans for more than a century. The aura of Ottoman invincibility is destroyed. The psychological importance of the battle should not be underestimated, even if its military, strategic place is lowly: an alliance of the Papal States, Spain, Genoa, Venice and the Knights of Malta had seemingly turned the tide of Islam once and for all. A fresco of the battle by Antonio Danti can be found in the Vatican, celebrating the glorious triumph of Christendom.

With massive effort, however, the Turks rebuild their shattered fleet including in it eight of the largest warships ever seen in the Mediterranean, "galleons", following merchant ship designs already seen in Western shipyards. The Turkish survivors had learned from what they had seen the galleasses do at Lepanto. A year after their defeat the Ottomans can again force the Westerners out of much of the eastern Mediterranean and consolidate control of the north African coast. Still, by the end of the century the era of successful Ottoman military action and expansion of the Empire is over. In the Indian Ocean, too, towards the end of this 16th century the English and Dutch, displacing the Portuguese, begin to exercise armed control over East-West ship-borne oceanic trade, shutting out the Ottomans.

On the battlefield, with rising conservatism, the Ottomans were gradually falling behind the Europeans in military technology. Internal conflict arose in the military and in the bureaucracy. Less important battles than Lepanto (which S. E. Finer categorizes as "inconsequential") were won and lost. The strategic Yerevan (Erivan), capital of Armenia, was fought over again and again by the Ottomans and Safavids, the town changing hands fourteen times between 1513 and 1737.

The Ottomans under a new fighting sultan, Murad IV, restored for a time Turkish military prestige, recaptured Baghdad from the Persians in 1639, but suffered a major defeat at the hands of the Polish King Jan (John) III Sobieski at the second siege of Vienna in 1683. The Ottoman vizier, Kara Mustafa, an incompetent court favourite who was responsible for the siege and defeat, was strangled on the orders of the Sultan, Mehmet IV.

The defeat at Vienna was the decisive event swinging the balance of power in Europe in favour of the Europeans. The Turks were forced to cede territory and to open diplomatic relations with nations they had never before even recognized (being constrained to address the sovereigns of these states as "Sir my Brother and Good Friend..." in the custom of the times among equals). Mehmet IV's reign, ending in 1687 when he was deposed, formally ended the era of Ottoman sultans as rulers of the Empire and ushered in the era of remaining Turkish power in the hands of the Grand Viziers.

From the mid-17th into the 18th century, under Ivan the Terrible and Peter the Great, Russia had been modernizing rapidly, centralizing control and expanding, adopting European technology, and presenting a third military front to the Turkish Empire: Europeans in the west, Russians in the north, Persians in the east. In the 18th century the Ottomans were defeated three times by the Russians.

Until the beginnings of its indisputable decline in the 18th century the Ottoman Empire had always been predatory. Like all its Arab and Mongol predecessors, its purposes had been to acquire plunder, slaves, land and revenue. A secondary motive of a few of the leaders was to spread the Word of Allah. (But to Western eyes it was difficult to see how they could think that Allah, the Compassionate, the Merciful, would sanction spreading the Word to a solidly Christian continent by the sword, by rape and plunder.) If there were benefits arising from their actions – and there were – they were unplanned, unintended consequences. The spread of Islamic civilization south of the Mediterranean coast of Africa and deeper into south-east Asia was brought about by the example and persuasion of journeying merchants and Sufi missionaries. Into 8th century India it had been on the backs of the invading Arab horsemen. Spreading the Word had not been their objective. Plunder, land and slaves were.

To prevent any repetition of the eleven-year civil war between the sons of Bayazit I, his great- grandson the Conqueror of Constantinople had decreed the Law of Fratricide authorizing the legal putting to death of possible rival, family claimants to the throne. The immediate descendants of the Conqueror took little advantage of this edict. But Suleiman, much to his sorrow it was said, had two of his sons, half-brothers, executed for intrigue, and a century later, Murad III (r. 1574-95), twenty-eight years old in the year of his accession, had his five brothers strangled under the law. Sultan Murad fathered 103 children, 47 of whom survived him, 20 of them boys. On succeeding to the throne, his son Mehmet III (r.1595-1603) put to death his 19 living brothers, two of his own sons, and 15 pregnant slavegirls (nine according to another account) left over by the insatiable, recently departed Murad, to eliminate any threat to his rights to the throne. The slavegirls were believed to have been sewn up in sacks and dropped like garbage in the Bosporus, a not-uncommon practice of the times.

With time, while the population of the Ottoman Empire may never have exceeded 30 million, the geographic immensity of the realm, its record of military success, and the longevity of Osman family rule bestowed on them much of the weight and authority that the Abbasids of Baghdad had held in their early days, centuries before. Notwithstanding attempts by Ottoman sultans, however, to marshal the Islamic world under their religious leadership, they never succeeded, even though at the surrender of Mecca and Medina during the early 16th century conquest of Egypt and western Arabia, the Ottomans prevailed upon the Sharif of Mecca, the Guardian of the Holy Cities, descendant of the Prophet's grandson Hassan, to acknowledge Sultan Selim the Grim as Caliph.

The Ottoman system suffered from the failings of *dirigisme* and heavy handedness. It was destructive of enterprise, damaging to commerce, forbidding of originality, while Europeans were beginning to find ways of circumventing the old restrictions. Inability to expand the empire much further into Europe after Suleiman's death denied the Turks what for them was the essential booty of conquest.

Inflation caused by the arrival through trading operations of mountains of American silver from Europe in the 16th century could not be overcome. Taxes had to be raised more and more, ruining trade, driving merchants out of business. Among others to suffer were the peasants whose crops and livestock were foraged by marauding unpaid soldiers living off the land. Islamic business partnership customs and regulations in the 15th century, until revision in the 18th, interacted with inheritance law to keep enterprises small, blocking the establishment of the large, predatory trading companies found in the West.

Upon the death of a partner in a merchant enterprise, the partnership was often dissolved so that the deceased's estate could be divided fairly among the family members according to Koranic prescriptions. Ignorance of the principles of economics heightened the difficulties. Imports of western goods were desired while exports were often prohibited. In renewal of old Arab practice, trading bases on Ottoman soil, bases with extra-territorial rights, tax concessions and privileges, known by the French term of *capitulations*, were granted to European merchants from Suleiman's time. French traders, backed by their King François (Francis) I, were the first to negotiate these agreements early in the 16th century, but old Genoese trading rights in Byzantine Constantinople had also been renewed by Mehmet the Conqueror in the mid-15th.

Beyond the state bureaucracy and the small, largely Christian and Jewish commercial bourgeoisie, no middle class had by the 16th century developed in Ottoman lands. Nor it seems had one ever arisen in the earlier Arab empires.

The printing press, a facility essential for progress, was banned in the Ottoman empire by Selim the Grim for sowing the seed of dangerous opinion. By this time there were 150 printing presses at work in Venice alone. And after being among the early adopters of the bronze cannon, the Ottomans were slow to recognise the advantages of the much less expensive, re-engineered cast-iron cannon, and therefore to afford to arm many more fighting ships with this battle-winning weapon. They were backward also in developing field guns for land warfare. Nor did the Ottomans quickly adopt the new ocean-capable sailing ships, continuing to rely later than Spain on slave-propelled galleys. Cultural conservatism was at the root of the Ottomans' long fall. In essence, they sacrificed the prospect of more successful commercial enterprise and a more assured future for the empire on the pyre of religio-cultural orthodoxy.

In 1950, in *Islamic Society and the West*, H. A. R. Gibb and H. Bowen wrote the following brilliant epitaph for the Ottomans: "Lacking any real consideration for the welfare of the subjects, losing little by little any moral ideals which might have inspired them in the early stages, the officers of the [Ottoman] administration were, by their very virtues, led insensibly to adopt a cynical view of their functions and responsibilities. Their world was divided into governors and subjects, the latter of whom existed, by divine province, to supply the needs of the former...By the beginning of the 18th century it had become the established practice to give promotion by favouritism and bribery, and to put up to auction offices (not only administrative, but also judicial and theological), lands, and concessions of all kinds. Cynicism had taken such root that it had ceased to be immoral and had become second nature. To maintain discipline over the Turkish soldiery, when its natural foundations in respect for superior ability were absent, became an all but impossible task. The impotence of the Pashas to prevent abuses, and the probability that they would be condoned at a price, encouraged lawlessness and rebellion, which gradually became more violent and widespread. Yet such was the talent of the Turkish governing classes, and so ingrained their conviction of superiority, not only among themselves, but also in the minds of their subjects that (apart from the turbulence of the Janissaries) it was not until the middle of the (eighteenth) century that the system began seriously to be challenged and to show alarming symptoms of breakdown."

The Ottoman dynasty lasted for 644 years, 1281-1924, generally father-to-son. By coincidence, the Arab caliphate of Asia Minor had lasted practically the same length of time, 627 years, 632-1258, under the Rightly Guided Caliphs and the two Meccan dynasties, the Umayyads and the Abbasids.

What is remarkable in all this is the part played in the formation of Middle Eastern, north African, South Asian and south-east European polities by descendants of Turkic tribesmen barely evolved from nomadic paganism. Be that as it may, the baneful consequences of the Ottoman invasion and domination of Christian south-east Europe in the 14th-18th centuries, radically distorting its social structures while impoverishing and brutalizing its people, are still being felt. Today, the Balkans are a cockpit of historical grievance, of nationalism of a virulence existing nowhere else in the EU, prideful religions hostile to others, political fragility, corruption, organized crime. This where the terms "Balkanization" and "ethnic cleansing" come from.

By way of comparison, at the other end of the continent, in Spain and Portugal, the consequences of the 8th-15th century Muslim domination of what had also once been Christian lands can be viewed as beneficial, a blessing to Europe and civilization in general. If Iberia were slower than northern Europe to make social and economic progress after the expulsion of the Moors, which it was, it was not because of the centuries of dominant Muslim presence.

Ottoman Sultans, 14th-16th Centuries

Sultan	Ruled	Notes
Osman Ghazi	1281-1326	Founded dynasty
Orhan	1326-61	Expanded into Balkans
Murad I	1361-89	Crushed Serbia in Kosovo
Bayazit I "the Thunderbolt"	1389-1402	Defeated Europeans at Nicopolis
(Interregnum)	1402-13	Civil war among brothers
Mehmet I	1413-21	Reconstructed Ottoman state
Murad II	1421-51	Consolidated state
Mehmet II "the Conqueror"	1451-81	Conquered Constantinople
Bayazit II	1481-1512	Welcomed Jews from Spain
Selim I "the Grim"	1512-20	Captured Syria and Egypt
Suleiman "the Magnificent"	1520-66	Empire builder supreme. Laid siege to Vienna, 1529
Selim "the Sot"	1566-74	Lost the battle of Lepanto
Murad III	1574-95	Had his brothers strangled
Mehmet III	1595-1603	Mass murderer of family

The Rise of the House of Saud:

In the 18th century, under weak, ineffective largely absentee Ottoman rule, poverty-stricken Arabia was fertile ground for fundamentalist Islam. Following their adoption in 1744 of the forbidding creed of Mohammed bin Abdul Wahhab (in which veneration of saints, ostentation in worship, dress, behaviour or architecture, pilgrimage to any site other than Mecca, music, dancing, hashish, wine, wearing charms and practising magic was forbidden, and the head to foot veil was mandatory for women) the powerful Arabian clan headed by Mohammed bin Saud gathered strength and willing followers. From their headquarters in Diriyah in the central Nejd, the "Wahhabis" – as they would become known in the West – ranging widely across the Arabian Peninsula and imbued with spiritual fervour, converted bedouins and oasis villagers alike to their beliefs, killing those who refused the new, Wahhabi interpretation of Allah's will.

Claiming to have been appointed to restore Islam to its original pristine state, in 1801-02, with eight or ten thousand camel- and horse-mounted warriors, the Wahhabi-Sauds attacked the holy Shiite city of Karbala in Iraq, near where the Prophet's grandson Hussein had been beheaded in 861, killing a thousand people (some sources say two thousand) because the Wahhabis considered Shias to be heretics and idolators. The raiders destroyed Shiite mosques and holy places, and made off with everything of value they could carry. Time and again in the following years, under the cloak of purist Islam, the Wahhabis raided Mesopotamian and Syrian towns, sometimes successfully, though often failing when the target was a fortified town.

In 1803 the Wahhabis captured Mecca and Medina in the Hejaz, laying the foundations of the first Saudi state by destroying the many Shiite and Sufi shrines dedicated to Islamic saints, including a shrine over the tomb of Fatima the Prophet's daughter. However, threatened by the approach of Ottoman forces and weakened by disease, the Wahhabis abandoned their positions and returned to Diriyah. Their leader Abdul Aziz, son of the co-founder of the sect Mohammed bin Saud, was murdered by a Shia fanatic soon after returning to Diriyah, in revenge presumably for the destruction of the Meccan shrines. Nevertheless, led by his son Saud, an avowed Islamist, the Wahhabis fought their way back to Mecca in 1805, defeating the just arrived Ottoman garrison and seizing their 2,500 valuable firearms.

With further success in local wars, including establishing control of Qatar and Bahrein, by 1811 the alliance of the Sauds and Wahhabs had extended its rule to all of Arabia except Yemen. Emir Saud bin Abdul Aziz was then able to live royally for several years in his home town of Diriyah with revenues from trade and tribute, and the conveniences of hundreds of slaves, male and female.

The Wahhabis recaptured Mecca in 1805. In the same year the Ottoman sultan appointed the Balkan Muslim, Mohammed (Mehmet) Ali, as his viceroy – Pasha – of Egypt. When the Wahhabis reoccupied Mecca the zealot Saud prohibited Ottoman pilgrim caravans journeying on the hajj to the holy city. The fundamentalist Wahhabis considered the Turkish Ottoman subjects, although Sunni co-religionists, as ungodly deviants from the true faith whose presence would defile the holy place. But then, by ending toll-paying Turkish pilgrimage to Mecca the Wahhabis devastated the economy of the Hejaz, affecting particularly the poor and the bedouins. Despite their doctrine of helping the poor, most of the spoils of conquest had gone to the Saudi and Wahhabi clans. As a result, poor tribesmen rose repeatedly in local rebellion. To top it all in 1810 Arabian trade with the "heretical" north, Iraq and Syria, was banned by the uncompromising Emir Saud.

The Ottomans, although generally leaving Arabia to its own devices and internal politics, were still vexed by all this, and had Mohammed Ali Pasha of Egypt send a younger son of his, Tusun (Tursan), with 8,000 men to the Hejaz in 1811 to re-establish order. (It was at the feast in Cairo to celebrate the departure of this force to Arabia that Mohammed Ali had the Mamluks massacred.)

The Wahhabis turned out to be superior in numbers and military tactics, and defeated the Egyptian army. Negotiations followed and failed. Non-crucial victories were won by both sides in subsequent engagements, followed sometimes by the killing of prisoners. The Pasha then sent his eldest son Ibrahim from Cairo to command the Egyptian forces. Planning his campaign skilfully, Ibrahim overcame the Wahhabis in 1818-19, driving them back into the desert, destroying Diriyah and capturing the Saudi leader Abdullah, successor to his father, Saud. Abdullah and his chief Wahhabi clan lieutenants were sent in manacles to Istanbul where the Turks cut off their heads. The first Saudi state had lasted thirteen years. But Wahhabism was not finished.

With typical Ottoman mismanagement and corruption, coupled with pillaging by the Egyptian troops, Arabia descended into tribal anarchy. Turki, the son of the beheaded Abdullah, established a new base for himself in 1821 in Riyadh, a few miles from the ruins of

Diriyah. The Egyptians attacked, killing most of the new Wahhabi garrison. Turki escaped, raised new forces from loyal tribes, and in 1824 besieged the Egyptians in turn in Riyadh, forcing them eventually to retreat to their bases in the Hejaz, 500 miles away. The well-regarded Turki then governed the revived but smaller Saudi domain until he was assassinated in 1834. The assassin, one Mishari, was caught by Turki's son, Faisal al-Saud, and suffered the consequences.

Enter the al-Rashids:
In 1835 Mohammed Ali Pasha, still ruling Arabia in the name of the Ottoman sultan, sent in another contingent of troops. When these Egyptians were also bested by the Arabs, they came back with an even larger force. Emir Faisal al-Saud, impressed and fearful this time, offered 5,000 camels for the Egyptians to withdraw. The Egyptians demanded 15,000. In the ensuing battle in 1837 the Egyptians were beaten again, causing them in 1838 shamefacedly to have to accept Faisal's control of eastern Arabia. Treacherously, however, the Egyptians had recognized a rival Arab tribe, the Shammar, based in the town of Ha'il in the hilly area of the northern Nejd 450 miles from Riyadh and headed at the time by Abdullah bin Rashid, scion of an ancient family. They were implacable foes of the al-Sauds. With Rashidi support the Egyptians were able to capture Faisal in 1840. Faisal, the great-great-great grandson of the co-founder of the Wahhabi sect, was taken as prisoner to Cairo. End of the second Saudi polity. This one had lasted sixteen years.

At the same time as these events, Egyptian military advances towards the south in the Hejaz, towards Yemen, caused the British – approaching their peak of power in 1839 – to seize Aden to protect the Bab el-Mandeb southern entrance channel to the Red Sea and some of the sea lines to India. The next year, British power, brought to bear upon him, persuaded Mohammed Ali to withdraw his forces from Arabia. In 1839 Britain was the world's sole super-power.

In a series of moves under different needs and circumstances, Britain had taken control of the island of Hormuz at the entrance of the Persian Gulf as early as 1622; in 1639 they had secured a trading base in Basrah in Iraq, at the top end of the Gulf. By 1764 they had a consul there armed with a letter of credence initialled compliantly by the Turks, giving the British power to protect their commercial interests militarily. As a result of this the British were able to support trade and suppress piracy in the Gulf and eventually to win control of much of the seaway, through the Perpetual Maritime Truce of 1853. These activities in the Red Sea and Persian Gulf were aimed principally at protecting British communications with India. The seaway routes to India were of vital importance to the British.

(When Britain had seized Aden, the Arabians and the British had not been Egypt's only problems. In 1838 Mohammed Ali had stopped paying tribute to Istanbul, provoking Ottoman Sultan Mahmud to declare war on him. But that's another story.)

Faisal bin Turki bin Abdullah, seventh Emir of the Saud-Wahhab symbiosis (his grandfather's brother or distant cousin, Khalid bin Saud, considered by contemporaries to have been an Egyptian puppet, had reigned in 1839-41 as the sixth) escaped from imprisonment in Cairo in 1843 and regained control of parts of the Nejd and the Al-Hasa Persian Gulf coastal area, overturning a usurper Ibn Thunayyan who had seized Riyadh in 1841. Ibn Thunayyan was locked up and died. Faisal bin Turki ruled despite widespread bedouin unrest until he died at the age of seventy in 1865.

After Faisal's death, although he had declared his son Abdullah as his successor, Abdullah's half-brothers Saud and Abdul Rahman contested the succession. Inter-family and internecine strife erupted, tribal groups and the Ottoman Turks becoming involved militarily. Saudi clan power and prestige deteriorated. Allies deserted. And in 1869 the Suez canal, built by French archaeologist, engineer and businessman Ferdinand de Lesseps, and financed largely by French investors, was opened, radically altering the political dynamics of all the Middle East.

In 1871 Saudi Emir Faisal's son, Saud, marched on Riyadh with a nomad tribal force and defeated his brother Abdullah, but had difficulties in maintaining the support of the bedouins. A few years later Saud was wounded in battle and died soon after, but apparently of smallpox. (As often in Arab histories, some accounts say he was poisoned.) Saud's half-brother Abdul Rahman then became the ruler of Riyadh and the Saudi territories, but for only a year before being overthrown by Saud's sons who installed one of their own, Abdullah (the fourth Saudi emir of this name) in charge. Abdullah IV reigned for fourteen years until his death in 1889, and was succeeded by his brother, another Abdul Rahman.

The British, although participating little in the Suez Canal enterprise at the start, were eventually among the main beneficiaries. With Egypt beginning to suffer the effects of disastrous financial misjudgement from the 1860s, approaching bankruptcy by 1875, British Prime Minister Disraeli was able to buy for Britain the Egyptian state's 45% share of the shares of the Suez Canal Company. Then, in 1882 imperialist Britain landed armed forces and took political control of Egypt. As Lord Cromer, the British Viceroy, pointed out at the time, "We don't really want the damn place but if we don't someone else will grab it and the whole balance of power will be mucked up."

In 1876 (some accounts say in 1880) a son named Abdul Aziz (Abd al-Aziz) was born in Riyadh to Abdul Rahman II and Sara bint Ahmad al-Sudairi, a son who one day would become king of the first country in modern times to be recognized internationally by a family name, Saud. Meanwhile the Shammar tribe of Ha'il, led by Mohammed, a son of Abdullah bin Rashid, is gaining strength.

In 1888 the al-Rashids ride out from the Jebel Shammar hills and take the Saudi capital of Riyadh. And during a decade of turmoil they take the rest of Abdul Rahman's lands in central Arabia and the Persian Gulf coast. The dispossessed Saudi ruler then takes his family into exile in Kuwait under the protection there of its ruling al-Sabah family with whom he has brotherly relations. Of the fifteen Emirs of the Saudi dynasty to this date, nine had been assassinated, executed or deposed, many of them by family members.

Abdul Rahman's son, Abdul Aziz, grows up from the age of fourteen in Kuwait, with access through his father to the Kuwaiti Emir's daily *majlis* where he learns the basics of statecraft and much about the world. At the age of about twenty-five in 1902 Abdul Aziz, already a formidable fighter, steeped in his family's patrician if chequered history, and by then much experienced in raiding Rashidi assets in Arabia, with only twenty men, most of them half-brothers, cousins and slaves – although he has a 200-man reinforcement nearby – attacks the lightly protected city of Riyadh in the early hours of a January morning, killing several of its guards together with the awakened Rashidi city governor, named Ajlan, who is caught fleeing the scene. On bringing in the reinforcements, the city surrenders to Abdul Aziz. The Sauds have recovered Riyadh.

Following this coup, former allies of his father rally once more to the Saudi banner. Quickly in the next months, extending to about two years, Abdul Aziz recaptures a large part of the Nejd. The al-Rashids appeal for help from the Ottomans, their liege lords, who come in force, and in June 1904, armed with battlefield tactics and equipment sold to them by the French and British, the Turks resoundingly defeat the Saudis, killing many of them. Abdul Aziz escapes, however.

As always, with nothing else to gain, and short of supplies, the Turks leave the field, returning to their bases in the Hejaz and to the north. As soon as they do the Saudis regain the offensive, but arduously, with plans and schemes, negotiations and war, local victories and defeats; and it is only years later, by 1912, when the Ottoman empire is in its death throes that Abdul Aziz is able once again to establish control over a large part of the Nejd. (The Ottomans had lost Greece to independence in 1832, Bulgaria and Romania in 1878, and the rest of the Balkans in 1911-13.)

Through serial, and doubtless carefully planned, polygamy Abdul Aziz is able during this first decade of the 20th century to extend his dominions much more widely across the Arabian Peninsula, cultural norms and Islamic law permitting short term marriage to and divorce from, in this instance, daughters of regional tribal chiefs simply by public declaration. Through to the late 1940s, between them, these girls, many of them alarmingly young, provide Abdul Aziz with fifty or more sons (accounts of the number vary widely) all of whom are legitimate and recognized by their proud father; the fathers of the mothers, honoured by having their daughters taken by this noble figure, generally remain loyal and eventually are well rewarded, becoming allies and "family". Abdul Aziz, an audacious, inspired leader, thus talks, fights and breeds his way to a new state in Arabia.

For hundreds of years the descendants of Mohammed the Prophet's Hashemite clan had been the guardians, the Sharifs, of the holy places of Mecca and Medina, titled and responsible but just as powerless for much of the time and for most of them as had been the Abbasid caliphs in Baghdad under the Seljuks or in Cairo under the Mamluks. No ruling political power during these centuries evidently found it wise or necessary to try to unseat the Hashemites. As from 1517 the Turks had (nominal) suzerainty over the Hejaz, appointing both Sharifs and governors, emirs, to administer the region.

In 1908, Turkey, still the ruling power of the eastern and western flanks of Arabia, appointed Hussein bin Ali, a Turkish-speaking Hashemite born in Istanbul, to the position of Sharif and, according to some accounts, Emir, thus apparently conferring on him an additional degree of administrative power and responsibility.

In this same year, 1908, the Turks inaugurate the 800-mile German-engineered Hejaz Railway from Damascus to Medina (the bedouins prevented it extending to Mecca), while Abdul Aziz al-Saud is busy trying to strengthen his own state in the east and skirmishing with his rivals in the Hejaz and Jebel Shammar.

In 1910 serious conflict breaks out again between the Sauds and Sharif Hussein. The Hashemite Sharif is supported by the Turks and the al-Rashids. Turkish reinforcements are quickly brought in by the new railway, but neither side gains a convincing victory (the Saudis perhaps having been secretly armed by the British who have been the dominant foreign power in the Persian Gulf for a century).

The First World War starts in 1914. In pursuit of its long established policy of protecting communications through the Middle East to India, to buttress resistance to the Turks who are allies of Germany, and to further other murky interests against Russia, while maintaining close links with Sharif Hussein, the British offer qualified protection to his enemy Abdul Aziz and sign a treaty of friendship with him in 1915, giving the British a measure of control over his foreign policy.

The next year, with war raging in Europe, Sharif Hussein of Mecca, then in his sixties, is persuaded by the British to lead and to act as spokesman for the Arab Revolt of his Muslim brothers of Arabia and what are now Syria, Iraq, Jordan and Lebanon against the Turks, in return for which the Arabs would after the war be rewarded, the British suggested, with a united kingdom stretching from the borders of Egypt to the borders of Persia. Sharif Hussein becomes the official leader of the revolt. But at the same time, in the secret Sykes-Picot accord, the British and French agree (with a nod of assent from the Russians who have been consulted) to carve up the Middle East, north of Arabia and south of Turkey, into British and French areas of influence or control after the War. The Arab Revolt is then launched and succeeds.

In 1917, Turkish power having gone from Arabia, Sharif Hussein is able to proclaim himself "King of the Hejaz", thereby never again having to suffer the indignity of being "appointed" by anyone but Allah. Lawrence of Arabia, who blew up the Hejaz Railway, wrote describing him as "...conceited to a degree, greedy and stupid"; but in the complexities of Middle Eastern and European politics Hussein receives international recognition as monarch of western Arabia.

In 1921-22 under repeated British urgings, shipments of weapons from them, and a regular stipend of £5,000 a month – never enough for Abdul Aziz – the Sauds march on and finally extinguish the then politically isolated al-Rashids, led by their last Emir, Mohammed bin Talal.

(To digress: following the admirable ancient Arab practice of taking in marriage womenfolk of defeated enemies giving support to otherwise defenceless widows – the Prophet Mohammed had married two or three widows – in 1923 Abdul Aziz marries a Shammari princess, his eighth wife, having by this time dismissed at least four earlier wives. The princess was Fahda bint Asi al-Shuraim, widow of no less a Rashidi notable than Emir Saud bin Abdul Aziz, the antepenultimate leader of the Shammaris of Ha'il. This Rashidi Emir Saud had been murdered in 1920 by his cousin in a family dispute. Princess Fahda – "Princess", there are no "Queens", only Kings – was the mother of today's King Abdullah of Saudi Arabia, born in 1924.

Again, Watfa, one of the daughters of the last al-Rashid Emir, Mohammed bin Talal, married Prince Musad (Musaid), fifteenth son of King Abdul Aziz in about 1945. Their son, the American-educated – at Berkeley – Prince Faisal, shot and killed his uncle, King Faisal bin Abdul Aziz, on March 25, 1975 for reasons that have not been completely elucidated – *plus ça change*. The assassin was officially declared insane, and was publicly beheaded in a Riyadh shopping centre car park on June 18 of that year.)

And again, although the record is fuzzy, it seems that at about the time Abdul Aziz's son Musad married Watfa bint Mohammed bin Talal – presumably in the mid-1940s – the King, then sixty-five to sixty-eight years old, had married her sister Jawhara bint Mohammed bin Talal.

Picking up the narrative, in March 1924 the Caliphate of Turkey is abolished by Turkey's now republican National Assembly. King Hussein of the Hejaz, seventy-two years old at this time, immediately proclaims himself "Caliph of all Muslims" and "King of all Arabs", *Malik bilad al-Arab*. Not much notice is taken by the Great Powers of this latest proclamation from the king of the still resource-poor Arabia, but the proclamation catches the attention of Abdul Aziz al-Saud who is not pleased.

The Saud sends his forces against the King and with not much effort succeeds in driving him from Mecca and Medina, putting an end to Hashemite tutelage of the Holy Places, and gaining control of the Hajj with its thousands of pilgrims annually, and the tolls they pay. Most of the pilgrims are of course adherents of Sunni sects other than Hanbali, some of them even Shias. Since that moment the Sauds have been the custodians of the Holy Cities.

Overthrown King Hussein retires to his summer estate in Cyprus. Britain, the main Western power in this affair, who had maintained cordial relations with both Hussein and Abdul Aziz, had turned a blind eye to the Saudi aggression. The next year, 1926, Abdul Aziz proclaims himself King of the Hejaz. Local conquests and consolidation by the Sauds in central and southern Arabia continue, and in 1932 still with support from the British, Abdul Aziz declares himself King of "Saudi" Arabia. A couple of years after this (six in fact), the Americans find oil for him, and the fortunes of Abdul Aziz and Wahhabism are raised to the heavens.

In the aftermath of World War I, British and French areas of influence were established, Britain in Iraq, Kuwait, Transjordan (Jordan) and Palestine – under League of Nations' mandates, France in Syria and Lebanon. No state uniting the Arab peoples between Arabia and Turkey was created. But one of King Hussein's sons was made King of Transjordan, another King of Iraq, another King of Syria. Of these only the Hashemite Kingdom of Jordan survives into the 21st century.

(The British connection did not disappear. The mother of the present King of Jordan, Abdullah II, is the Englishwoman Toni Gardiner, daughter of a British army officer.)

The bloody violence of Saudi Arabia, in contrast to the rather more tranquil histories of the littoral states of Kuwait, Qatar, Bahrain, UAE and Oman with their fishing-pearling-international trading-entrepôt-based economies, seems to have been rooted in the barrenness of the Arabian hinterlands coupled with population growth beyond the capacity of their resources to support, just as it had been 1,200-1,400 years before. Famine was an all too frequent occurrence, and in much of historical Arabia adequate food supplies and other necessities could be acquired only by taking them forcefully from others.

(Of interest, one notes here that the ruling family of the relatively untroubled Qatar are devout Wahhabis, and that Hanbali/Wahhabi minorities are spread throughout the fairly tolerant UAE.)

Finally, in 2006, Talal Mohammed al-Rashid, son of the last Emir of Ha'il, Mohammed bin Talal, set up a group in Paris in opposition to the Sauds, accusing the autocratic ruling clan of Saudi Arabia of plundering the wealth of the nation.

14

The Foundations of Western Civilization – the Roots

Preparing the Ground for Change – The Renaissance – The Black Death – The Aftermath

Preparing the Ground for Change:
Although not widely disseminated before the 11th century, scholarship and technology began seeping out of the Middle East into Europe from the 8th. Charlemagne's exchange of ambassadors with Harun al-Rashid was one of the vehicles for this. Voyaging merchants were even more important agents for the transfer of materials and knowledge. And Byzantium's constant contact with the Muslim world and its own rich scholarly and artistic foundations provided many channels for the communication of information to the 9th century's still benighted Europe. Arab merchant and corsair activity in the Mediterranean from the 8th to the 12th centuries greatly increased the flow – the magnetic compass, the ancient astrolabe, astronomy, cartography, medical science and much more. But with the taking of Toledo in 1085, the founding of the Norman countship in Sicily in 1090, and the settling of the crusaders into the Levant by 1100, the flood gates were opened. Everything of practical value that the Muslims had invented, discovered, inherited or borrowed from the Orient or Byzantium found its way into Europe. Greek philosophy and classical ways of thinking and questioning received opinion, rejected by most Muslims, were warmly welcomed in some quarters of the West. Commercial advantages and privileges

won by and granted to Italian traders in the Mediterranean after 1100 increased the flow of knowledge, while valuable nutritious sub-tropical foodstuffs cultivated by the Arabs were transplanted throughout Mediterranean Europe, adding to Europe's store of resources.

The Renaissance:

Always in the past, poetry, architecture, science and scholarship had been encouraged and financed by rulers who had been able to arrogate to themselves most of the economic surpluses of their communities. Rulers were all deeply involved in business. So too was it that the 13th-14th century commercial success of the dozen Italian city-states and counterparts in contemporary France and the Low Countries provided their rulers with the wherewithal to finance the flowering of classical culture known as the Renaissance *(Rinascimento)*. Ancient Greek and Roman scholarship had been kept alive in Byzantium where the glimmerings of a revival of art had first been seen. But it was in Ravenna early in the 14th century that the luminary, Dante Alighieri, sponsored by princely patrons, completed writing a novel kind of epic, *The Divine Comedy*. This was to be the start of a revolution in literature. Simultaneously, in Florence, Dante's friend Giotto di Bondone, the first artist to break free from the flat, stylized Byzantine art that still dominated the contemporary works of painters such as Siena's Duccio, began painting people engaged in ordinary daily activities. In doing so he brought a new form of expression to painting, three-dimensional realism, perspective. And, Florence, rapidly becoming the most civilized city in the world, emerged as the seed-bed of the new movement. Then, this embryonic revolution in art and scholarship, supported by a flow of technological progress, was suddenly halted by the most lethal event in recorded history.

The Black Death:

In 1347, soon after Orhan the Ottoman had first crossed the Dardanelles, and Egypt was falling into turmoil following the death of the last powerful Kipchak Sultan, galleys put into the harbour of Messina in Sicily with deathly sick men at the oars. They had come from Kaffa (today's Feodosiya) a Genoese port in the Crimea under siege by the Mongols of the Golden Horde. The besiegers had catapulted plague-infected cadavers over the walls at the defenders. The sailors suffering severe pain had horrendous black festering lumps in the armpits and groin. Most of these men died within a week. Others coughed and spat blood. These died in a few days. News of a terrible plague in the Orient had reached Europe the previous year, yet had raised little alarm. News like that was not uncommon. Other infected ships carried the pestilence into Genoa and Venice, and into the Levant at the Mediterranean ports. It reached Mesopotamia along the Silk Road caravan routes from the steppes of Asia. The next year it arrived in France, Germany, Spain and England. It was the Black Death, a triple epidemic of the deadly bubonic plague, the even more virulent pneumonic plague and septicaemic plague, a nightmarish brew. The bacillus of the bubonic and septicaemic pestilence, *Pasturella pestis*, lived alternately in the stomach of fleas and the bloodstream of rats. It travelled aboard *Rattus rattus*, the small black rat that lived on ships and, on land, lived in the towns in the common sewer rat. Pneumonic plague was airborne, spread by breath. Mortality among the people ranged from 10% to 90%, towns suffering more than the countryside. In enclosed places, monasteries and prisons, if one person sickened everyone died. The plague swept from India and China to Ireland and Iceland. One-quarter to one-third of the population of Europe was lost, 20-25 million people. The great cities of Italy, France and Spain were emptied. Italy suffered perhaps the most, with its many large towns. Boccaccio wrote that 100,000 died in Florence (but this was more than the total population of that city.) Petrarch's beloved Laura may have been among the victims (had she been more than a figment of imagination), and it is recorded that twenty of the twenty-four doctors of Venice died. In Marseille, an English observer wrote, "Not one of the hundred and fifty Franciscan friars survived to tell the tale. And a good job too!" Miraculously, one patch of rustic southwest France, from Dax near the port of Bayonne to Lourdes, seems to have escaped the Plague, perhaps the only part of western Europe to do so. The people of Europe had no idea how the plague was transmitted. Poor sanitation everywhere provided an environment in which rats could flourish. (After all, had rats not always lived with people?) Italy was toppled into near-anarchy. To add to the devastation, the earthquake of 1348 caused widespread destruction from Naples to Germany.

Barbara Tuchman recounts how in 1348: King Philippe VI "the Fortunate" of France sought the opinion of the medical faculty of the Sorbonne on the affliction that seemed to threaten the very survival of mankind. With careful thesis, antithesis, and proofs, the good doctors ascribed it to a triple conjunction of planets Saturn, Jupiter and Mars in the 40th degree of Aquarius which had occurred on March 20, 1345. This verdict of some of the wisest men of Paris became the official explanation and was accepted by the authorities almost everywhere. Perhaps King Philippe should instead have consulted the Arab physicians of Granada.

In the *Decameron* in 1358, Boccaccio wrote, "Some say that it descended upon the human race through the influence of heavenly bodies, others that it was a punishment signifying God's anger at our iniquitous way of life. But whatever its cause, it had originated some years earlier in the East, where it had claimed countless lives before it unhappily spread westward, growing in strength as it swept relentlessly from one place to the next."

Many of the commonfolk saw it as the wrath of God for the sinfulness of Man. Others were certain it was the Jews who were responsible and took retribution against them. In many towns, particularly in Spain and Germany, Jews were penned into their synagogues and burned alive. Those among the German Jewry who escaped fled to a haven of relative tolerance, Poland, which became the main refuge for Jews in Christendom – the Ghetto, in the new town of Warsaw. The Plague remained endemic in the West for hundreds of years, outbreaks continuing to be accompanied by religious hysteria. The last major outbreak in Europe was in 1816.

The savagery of life in the Middle Ages magnified all the emotions of day-to-day living. Everywhere was ablaze with religious fear and fervour, barely suppressed exhilaration, burning passion just below the surface. The mood of the people seesawed from hopelessness to exultation, from pitiless inhuman cruelty to loving, caring kindness. On the whole, children appear to have been left to survive or die without much concern by their parents until the age of five or six when they became "people". That was how the Good Lord had ordered it. Certainly, the death of a young child was not the devastating event it would be for parents today. Children died all the time. What psychological effect this may have had on people's character can only be guessed at. It also illustrates the profoundly callous attitude towards life and suffering everywhere in the Middle Ages. The acceptance of the most horrifying punishment meted out to wrong-doers is beyond belief today. Everywhere, blood and cruelty haunted the medieval world.

The Aftermath:

The late Middle Ages were still a time of ubiquitous hardship. They were still the times of magic, miracles, fairies, witches, astrology, the black art of necromancy. And for the common man there was no expectation of relief. The Renaissance had gone into hibernation during the Plague. But the socio-economic consequences of the cataclysm that had befallen mankind were far reaching and it was a decisive point in the erosion of the feudal system in the West. The Plague accelerated discontent with the Christian Church. Minds were opened. Once people saw the possibility of change in the old ways, the end of the age of unquestioning submission came into sight. The major population centres of northern Italy were already beginning to recover from the Black Death by the late 1300s, strengthening their economic position by drawing in labour, wealth and expertise from the countryside. *Torre* (tower) building resumed.

A long period of conflict between England and France had begun about 1337 and lasted with interruptions until 1453. This was the Hundred Years' War, noted in England for the battlefield successes of its longbowmen at Crécy, Poitiers and Agincourt. It had been what Norman Davies called an orgy of endless killing, witless superstition, faithless chivalry, magnified by the treachery and unscrupulous behaviour of rulers and prelates.

The Plague was an important society-deforming event in the early years of the war. Disorder was everywhere in Europe. In 1410 there were three Holy Roman Emperors, three Popes and two kings of France. The English burned the innocent, nineteen-year-old peasant girl Jeanne d'Arc in the market square of Rouen, after which the heat of battle cooled. Still, by the time it was over nobody could remember what it was all about.

For France the war which it won on points finally removed England's foothold on the continent; even so, it was an experience that France was not anxious to repeat. French power expanded afterwards but its population had been laid waste. For the loser, England, the war was crucial for the formation of a national identity that had not existed before, and the arising of a sense of Englishness, strengthening it for future centuries:

> This royal throne of kings, this scept'red isle
> This earth of majesty, this seat of Mars
> This other Eden, demi-paradise

This fortress built by Nature for herself
Against infection and the hand of war
This happy breed of men
This precious stone set in a silver sea
Which serves it in the office of a wall
Or as a moat defensive to a house,
Against the envy of less happier lands, –
This blessèd plot, this earth, this realm, this England.
(Richard II, Act II scene I)

The population of Europe in the mid-14th century, before the Plague, had been approximately 75 million. Estimates a century later put the number at only about 50 million. But, shrugging off the calamities of the 14th century, by the early 15th six cities in Italy/Sicily had populations of more than 100,000, and two cities in France, two in Iberia, two in the Low Countries. With change in the demographic framework of the continent people had begun to move to the towns for a better life. Wealth became concentrated in fewer hands, facilitating its mobilization. A new wealthy elite arose in northern Italy based on growing trade and industry. An Italian merchant who died at this time left 100,000 documents of commercial correspondence with agents across Europe and the Maghreb. The influential Medici family of Florence became bankers to the Holy See, highlighting the need for such a service. In the countryside surviving peasants were able to accumulate extensive areas of land as relatives had died of the Plague. Other parts of the West also benefited from the new economic climate. English cloth exports expanded, as did Spanish wool exports. The Hanseatic League was founded in Germany, coming to dominate north European markets, the Baltic and the North Sea, in fish, cereals, milk products, timber, minerals and furs. New fortunes were founded. And by 1480 a banking operation had been set up in Germany.

The Guns-and-Ships revolution of the late 1400s, giving rise to both the crossing of the Atlantic in the 1490s and the Cape route to India with the capture of much of the spice trade, put an end to European backwardness. For the Arab world, however, economic decline of long duration was quickened, and the material void between the West and the Arabs widened.

At this time at the end of the 15th century few of the ancient superstitions of the West had been discarded. According to popular belief no-one since the schism of Christendom in 1054 had entered Paradise.

The century was still a time when European men, those who dared, had to struggle to confine the power of the Church to the sphere of religion and to the realm of private conscience. Bigotry, intolerance and irrationality persisted with their strangle-hold on Christian mankind. Since 1215 confession and penance had been obligatory. Praying was a daily ritual just as much in Christendom as it was in the Muslim world. Relics of the saints were worshipped everywhere. Pilgrimage to the holy places was a universal obligation. Worst of all, the fallen angel, Lucifer, was striving to dethrone God.

As late as 1490, the Pope, Innocent VIII, could announce that: "It has lately come to our ears that many people of both sexes have abandoned themselves to devils, incubi and succubi, and by their incantations, spells, conjurations and other accursed charms have slain infants in their mothers' womb, have blasted the produce of the earth, the grapes of the vines, the fruits of the trees. The wretches, furthermore, blasphemously renounce the Faith which is theirs by baptism, and at the instigation of the Enemy of Mankind they do not shrink from perpetrating the filthiest excesses to the deadly peril of their souls."

Paradoxically, it was the Roman church, the monasteries and their kin, the universities, which were the well-spring of reform, preparing the way. It was in these institutions that learning took place, scholars were made, ideas germinated. Thomas Aquinas, a priest, was among the earliest of the reformist scholars in the mid-13th century. Dante was educated by Florentine priests in the late 13th. Petrarch was a priest in the early-mid-14th century. And many of the later reformers, like Erasmus, were priests or lay scholars educated in monasteries or priestly colleges.

15

The Foundations of Western Civilization – the Branches

The Renaissance – The Reformation – The Discovery of America and the Spanish Empire – The Scientific Revolution and the Enlightenment – The Little Ice Age

The Renaissance:
With the gathering of pace in the early 1400s the reawakened Renaissance began to revive art and poetry and pleasure for the small though growing leisured class of Europe. At this time, faced with continuing threats from the warmongering Ottomans, many of the academicians of Byzantium accepted invitations to relocate to Florence. They arrived between 1397 and 1438 bringing with them priceless ancient Greek scrolls and codices, and evolving ideas about art and architecture, making an outstanding early contribution to the Renaissance. They introduced Homer, Plato, Pythagoras and Socrates to Western Europe. The works of the ancients were then resurrected by Italian men of letters, Homer's *Iliad and Odyssey*, Virgil's *Aeneid*, Ovid's *Art of Love*. And Biblical scholarship began to be re-examined from original manuscripts under the spotlight of scientific philology. Secular subjects and scenes began to be painted, mundane choral music composed, and vernacular literature written. Gothic styling in architecture was overtaken.

European literature had been hampered to the beginning of the 16th century by the Latin language, even though the masterpieces of the

Middle Ages had been written mainly in the vernacular. But when the vernacular on the back of the printing press began spreading reading across Europe in the second half of the 15th century, the cultural revolution was immeasurably fortified. Literature would no longer be about the lives of saints, manuals of prayer and spirituality, and how to die with dignity. It would begin to cover human life and love, idealism and realism, people's character, experiences, hopes and aspirations.

With humanism and the legacy of classical times at its heart, the Renaissance introduced new ways of thinking and living. It placed Man, began to place Man, at the centre of day-to-day life, not God. With the Renaissance there appeared, too, the liberal questioning of received wisdom and the firmer establishment of scepticism in religion. Humanism gave Man stature, and for the first time in history civilized people began to feel no need for religion, priest or lord to provide opinions or beliefs. Such ideas had never before been voiced or even thought. Only in parts of Christendom was any of this taking place. This faculty has been described as independence of mind. John Stuart Mill called it freedom of judgment. No such independence existed in the world of Islam where man had to be denied his freedom of thought in order to save his soul. In Islam, still the religion of unquestioning submission, there was no place for free, independent thinking.

The Renaissance was not a widely supported movement, nor was the common man even aware of it. It was comprised of a few scholars and artists, perhaps a hundred or so at any one time in the early decades, encouraged and sponsored by a like number of princely patrons and wealthy merchants of Italy, notable among whom were the Medici, the Sforza and the Visconti families, and a few Popes.

Animated by classical design concepts arriving at the time with the immigrant Byzantine scholars, in the early-mid-15th century the Florentine architects, Filippo Brunelleschi and Leon Battista Alberti, gave a humanist and newly scientific basis to architecture. In doing so they raised the construction of buildings to the cultural level of literature and the architect to the status of intellectual.

If any single individual could however be credited with spreading the new ideas it would be a Dutch priest from Rotterdam, Gerhard Gerhards, "Erasmus", perhaps the most talented scholar of the early 16th century, and the first great Western practitioner of newly scientific philology. His *Praise of Folly* (1509) which was banned, Indexed, by the Papal authorities, was read by "everybody". It warmed the hearts and cleared the heads of those who did, as also were those of the privileged who could marvel then at twenty-seven-year-old Raphael's *School of Athens* fresco in the Vatican Palace, with Plato, Aristotle, Socrates, Pythagoras (and Raphael himself) holding court, portraying the newly secular civilization.

16th century philosophy was not just wise thoughts, mathematics and astronomy, it was the starting point of another fundamental society-reforming discipline, political science, when in 1513 Niccoló Machiavelli, its supreme exponent of the time, wrote *Il Principe*, the art of government – influenced one wonders by Nizam al-Mulk's *Siyasset-Nameh* ?

In 1532, the onetime monk, law student, physician, and humanist, François Rabelais, published his satirical, ribald *Pantagruel*. Two years later he brought out the equally irreverent *Gargantua*. The authorities would have none of it, and his works were condemned by both civil and priestly tribunals.

In 1540-80, the third great *Rinascimento* architect, Andrea Palladio, the most influential architect in history, designed palatial villas for the rich, on classical Roman principles. In launching a revolution in home design he made private homes look the way many of them do today.

The Renaissance was characterized in addition by the reawakening of interest in scientific matters. Muslim scholarship and Hispano-Islamic and -Judaist culture provided the foundations from which the scientific advances of the Renaissance were made. Muslim and Jewish physicians and their medical theory and practice were the bedrock of European medicine. The science of pharmacy was developed by these men from roots reaching back to the days of Harun al-Rashid. By the time al-Ma'moun came to power, pharmacy was an established profession in Iraq. Purified alcohol was first used as an antiseptic agent in Europe in Moorish Córdoba. Inhalation anesthesia using opiate-soaked sponges placed over the face was conducted in 13th-century Muslim Granada. This use of opium originated in antiquity, brought along by Arab medical practice.

The late 15th- and early 16th-century researches of Western scientists, the musings of its philosopher-priests, the themes of its writers, the works of artists, and the enlightened policies of a few Christian rulers were still however barely escaping the conservative hold of the Church. This was a millennial struggle, and the 16th century was little more than half-way through it. Pope Leo III's 9th-century notion – expressed in his crowning Charlemagne as Caesar – of the Holy Roman Emperor's joint and parallel authority with the Holy See's, would be followed by many centuries of pontiffs striving to exercise day-to-day control over worldly affairs.

The Reformation:
Early in the 16th century while Michelangelo, having just finished sculpting *David* in Florence, was frescoing the ceiling of the Sistine Chapel under the watchful eye of the Pope, Giuliano della Rovere, and Leonardo was labouring under the urgings of his patron, the perfect despot, Ludovico Sforza, to perfect the *Mona Lisa,* a German Augustine monk, Martin Luther, tormented by the moral decay and the political antics of the leadership of the Church of Rome, spoke out against the Papacy.

Already in the 1490s in Florence the fanatical friar Girolamo Savonarola had preached hellfire on the misdeeds of the Church. Luther based the authority for his revolt on biblical scriptures which ordinary people could then read for themselves in vernacular translation from Latin. In 1513, as Machiavelli's *Il Principe* was being published, and the Ottomans were strengthening their grip on southern Anatolia, Luther obtained the Chair of Saintly Scriptures at the University of Wittenberg in Germany from where he denounced the corrupt practice of selling "indulgences" – certificates guaranteeing relief in Purgatory from punishment for sin on Earth. Worse, priests were selling licences for concubinage.

Luther, an intolerant man, had no time for the humanists of the day. Rome to him was Sodom and Gomorrah. In 1517 he (is widely believed to have) nailed to the door of the Wittenberg church his *Ninety-five Theses* pointing to the abuses of the Church, calling for the removal of the spiritual authority of Christendom from Pope Leo X (Giovanni de Medici) and from the Holy See.

Months earlier the Ottomans had finally destroyed the Mamluk empire and had removed the governorship of Islam from the hands of the Mamluks and the Arabs. And a few months later, Thomas More, English jurist and humanist, was to publish his concept of the ideal state, *Utopia*, strikingly unlike the existing condition of European society and faith.

The Papacy faced Luther's challenge crippled by the widespread perception that popes were cynical participants in the complex web of Italian politics. As indeed they were. The *Ninety-five Theses* were the opening shot in the movement, later to be called the Reformation, to reform the Church, its doctrines and practices. The causes of the Reformation were moral, doctrinal, economic, political and complex. The key to the propagation of Luther's ideas was the revolution in information technology, Gutenberg's "hot metal" printing press. After this machine appeared, texts for publication could rapidly and relatively inexpensively be mass produced anywhere. By the 1470s the printing press was spreading quickly across Europe. Caxton set up the first English one in London in 1476. It reached Stockholm in 1526 and Moscow in 1555.

The importance of the printing press cannot be exaggerated. The introduction of this machine with its movable and interchangeable type face was a foundation stone of modern industry and civilization, more important among the giant forward steps of the West's 15th century than even the Guns-and-Ships revolution. The printing press powered the Reformation and the Scientific Revolution soon to follow.

A wave of protest against the Church followed Luther's denunciation. In 1520, the Pope inevitably excommunicated Luther and banned his writings. Soon after, however, King Gustav Vasa of Sweden confiscated all of the extensive Church lands in his country and subordinated Church to State while realigning the established religion towards Lutheranism. The clergy were made civil servants.

In 1529, Henry VIII, Catholic King of England, determined to escape Roman highhandedness (the Pope had refused to give him a divorce from Catherine of Aragon). Occupied as they were with doctrinal and dynastic matters, many of the leaders of western Europe reacted with a shrug to the simultaneous siege of Vienna by the Ottomans, led by Suleiman the Magnificent.

Prominent in the Church's resistance to the Reformation was the scholarly puritan Society of Jesus, the Jesuits, founded in 1534 by a Basque veteran soldier, the more papist than the Pope, Ignatius Loyola. It was Loyola who initiated the bloody but unsuccessful Counter Reformation.

In 1536, a French reformer Jean Calvin, confirmed partisan of Lutheran ideas but even more radical and uncompromising, published his *Institution of the Christian Religion*. Soon afterwards, Henry VIII dissolved the English monasteries, confiscated their real estate and distributed much of it among his noble vassals. In 1541, with the reform movement then known as Protestantism, Calvin set up a puritan Protestant society in Geneva. After this, the spreading of reform was unstoppable, notwithstanding or indeed because Calvin's writings were also Indexed by the Pope, Pius IV. Rebellions and religious wars broke out everywhere in and between the Christian countries while Suleiman continued to threaten Europe with his advances in the Balkans. Fortunately for Christendom, Suleiman, the greatest Ottoman, died in 1566 and was succeeded by his incompetent son, Selim "the Sot", addicted to sexual and alcoholic pleasures.

Protestantism arrived at a sort of compromise with Catholicism in the mid-16th century in certain countries – Germany, parts of Scandinavia, Switzerland and Italy. Sweden alternated for decades between Lutheran and Catholic practice. And, by 1600 (the year that *Hamlet, Prince of Denmark* was first performed), England, Scotland, Holland, Denmark, northern Germany, Norway, Sweden, Prussia and the Baltic States had in the main adopted one or more of the several Protestant churches that had appeared. In the course of time these would number in their scores from Adventist and Anabaptist to Wee Free, Wesleyan and Zwinglian.

Spain, Portugal, much of France, the Belgian part of the Low Countries, southern Germany, Italy, Austria, Poland and Ireland remained Roman Catholic. Some areas of France were mixed Catholic and Protestant. Ottoman lands in the Balkans were mixed Muslim and Orthodox. After the fall of Constantinople to the Ottomans in 1543, in the eastern regions of Europe there arose an autonomous Orthodox church in Russia, and a new Greek Catholic church, the Uniate Church, in what is today's western Ukraine. The Uniate Church recognized the Pope's authority but was independent of Rome and retained from the Orthodox Church a married clergy.

The English fundamentalist Puritans, who considered the Protestant Church of England to be "Catholicism without the Pope", landed in Plymouth, Massachusetts, in 1620, in the bitter cold of the Little Ice Age. Half of them died in that first terrible winter of 1620-21.

Religious civil wars and persecutions continued in Europe until about 1660 when the European map of faiths took on a more permanent appearance. By this time, the success of evangelization had made it difficult for rulers of different conviction to challenge the religious beliefs of their subjects. Little has changed in the religious map since the late 17th century although the French Calvinist Huguenots were mostly driven out of France by Louis XIV in 1685 amidst a reign of terror. This turned out to be to the immense benefit of Germany, England and South Africa, whither fled some 200,000 Huguenots, many of them skilled craftsmen.

All over Europe religious ardour affected the evolution of the arts. In Catholic countries, particularly, perhaps because of a perception of need for emotional release from the stresses of the times, demands arose for ostentatious theatrical display in music and play acting, as well as in architecture. In the mid-16th century, Mannerism in Italian painting began to succeed the High Renaissance art of the two earlier geniuses Leonardo and Raphael, and initiated a trend in the 17th century for which the term Baroque was coined – by art historians in the 19th. The Protestants, in contrast, were often austere in their newfound faith, and restrained if not melancholy, like the Puritans and Anabaptists.

In c. 1570, Giovanni Palestrina began to compose his religious music with more potency. At the turn of the century, the violent, quarrelsome teenager Michelangelo Caravaggio, a pardoned murderer, launched a theme of revolutionary realism into painting. Peter Paul Rubens, the greatest Fleming of the day, followed with his remarkable vitality, and then the Spanish artist, painter to the royal court, Diego Velazquez, came upon the scene.

By 1607, Claudio Monteverdi with his *Orfeo* was in full Baroque theatrical flow, and many builders were following the Spartan external but sumptuous internal styling of the Gesù Church of Rome. There came also a reaction to the Puritanism of the Calvinist and Jesuit die-hards in the form of a sharp fall in moral restraint in high society. (This was well illustrated by the hard living Friedrich Augustus, King of Poland, famously father of some 300 children, about whom an English wit, commenting upon the vigour with which the king discharged his royal responsibilities, declared that "Friedrich left no stern unturned".)

By underlining the need for Bible-reading, the new version of Christianity gave literacy another unexpected stimulus. By challenging many of the old social ways and craft practices and rituals, it breathed new life into business enterprise. By dividing the Western Christian world into two irreconcilable ideals, Protestantism prodded the Church of Rome into much needed, and in the final analysis, welcome reform. The Catholic Church did well from the Reformation, strengthening its position in many respects by the mid-17th century within its remaining realms – spiritual, geographical, financial.

After the 1530s, there were three Christian orthodoxies: Orthodox, Catholic and Protestant. The mainstreams of all three differed from Islam in having divine revelation and intervention play little part in doctrine (*pace* the miraculous virgin birth, the Holy Trinity, the purported instances of revelatory events in the Bible, and the beliefs of creationists.) For all three the Bible consists of accounts of the words and deeds of Christ. All make some separation between the celestial and the temporal. The autocracy of the papacy in the 17th century at least over central Italy was still as absolute as that of Ottoman Islam over its lands. Even so, by dealing a fatal blow to the unity of Christendom – not suggesting it was ever really united – the Reformation replaced "Christendom" with "Europe", a continent of many and varied faces and a spectrum of distinct cultures, but all with the same supple Christian roots, the European character.

One of the founding ideas behind Western pragmatism and scientific civilization was expressed c. 1600 by the English philosopher Francis Bacon (who still believed that some knowledge derived from revelation) when he wrote: "Henceforth in human affairs what is most useful in practice will also be the most correct in theory"; truth itself could be defined in terms of practicality, a concept unutterable in the Islamic world.

Out of religious disunity there arose strengthened nationalism and diversity; out of diversity there grew fragmented, decentralized, unsupervised commerce, industry, art and scientific investigation questioning many of the old beliefs. In particular, science was liberated, began to be liberated, from the confining hands of the institutional Church and of old ideas. This was the beginning of a blossoming European civilization. The make-up of Europe's unique, free-thinking, individualist identity began to appear – an identity that Alberto Moravia would one day call "a reversible fabric, one side variegated, the other side a single colour, rich and deep." Only such a Christian culture could ever produce a Descartes, a Montesquieu or a Rousseau.

The Discovery of America and the Spanish Empire:
Christopher Columbus' discovery of the New World in 1492 on behalf of the rulers of Castile and Aragon, apart from changing everything, would have an immediate economic effect. The immediate successors of Columbus, Spanish gentlemen adventurers, came across and laid claim to vast treasure – silver and gold – which would spur the economy of Europe for a century, a Europe beginning to be refreshed by the Renaissance and already in a stage of economic growth through expanding trade. The effects of the arrival of these riches on Europe were like the effects of plunder and tribute on the Arab caliphate after

the death of the Prophet. New foodstuffs also were brought in from the New World, helping to nourish the population increasing in the early part of the century. It was during the 16ᵗʰ century that the standard of European living became comparable to what it had been under the Romans 1200 years before. Still, the 16ᵗʰ century was seriously disturbed by religious strife issuing from the Reformation and the imperial ambitions of kings and princes, producing almost incessant warfare, peasant revolts and insurrections.

In 1504, Isabella, regnant Queen of Castile, died, and her daughter Juana "the Mad" inherited the throne although Juana's father Ferdinand of Aragon continued to govern. Upon Ferdinand's death, Isabella's and Ferdinand's 16-year-old son Charles of Ghent became King Charles I (Juan Carlos) of Spain and of its possessions in Sardinia, the Maghreb city-states of Melilla, Oran and Tunis, the kingdoms of Naples and Sicily and the Americas. (Charles' mother tongue was Flemish; he also spoke Spanish, French, and Italian, and German to his horse.)

When his Habsburg grandfather, Holy Roman Emperor Maximilian of Austria, died, King Charles of Spain inherited – as was his right – the countries of Germany, Austria, western Hungary, the Netherlands and Franche-Comté, an eastern province of France. He was nineteen years old. In order to exercise fuller control over his Europe he enlarged his army by raising taxes, particularly in Spain, causing the people to rise in revolt which he put down fearlessly.

In 1521, Charles went to war with France, Spain's foe for hundreds of years, capturing and for a time in 1525 holding King François I. (François I was the cultivated man of pleasure who made common cause with Suleiman the Magnificent under the *capitulations*.) The population of all of Spain at this time was about 6 million. France had 15 million. At this moment few of the riches of the Americas had arrived in Europe, and Charles had been obliged to finance his military adventures through taxes and borrowings. However, silver and gold were discovered by the Spanish explorers in both Mexico and Peru. Hernán Cortés declared upon landing in America: "I came to get gold, not to till the soil like a peasant." Spanish gentlemen did not dirty their hands.

By the 1520s, while the Reformation was beginning to gather pace and the High Renaissance was beginning to be distorted by Mannerism, Cortés with a few hundred men had conquered the Aztecs of Mexico. By 1533, the Pizarro brothers with 180 men had seized the Inca empire of Peru. And by 1540, a flood of silver was pouring out of Mexico and the Pelosí mine of Peru (now in Bolivia) through the port of Seville into the European economy, making increased credit available for merchants and invigorating the continent's finances, banking, trade and industry.

The Spanish Netherlands' city of Antwerp (in today's Belgium) had been established by the Portuguese as a banking centre in the very early years of the 16th century, supporting their near-monopoly of spice and other luxury imports into Europe. Later, the city became the distribution point for silver from the Americas, and Antwerp became for some eighty years the powerhouse of the European economy. Simultaneously, Venice with its 1.5 million population, long the dominant European home base for the spice trade, began to suffer serious decline as Portugal strengthened its hold on this trade. With low interest rates, free capital movement encouraged by Netherlands' and English banks, a secure international payments system, and a flow of savings from the growing middle class of Europe willing to accept interest payments from the bankers, dividends from entrepreneurs and profits from equity partnerships, capitalism was placed on a firm footing.

In the Europe of the 1500s, few of Ibn Khurradadbeh's 9th-century list of exports to China, an important market, were still traded – "eunuchs, slavegirls, boys, brocades, castor skins, marten and other furs…" And 16th-century Europe manufactured little that the Far East desired. Ming Chinese arts and crafts were of notably higher quality (the Ming dynasty had overthrown the Mongol rule of the Great Khanate in 1368) and India was the source of many desirable products. To obtain the products of the East – ceramic, industrial, mineral, herbal, ornamental, silken – Europeans often had to pay in bullion. Counterbalancing exports were often not acceptable. When it became available in huge quantity about 1550, silver financed Europe's deficits with the Orient. Much of the silver coming from the Americas then ended up in China, India and the Ottoman lands.

With the opening up of the oceans by the new ships, international trade was transformed from the limited medieval luxury kind to mass transport of bulky cargoes – timber, grain, fish, metal products – commerce financed by the banks. Trade became effectively monopolized by the great trading companies, England's Muscovy Company founded in 1565, the Levant Company in 1581, and the fabled East India Company in 1602. With their Dutch and French counterparts, these buccaneer traders overtook the Portuguese and many of the Italians and Arabs, and gained control of a large part of the international merchant business by the end of the 1600s, often by forcing local competitors out of business. Meanwhile, in the Americas, imperial Spain, Portugal, England, France and the Netherlands traded in and exploited African slaves, abetted in these profitable activities by professional Arab slavers and their native African business partners.

By the mid-16th century, the torrent of American silver had already changed Europe's economy. By this time though, King Charles of Spain had been at war five times with France. Much of the financing for these wars had been raised from the banks. As a head of the most Catholic House of Habsburg, the most powerful family in Europe, Charles had fought the 1525 Peasants' War in Germany. In 1527, his German mercenaries, recently converted to Lutheranism, had sacked Rome to unite the Papal States with his lands, massacring the monks and raping the nuns, Pope Clement VII having conspired with the French against him. This attack had put an end to liberal philosophical writing in Italy and to the High Renaissance in art.

Following this, King Charles had defended Vienna in Suleiman's siege of 1529. In 1530, he had had himself elected Holy Roman Emperor, under the title of Charles V, being crowned in Bologna by the same subdued Pope Clement. But having failed to subdue the Reformation, Charles had fought the Protestant princes of Germany while continuing to attack the French. His many wars were ruinous to Spain and damaging to France.

Spain was seriously weakened by the bankruptcy of the state in 1557. Huge Spanish borrowings in the financial markets had sapped the monetary system leading, together with the flood of American silver, to inflation for the first time in European history. Subject to the same pressures, France went bankrupt in the same year.

In 1556, Holy Roman Emperor Charles V, fatigued after his exertions of the previous forty years, abdicated his Spanish kingdom and its possessions in favour of his son Philip and retired to a monastery. By then Charles' realms stretched from Europe and north Africa to the Americas and the Philippines. His son became Philip II, Catholic King of Spain and of its possessions and colonies, but not of Germany or Austria which went to Emperor Charles' brother Ferdinand I, the new Holy Roman Emperor. With the increased flow of American silver, Philip was able quickly to restore the finances of the Spanish state following the bankruptcy of 1557. In 1554 Philip had married

Mary Tudor, Catholic Queen of England, daughter of Henry VIII, but had assumed none of her sovereign prerogatives. Mary died young and was succeeded on the English throne by her twenty-five-year-old Protestant half-sister, Elizabeth, a woman of remarkable qualities who would change the character of England.

Philip, driven to enforce religious and administrative uniformity over his huge empire, launched a string of unenforceable policies and unwise actions. Like his father before him, Philip II spent much of his resources on the defence of Catholicism against the Reformation. He drove the Protestant Dutch into revolt, the persecuted Moriscos of Spain (pressured already by Queen Isabella in 1502 into conversion to Christianity) again into rebellion, and his unpaid Spanish troops in Antwerp into mutiny. For a few fabulous years Spain had been the greatest power on Earth when possession of American silver enabled it to field the best army in Europe. Catholic Spain, just emerged from four hundred years of war with the Muslims, had launched itself into another hundred with Protestants. Neither Charles nor Philip had any idea how to cope levelheadedly with the widespread desire for confessional change or with the unexpected acquisition of wealth.

In 1565, the Protestants of Spanish Holland petitioned King Philip for religious toleration. When he refused rioting broke out. In the next year, two of the Protestant leaders, noblemen, were beheaded in the Grand Place of Brussels and their heads sent malodorously in a box to Madrid. Another of the leaders, William of Orange, escaped to England and a general revolt against Spain erupted in the Netherlands. The Spanish hanged dozens of revolutionary Calvinists in Haarlem, Holland, for heresy. The revolt continued intermittently for decades, the Dutch being helped periodically by the French and the English, for their own purposes, it must be said.

(William of Orange's adulterous second wife's lover later became the father of Rubens, the greatest of the Flemish artists. William's great grandson became King William III of England. This last William was the inspiration for the Orange Order of Ulster founded in 1795 to guard and preserve Episcopalian power in Northern Ireland. The drinking toast of the Ulster Orange Order is: "To the glorious, pious and immortal memory of the great and good King William who saved us from popery, slavery, knavery, brass money and wooden shoes. And a fig to the Bishop of Cork"!)

In 1570 Pope Pius V excommunicated Elizabeth of England. Three months later a Papal Bull was issued against Elizabeth giving special licence to her subjects to take up arms against her, absolving Roman Catholics from their sins in doing so: "Elizabeth the pretended Queen of England, a slave of wickedness, lending thereunto a helping hand, with whom, as in a sanctuary the most pernicious of all men have found a refuge. The very woman having seized on the kingdom, and monstrously usurping the supreme place of the Head of the Church in all England, and the chief authority and jurisdiction thereof, has again brought back the said kingdom into miserable destruction, which was then newly reduced to the Catholic faith and good fruits...We do out of the fullness of our Apostolic power declare the aforesaid Elizabeth, being a heretic, and favourer of heretics, and her adherents in the matters aforesaid, to have incurred sentence of anathema, and to be cut off from the unity of the body of Christ." The Papal Bull solemnly conferred Elizabeth's throne of England on Philip II of Spain.

In 1578, the twenty-four-year old King Sebastian I "the Desired" of Portugal was killed on crusade in Morocco. With this came the end of Portugal's seventy-year near-mastery of world trade. Then, Philip of Spain took the Portuguese throne to add to his collection, under the pretext that he had inherited it from his mother. Spanish power reached its own peak in the 1580s, but vanity, extravagance, determination to overturn the Reformation, and wasteful competition with France led to the failure of Philip's reign. The Spanish state again over-extended itself in 1585 and once more the unpaid troops in Antwerp mutinied. So the bankers of Antwerp moved to the safer Amsterdam; many had already done so after the mutiny of 1576. But later, with all the Netherlands sunk in religious war, their war of independence from Spain, the banking industry moved back to Genoa from where Europe's money business was managed until the 1650s.

In 1588, Philip sent his Invincible Armada of three-masted, square-rigged galleons (*Grande y Felicisima Armada*) in a glorious crusade against the enemies of the faith, to return the heretic Elizabeth's Protestant England to the fold of Catholicism, and to avail himself of the rights to the English throne conferred on him by the Holy Father.

Spain, a Mediterranean power, still fought at sea with outdated age-old Mediterranean naval tactics, like the Italians, the Ottomans and the Mamluks before them. The Armada was an army of soldiers embarked on giant ships, expecting to board and fight the English hand to hand at sea, as in the old days, before conquering them on land. It was a poor match for England's nimble, newly-evolved, sneaky ways of fighting in the open sea with the new ships, and fire ships. (Even though fire-ships set fire to none of the enemy, the Spanish formation was scattered and failed to rendezvous with the necessary land-based component of the expedition.) And on this occasion the English were abetted by the weather. Just seventeen years earlier, the Spanish and their Italian allies had beaten the Turks at Lepanto, all belligerents then still employing 2000-year-old naval tactics and oar-propelled galleys.

The outmanoeuvring of the Spanish fleet by Drake's and Hawkins' and Lord Howard of Effingham's little ships ended Spain's supremacy at sea and raised England with barely two-and-a half million people to the status of a major maritime power. At the end of the century Philip II went bankrupt again. "There was misery amidst splendour and an overpowering sense of disillusionment. Philip, like Don Quixote," wrote Miguel de Cervantes, a few years later, "had been tilting at windmills." (Cervantes lived through all this after being wounded, losing the use of his left hand, as a soldier at Lepanto, and later surviving five years as a slave of Barbary pirates in Algiers.)

In 1598 Philip died, leaving an immense kingdom crippled by debt after seventy years of almost continuous warfare and the erection of monumental buildings like the sombre El Escorial, near Madrid. A decade after Philip's death, Catholic Spain ruled then by Philip III, the last of the Spanish Habsburg monarchs, expelled many (perhaps 275,000) Moors and *faux* Moriscos with disastrous consequences for agriculture. Silver remittances from Spanish America began to be gravely reduced in the 1620s. After the golden years of discovery, victorious warfare and expansion of empire, Spain's economy stagnated, with low investment, little technological innovation and hedgehog conservative governance. And Philip II's successors failed dismally to prevent the independence of the Republic of Holland in 1648, Spain's most valuable dependency, after eighty years of struggle.

In 1640 the Portuguese rose against their Spanish masters, seeking to recover their independence. They won, although their independence remained unrecognized until 1668. These losses signalled the end of Spain as a world power. Spain had passed from grandeur to decline in little more than a century, just as had the Abbasid caliphate in the hundred years from 750 to 850. Spain had employed the unexpected flow of wealth from the Americas just as the caliphs had managed the rivers of income from the plunder and tribute of conquest. Paradoxically, Spain enjoyed a golden age of art and culture after the death of Philip II in 1598, with the second part of *Don Quixote* being published and Velazquez reaching his prime. Islamic culture had also prospered for a time in Egypt and Spain in the wake of the political and economic demise of the Middle Eastern Arabs.

By the beginning of the 17th century, except for Genoa, none of the Italian city-states was any longer a power to be reckoned with in Europe; Venice had faded and even Genoa had little remaining military muscle. With the shift of the West's economic centre of gravity from the Mediterranean to northern Europe, the North Sea and the Atlantic seaboard came the transfer of the cultural leadership from Italy, Rome and Florence to the Protestant north and northwest. Rubens left Italy and returned to Amsterdam, and his gifted pupil, Van Dyck, set up his easel in England.

Upon gaining independence, as a haven of relative tolerance, the Dutch Republic attracted bankers, artists, philosophers. The Jewish lens grinder, Baruch (Benedictus) Spinoza, whose Portuguese Marrano parents had fled the terror of the Spanish Inquisition only to have their secular son vilified and expelled for heresy at the age of twenty-three by Amsterdam's Jewish community, was described by Bertrand Russell as "the noblest of the great philosophers". Spinoza believed that "Minds are conquered not by arms, but by love and magnanimity." "The alleged will of God" he said, "is the refuge of ignorance." Spinoza argued against the influence of clerics in government as their commitment to further their one version of truth against all others led inevitably to conflict. But, of course, his humanist view of the innate intellect of man needing no appeal for guidance to divine revelation led to his denunciation as a godless immoralist.

Great painters – Rembrandt, Vermeer, Frans Hals – set up their studios in Holland. The economy of independent Holland, its social structure and ethos allow the modern person to consider it the first modern state, even if Holland's power waned after fighting England for commercial reasons three times in the second half of the 17th century.

The supremacy of France as a continental power in Europe began to reappear with the death in 1661 of its *éminence grise*, Cardinal Mazarin, allowing the twenty-three-year-old Sun King Louis XIV to spread his wings and begin calling the tune in the continent with what would become Europe's mightiest army.

It has been said that Catholicism imposed such restrictions on its society that progress was hampered more than it was under the sombre but more liberal Protestantism, and that Catholicism's influence on its community was much the same as that of the Mosque on the Muslim community.

In the 17th century, while in northern Protestant Europe agricultural productivity increased dramatically and trade and industry prospered, in mostly Catholic southern and Orthodox eastern Europe improvement was slow, both in the level of industrial productivity and in agricultural techniques. Most advances in productivity depended upon breaking the old oppressive feudal relationships between master and man.

Northern France was different from the south, the *Pays d'Oïl* from the *Pays d'Oc*. When the peasants exchanged their traditional feudal labour services on their lords' land for money rent in England, the Netherlands and parts of the *Pays d'Oïl*, southern Europe often accepted restrictive share-cropping tenancies. In eastern Europe, in an even more troubling counter-trend, feudal conditions grew until they approached slavery for the country folk. This was why the industrial revolution came so late to eastern Europe. It was only in 1812 that feudalism was abolished in Sicily, and as late as 1815 the peasants, the mainstay of the economy, were not free in parts of the Italian mainland, Spain, Portugal, most of Hungary, the Balkans and Russia. Serfdom persisted in parts of Russia until the final Emancipation of 1861. In these differences lay the differences in standard of living between western Europe and eastern and southern Europe. The differences continued into the 20th century. Mass tourism, the expansion of the European Union, the CAP and the collapse of the Soviet Union are redressing the balance.

Before 1500, the frontiers of most countries across the globe were indistinct, fluid. Still, rivers, mountain watersheds, deserts, seashores often marked transient limits of the rulers' powers. After globalization of trade began in 1500, the major states of Europe set their territorial borders. They exercised sovereign rights within those borders. Except for England they maintained standing armies. They had professional bureaucracies, systematic tax-collection, extensive trading networks, and permanent embassies abroad. After 1600, Europe, the French in particular, reinvented the State. The nation-state appeared, united by language, common descent and culture. The nation-state faced others striving for supremacy which was often denied because counterbalancing alliances among the weaker thwarted the intent. This balance of power had been developed by the Italian city-states in the 13th and 14th centuries from ancient Greek models.

The new, largely maritime states were belligerent, piratical, cannon-armed and rigged for supremacy at sea. Like many before they were wedded to violence. From 1750, the West was ascendant on the world scene, even if, in 1700, the West had been barely ahead of parts of China, the Ottomans and India in standard of living and technology. (In 1640, when Shah Jahan – ninth generation in direct line of descent from Tamerlane and thirteenth in a female line from Genghis Khan – had been building the Taj Mahal, India had still been producing the world's finest quality steel, crucible wootz steel, and China still had the world's largest national economy.)

By the mid-18th century, however, the new merchant capitalism had turned Europe, with all its acquired material and philosophical advantages and the textured diversity of its Christian culture, into the economic dynamo of the world. In wealth, power and progress the West then rapidly left all other regions of the world behind.

The Scientific Revolution and the Enlightenment:

Almost everything that distinguishes the modern world from earlier times is attributable to science, which achieved its most dramatic advances after 1600. Science became the all-absorbing intellectual activity of the 17th century with the wide adoption of the scientific-experimental method – systematic, recorded, observation and measurement, and repeatability of results. Herbert Butterfield (1949) called the Scientific Revolution the most important event in European history since the rise of Christianity, "reducing the Renaissance and the Reformation to the rank of mere episodes and marking the real origin both of the modern world and of modern mentality".

During the 1500s, Europe was still absorbed in theology, and men of good will were striving still to escape the world of good and evil, angels and demons, paradise and hell-fire. In 1509, the portable timepiece which became an essential tool both of gentlemanly living and science was invented by the German locksmith Peter Henlein: things were getting measured, including time. The basis of science, as always before the 19th century, was astronomy and its allied disciplines of mathematics, physics and optics. With regard to the philosophical exercise of mathematics – in which no progress had been made for centuries – between 1540 and 1545 three Italian mathematicians Scipione del Ferro, Nicolo Tartaglia and Girolamo Cardan found an answer to one of the most weighty unanswered questions, how to solve cubic equations. (Though the modern-day Muslim writer K. Ajram – see bibliography – claims that: "The secret of cubic equations was solved with ease by Muslim mathematicians as early as the 10th century.")

Nikolaus Copernicus (1473-1543) did not discover that the Earth rotated around the Sun. The early Greeks, Aristarchus of Samos, had suggested this possibility. Abbasid astronomers under Caliph al-Ma'moun had also done so, with more conviction. Copernicus merely rediscovered it, with or without clues from the ancients. But with Copernicus, mathematics began for the first time to be used to describe natural phenomena quantitatively rather than qualitatively. Copernicus in his day was, not unexpectedly, largely disbelieved even though his scientific methodology was correct. And it was not until a century later that the German Johannes Kepler (1571-1630) laid the question of heliocentricism to rest in Europe. The telescope was designed at about the same time, in 1609. In 1609 also, Zacharias Janssen of Amsterdam designed the microscope.

Although K. Ajram maintains that logarithms were commonly employed in the Muslim world as a mathematical tool as early as the 13th century, the Scot, John Napier, is usually credited in the West with establishing them in 1614 (and with inventing the decimal point.) Whoever got there first, creativity, discovery, freedom of imagination were flooding Europe, even if of interest and direct benefit to only a few people, and notwithstanding the 17th century's many upheavals and conflicts.

A few years after Kepler, Galileo Galilei of Pisa (1564-1642) founded the science of dynamics. He discovered the importance of acceleration and explained the constancy of gravity by dropping weights from the Leaning Tower of Pisa. He made astronomical discoveries unquestionably beyond the works of the Arabs and the ancients.

Galileo, having heard that a German, Hans Lippershey, living in Holland had in 1608 invented the refracting telescope, made one for himself. (Lippershey may in fact not have been the first to assemble such a device, but only the first in the written record.) Among other observations in the night sky Galileo found Jupiter's four moons. Now, *everyone knew* there were only seven heavenly bodies – the Sun, the Moon and the five planets. Galileo was mistaken; his four moons of Jupiter were an illusion. On these grounds the clerics denounced the telescope as a devilish creator of illusions. Such was the mood of Italy and the Church in the 17th century that Galileo was summoned by the Inquisition, condemned and forced to recant some of his theories and disavow several of his observations. The Church's suffocating grip on science and education was long in loosening. The Muslim *ulema* had also centuries before completely smothered science and progress in their world for questioning that which must not be questioned. Just as King Charles of Spain had put an end to Renaissance philosophical writing, the Inquisition put an end to science in Italy until a reawakening in the 19th century, adding to that country's woes and damaging the Church itself. Unexpectedly, such folly strengthened the separation of the secular and the spiritual in Europe, a necessary condition for progress. While there were Protestant countries in Galileo's time where the clergy was just as bigoted and suspicious of science as the Catholic clergy, they had failed to win control of their countries. So it was under the more adaptable, reformed branch of Christianity that science and the acquisition of knowledge were finally liberated from some of the shackles of tradition.

We must remember that the 17th-century "philosophers" were the scientists, mathematicians, inventors of the time. In 1637, the French adventurer René Descartes (1596-1650) writing in French, not Latin – as learned writings in Europe had previously been – advanced analytic geometry, a great boon to architecture and engineering and the first step forward from Arabic and Euclidian geometry. He enunciated laws of refraction of light, restructured the foundations of modern science and is one of the founders of modern philosophy. He had the wisdom to settle in Holland, the one 17th-century country where much freedom to think already existed. The Protestant Dutch were business-like, industrious, reasonably tolerant of other religions. In order to reconsider the source of all his knowledge Descartes resolved to doubt everything, everything that he had learned through his five senses, everything he had learned from other people. His conclusion, his sole piece of certainty, was that if he was capable of thinking, which he was, he must exist: *Cogito ergo sum* – a basic tenet of modern philosophy, creating the rationalist Cartesian system.

The French mathematician, physician, philosopher, Blaise Pascal (1623-62), invented a mechanical digital calculator at the age of eighteen to help his father, a tax collector. He devoted much of his short life to physics. He enunciated a law of fluid pressure, invented the syringe, designed the hydraulic press and wrote works on philosophy. His *Lettres Provinciales* (1656) is referred to in Jesuit publications as a poisoned chalice. Pascal corresponded with his fellow mathematician, Pierre de Fermat, the pioneer of differential calculus (whose Last Theorem, which tormented mathematicians for centuries, was finally validated in 1995, by the Englishman Andrew Wiles.) Pascal's post-mortem *Pensées* has been described as the epitome of common sense.

In this mid-17th century, laissez-faire liberalism was still not out there in the community. In continued defence of government interference in the actions of people, the philosopher, Thomas Hobbes, (echoing al-Ghazali ?), described in his *Leviathan* of 1651 the modern state as a "monster composed of men" regrettably necessary because, "During the time when men lived without a common power to keep them in awe, they are in that condition called war where every man is enemy to every man. In such condition there is no place for industry, no navigation, no arts, no letters, no society, and continual fear of violent death. Then, the life of man is solitary, poor, nasty, brutish and short."

The mathematization of scientific description reached a new zenith with Isaac Newton (1642-1727). He, having "seen further by standing on the shoulders of giants", invented the reflecting telescope, defined laws of optics, extending Alhazen's 11th-century work on lenses, and discovered the laws of motion and gravity. With Gottfried Leibniz, Newton expanded Fermat's work on differential and integral calculus, the tools of higher mathematics. He thought of himself as "a boy playing on the sea shore…while the great ocean of truth lay all undiscovered before me." Newton's *Principia Mathematica* was the supreme scientific work of the 17th century. A founding figure of the Enlightenment, he gave a rational basis to the understanding of the working of the universe more or less unchallenged for 200 years until Albert Einstein came along.

The activities, the discoveries of these 17th-century geniuses set in motion a torrent of invention in Europe and America in the 18th century, the material nuts and bolts of civilization: the piano, the steam engine, mercury thermometer, diving bell, sextant, spinning jenny, flush toilet, circular saw, hot air balloon, torsion balance, bicycle, ball bearings, lathe, electric battery, bifocals, threshing machine, diving bell, lightning rod, parachute, cotton gin, cast iron plough and scores of mechanical improvements providing the technological framework of the Industrial Revolution.

Necessity and inventiveness, freedom of thought, available finance and expanding markets were already germinating the Industrial Revolution by the 1750s. Thinkers in the France of the earlier 1700s had already brought forth the Enlightenment in philosophy and politics, seen in the works of Voltaire, Montesquieu, Diderot, Rousseau. And art freeing itself from ancient cloistered conviction, brought excitement and new perceptions to society, with Watteau, Canaletto, Hogarth, Boucher, Reynolds, Gainsborough, Fragonard and Goya. But it was not until the French Revolution that the Catholic Church was stripped of its power to impose its will on much of European society, and even then Napoleon restored the Church's power over education in France until it was wrested away by lay society at the end of the 19th century, and confirmed constitutionally only at the beginning of the 20th.

The Little Ice Age:

Sediment cores taken in recent years from the ocean bottom west of Iceland and isotope evidence from polar ice cores show that the 1300s had the coldest climate experienced in Greenland during the past 700 years. Beginning at the opening of the 14th century or late in the 13th, a few decades before the Vikings had to abandon their northern Greenland settlements, the Medieval Warm conditions passed away, and European weather deteriorated, winters becoming longer, colder and wetter, summers shorter, eventually with severe consequences for agrarian communities in northern Europe. We now know from worldwide tree ring data and the many new tools of Earth Science investigation that for the second time in the Christian era the world was experiencing a radical fall in atmospheric temperature, a Little Ice Age, the glacial effects continuing until about 1850. In 1665, as Samuel Pepys was writing his *Diary* in London, people lit Christmas bonfires on the frozen Thames. Dutch canals stayed frozen for months. Farms in the higher latitudes of Europe had to be abandoned. The harvest failed in 1693 and millions died across Europe.

The most intensely frigid period in Europe, 1650-1700, coincided with a period of much reduced sunspot activity, named the "Maunder Minimum" after the English solar astronomer E.W. Maunder. Together with other theories, the suggestion has been made that this low level of activity caused global cooling. Although the evidence is not at all conclusive, the Little Ice Age seems to have coincided with a time of heightened volcanic activity when huge quantities of volcanic dust, sulphur dioxide and other gases were lofted into the upper atmosphere, reducing the amount of solar radiation reaching the earth's surface. This level of volcanic activity might also partly explain the icing phenomenon. The cooling in the northern hemisphere may on the other hand have been foreshadowed or would have been deepened by the considerable fall in population numbers resulting from the Black

Death. The Plague unquestionably caused a widespread and centuries-long return to forest condition of previously farmed land, and therefore a reduction in the carbon dioxide level of the atmosphere, possibly bringing on cooling. Wally Broecker in the 1990s contended that it was a slowing or cessation of the northward flow of the Gulf Stream in the Atlantic that allowed the southward shift of Arctic conditions into Europe and North America. None of these explanations would alone cover the worldwide phenomenon.

Global re-warming began in the 1800s, coinciding with a renewal of sunspot activity, population growth, forest clearance, and the relative quiescence of volcanic activity. The effects of the Little Ice Age added to the inflation of c.1550–1690 caused mainly by the influx of American silver, religious wars, many of which had been started by Spain, and the financial mismanagement of some European governments were dire, impacting upon agriculture, health, economics and social life. The effects on the economy of Europe were felt into the 19th century.

16

Islamic Education and Modernity

Education in the Early Arab Empires – 21ˢᵗ Century Education in Arabia

Education in the Early Arab Empires:
The early Arab empire created a cultural universe of art and learning in which literature, poetry, the sciences, architecture and medicine were particularly favoured. Schools were established in the mosques in Umayyad times. Financial aid was given by the Abbasids to places of higher learning in the major cities of the empire. The Fatimids of Egypt and the Mamluk sultans were behind the expansion of second-ary education. And the Seljuks launched the mass-education *madras-sas*. While treasured in its own right, teaching's main purposes, how-ever, were the dissemination of Allah's revelations to Mohammed and the describing and understanding of the wonderful things that Allah had created. The mosques were the first institutes of learning and the Koran and its received interpretations the only text books. Together they formed an encyclopedia of science, philosophy and ethics. The added purpose of Muslim schools was to prepare men for the after-world and to train theologians and lawyers, the *ulema* and mullahs to interpret and explain these purposes. A simple form of philology, the proper understanding of the words of the Koran, and religious studies were at the heart of the curriculum. Elementary science and arithme-tic were taught for practical use. But despite the encouragement of medical research, the detached philosophy prominent in the Greek

learning beginning to enter the Islamic world from the 7th century was frowned on as possibly questioning the truths that had been revealed to Mohammed. There was no room for scepticism in religion.

Some of the spirit of enquiry which had been the gift of classical civilization was nevertheless kept alive by the Arabs. Translations from Greek, Persian and Sanskrit into Arabic began under the Umayyads and expanded under the Abbasids well into the 9th century. Translation continued until the 14th century in Spain. Unfortunately, the early eruption of turmoil in the Arab heartlands caused loss of confidence among the leaders. Confidence required stability and prosperity. These shortcomings, together with the constant questioning of the religious legitimacy of the caliphs and unsuppressed rationalist enquiry into revelation made the religion turn in on itself in defence. So, from the exhilarating days of conquest when they were willing to study and learn from the cultures they had overrun, the *ulema* convinced themselves of the need to maintain orthodoxy by creating religious impediments to change. Many orthodox Muslim theologians argued that since all necessary truth was already in the Koran there was no need for philosophical speculation or broadening the scope of enquiry.

The rejection of rationalism and of the endeavours of the Brethren of Purity had a stifling effect on Arab civilization. The *ulema* who had once sought knowledge from everywhere, following the Prophet's command to "seek knowledge even unto China," were succeeded by men seeking knowledge only from conservative consideration of the Scriptures. Sunni Islam, a religion nominally without a priesthood, became priest-ridden. And the cost of Islam's withdrawal from reason was to drive teaching into the cold hands of petrified medievalism out of which at the same time Western thinkers were struggling to escape – as Pierre Abélard had written, "By doubting we come to enquiry, and by enquiry we grasp truth"?

At the end of the 10th century science was still being studied in the Muslim world, even if it was suffering from the growing disapproval of the *ulema*. But from the death of al-Ghazali in 1111 progress in many of the sciences in which the Middle Eastern Arabs had once been so adventurous slowed markedly – in physics, mineralogy, botany. The lifeblood of universities – research and uncluttered thinking – was draining away, even in Cairo. Only in medicine and mathematics was progress made after the 12th century, principally in Spain before the fall of the Almohads (although Al-Qalasadi introduced alphabetic letters as algebraic symbols in about 1470), in 13th to mid-14th century Persia under the Ilkhanate Mongols, and in Samarkand under the Timurid, Ulugh Beg, until the mid-15th.

For all that, belief in Koranic education was still widely held and deterioration in scholarship was by no means a clear trend even by the 12th century. As late as the late 12th, poets in Spain under the Almohads and the Nasrids of Granada could still make (restrained) fun of religion. And universities were still being founded in the mosques. The Abbasid Caliph al-Mustansir (not to be confused with the Fatimid caliph of the same name) founded the Mustansiriyah University in Baghdad in 1234, with a hospital and an attendant physician. (It did not survive the Mongol attack of 1258 but was later rebuilt and is there today). At great cost to Islamic culture, however, freedom of contemplative inquiry beyond the realms of medicine and mathematics died out in Spain with the deaths of Averroës and Yaqub al-Mansur in 1198-99. In an atmosphere of increasing radicalism in the 13th and 14th centuries, almost all that was left in the Muslim world of scholarship was learning by rote – seen still today in rows of boys in *madrassas*, nodding in cadence over their principal textbook, the Koran, committing it to memory.

Intellectual feebleness in the 13th-14th century Arab world was exacerbated by the absence of challenging cultural exchange with the rest of the world, with Europe and China and India. New thought and knowledge coming from outside were condemned as profane; for were they not the utterances of infidels? Cultured Arabs – with justification until the 13th century with respect to Europe – were contemptuous of the semi-barbaric people of Christendom.

(Many writers quote the 9th-10th century Baghdadi geographer, al-Masudi: "The peoples of the north" [probably Russia] "are those for whom the sun is far from the zenith; cold and damp prevail in those regions, and snow and ice follow one another endlessly. Warm humour is lacking in them; their bodies are large, their natures lack refinement, their manners are coarse, their minds are dull and their tongues heavy. Their religious beliefs are without substance. Those furthest north are burdened most with stupidity, grossness and brutishness.")

The mechanical printing press with movable type, which was invented by the Chinese, was handicapped by the 30,000-ideograph Chinese "alphabet". Printing by this and more primitive means had been in general use in China from 900, and had been particularly useful in spreading information about the many improvements in agricultural technology that were taking place. In the sophisticated 12th and

13th-century Arab world with the advantages of its improved 28-letter alphabet, development of mechanical printing might well have been expected. Also, it was the Arabs – the Almohad Moors – who had brought paper-making to Spain, Valencia, 400 years after the Abbasids had first learned how to make it. Experiments with the design of printing presses are believed to have taken place under the Almohads but seem never to have been pursued to any practical conclusion. In any event, there was no time for much progress to be made in this respect as the Christians were pressing so heavily upon them from the 1200s, and the authorities were against it, anyway.

Conviction of cultural superiority had blinded Muslims to progress in Christendom. Abd ar-Rahman bin Khaldoun (b. Tunis 1332 - d. Cairo 1406) renowned historian, geographer, judge, professor at Cairo's al-Azhar mosque-university, perhaps the last Islamic scholar of supreme distinction, wrote in 1377 (during the forty years of family in-fighting sultans, the Black Death, and chaos in Egypt after the death of the Sultan al-Nasir), "We learn by report that in the lands of the Franks on the north shore of the Sea, philosophical sciences are much in demand, their principles are being revived, the centres for teaching them are numerous, and the number of students seeking to learn is increasing." This he noted while lamenting that: "Learning has almost disappeared in north Africa." It *had* disappeared in Iraq and Syria where religious conservatism reigned supreme. And the bloodchilling Tamerlane would finish off Iraq and Syria a few years later. "God knows best what goes on in those parts," Ibn Khaldoun remarked about Europe.

In *those parts* the writings of the theologian Thomas Aquinas educated in Frederick II's already mainly-secular University of Naples, and regarded by many Europeans as the epitome of scholastic philosophy, had been available for a century. Dante Alighieri, the first humanist visionary seeking rational ways of solving human problems and concerned with humankind as responsible intellectual beings, had sixty years before completed *La Divina Commedia*. Boccaccio had written *The Decameron* with its alternately tragic and comic views of life. Petrarch had addressed his poetry to Laura, his idealized beloved. With Petrarch, the sonnet, risen from Arab origins in Frederick II's court, reached its highest expression.

In Florence, Giotto had arrived as the first revolutionary Renaissance painter, the new "personality" of European art. Aristotle's thoughts, conveyed to Europe through Muslim Spain, were stimulating new thinking on human existence itself. What is more, by that time, 1377, the Sorbonne in Paris was already an intellectual powerhouse with a teaching faculty of more than 500. It had had schools of mathematics, astronomy, medicine and philosophy as well as theology for many years. There were nine more at least partly secular universities in France. Roger Bacon (author of the first known written formula for gunpowder – in 1249) who quoted the wise men of Islam, was a teacher at the Sorbonne in the 1240s-50s. Kublai Khan's emissary Rabban Sauma had visited and greatly admired the Sorbonne. In Italy there were fourteen universities; in Christian Spain and Portugal, nine; and England had Oxford and Cambridge. From Ibn Khaldoun's words it is clear that by the 1370s, the self-imposed cultural isolation of the Arabs was effectively complete.

Middle Eastern civilization with its rigid cultural rules, mosque-based "universities" and inflexible dogma was paralysed in the face of commercial setbacks, paucity of raw materials, rapid population growth alternating with famine-induced population shrinkage, and the manifest need to lift its restrictions on education and philosophi-cal enquiry. Intellectually stagnant Arab civilization faded with the growth of a dynamic, ever-changing, ever-strengthening West.

With the introduction of mechanical printing by Johannes Gutenberg (c.1450) an opportunity arose for the Arabs to make up lost ground, to recover from some of their technological backslide. However, their leaders and the reactionary Sultan of the Turks, Mehmet the Conqueror, imposed a total ban on machine printing. In Cairo the Circassian Mamluks, wracked by political unrest, were frozen in the past. By that time, Egypt had been beset by decline for two hundred years, and Iraq and Syria had long been poor agricultural backwaters. Muslim leaders agreed that the printing press was ungodly and might further divide the Faithful already profoundly divided by sectarianism. The print-ing press was forbidden. Moorish Granada, the last refuge of Islamic culture, followed suit.

The handicap Muslims placed on themselves by rejecting this inno-vation (until the Turks licensed it in Istanbul in 1729, and then only under strict government supervision and censorship) is immeasur-able. Mohammed Ali, Ottoman-appointed Pasha of Egypt, brought printing presses to Cairo in the 1820s. Even so, the great majority of books printed in Egypt in Arabic were on poetry and matters of reli-gion, history and Islamic law, the subjects that had dominated learning in the 8th-10th centuries, and primary school and vocational training text books. The date in the West for printing with few restraints began with the introduction of the mechanical press in the late 15th century.

The concept of the novel, the fictional prose narrative, the origins of which are lost in the mists of antiquity, never existed in the Arab world before it appeared in 1914, from tentative 19th century beginnings in Egypt, with Mohamed Hussein Haykal's *Zeinab*, the first truly Arabic novel, (the *Alf Layla wa Layla* being Persian/Indian tales translated into Arabic). The 21st-century Arab is bearing the consequences of these three hundred years and more lost in an intellectual fog.

For spiritual and cultural reasons the Arab world had cut itself off from the lands across the Mediterranean. Over a period of centuries Islam had slipped imperceptibly into ignorance buoyed up by false pride and by Arab Islam's long-held sense of superiority. Westerners learned much from the Arabs, some of it of practical use, and adopted it as their own (often claiming authorship). The Arabs learned nothing from the West. Even the revival of military power under the Ottomans produced no liberation of thought or liberalization of attitudes. And even in the mid-16th century, Suleiman the Magnificent was no revisionist liberal thinker, notwithstanding his exceptional intellect.

From a high measure of scholastic achievement Arabs descended into near-ignorance. Challenged by climate and lack of resources they found no practical solutions for their economic problems when the flow of booty and tribute came to an end. From some degree of riches – even if inequitably distributed – under the Turks, the Arab Middle East and northeast Africa slumped into poverty, subsistence agriculture and fishing. From imperial power they descended into parochial, subservient impotence. It might fairly be argued that the Arabs had brought down this Dark Age upon themselves with their refusal to evolve with the times and to adapt to the deteriorating economic and military realities.

By some measures, Tripoli, Tunis and Algiers did better. After the demise of the Almohads in Spain c. 1270, the Moors continued with their maritime trading activities and, following their expulsion from Granada in 1492, the Barbary (Berber) Coast prospered for centuries from piracy and capture of European seafarers. (The Spanish writer Cervantes was one of them. Between 1609 and 1616, according to one account, seven thousand English mariners were caught and sold into slavery.)

21st Century Education in Arabia:

It is with alarm and a sense of *déjà vu* that one reads in the UN Arab Human Development Report of 2002, written by Arab intellectuals, that while their level of poverty is the world's lowest and spending on education is the highest in the developing world, "Writing [authorship] in the Arab world is in severe shortage and there is a dearth of translations from outside." The Report states that the twenty-two members of the Arab League with an aggregate population of 290-300 million (the same as the USA) now translate into Arabic from foreign languages an average of 330 books a year. Since the reign of Caliph al-Ma'moun in the 9th century the Arab world has translated for its own interest, amusement and instruction, a total of something like 100,000 books, about the same number that Spain (pop. 42 million) a country of middling size and prosperity in the European Union "now translates for itself in one year." In addition, "a large share of the (Arab) market consists of religious books…that are limited in creative content." Education in the Muslim world, handicapped by historical limitations of the fields of study, the age-old restrictive practice of learning by rote, and domination by the mosque, appears still to be little more than the broadcasting of Allah's revelations to Mohammed.

The Economist reported in 2004 that: "In the third year of secondary school, Saudi children learn that a good way to show love of Allah is to treat infidels with contempt. They hear that ideologies such as communism, Arab-nationalism and secularism are forms of the capital crime of apostasy. Yet nothing is quite as bad as pretending to be a proper Muslim, then sneaking off to perform rituals in tombs." Wahhabis consider praying at tombs, widely practised by Sufis and Shias, to be idolatry, a cardinal sin. "Anyone who does so forfeits his right to life and property; his women-folk may be taken and made slaves."

Up to the year 2004, among the 554 Nobel Prize laureates for the Sciences since 1901 and the new science of Economics since 1969, astonishingly, 135-138 of them, 25%, are Jews; another source says 155 are, and yet another identifies 169 Jews among the science laureates by 2005. There is only one Arab, the Egyptian, Ahmed Zeweil, Chemistry (1999) working in California. (The Arab world does on the other hand have a Nobel Prize for Literature, Naguib Mahfouz and three Prizes for Peace – Anwar Sadat, Yasser Arafat and Mohamed El Baradei.) The world's total Jewish population is 12-14 million, less than the city of Cairo.

A million educated Arabs, many of them free spirits harassed by fanatic vigilantes, have fled the Arab world to live in the West. (At the age of eighty-three, in 1994, the Nobel laureate Naguib Mahfouz was stabbed in the neck, in a Cairo street, by militants for criticizing Islamic extremism.)

The UN Report states as well that research in the Arab world is weak or non-existent; science and technology are dormant; the utilization of Arab women's capabilities through political and economic participation remains "the lowest in the world".

In 2004, Jaio Tong University of Shanghai published a list of the world's top 500 universities ranked by academic quality and performance. No university of an Arab country made the list. Of the world's fifty-two Muslim-majority countries, with their aggregate population approaching a billion, only Turkey made the list, with two. Israel with a Jewish population of 5+ million (and 1+ million Arabs) had seven on the list. (It is not without forethought that Warren Buffet is paying $4 billion for the Israeli high-tech engineering company Iscar Metalworking, his first investment outside the United States.)

Prior to the discovery of oil in Saudi Arabia by Americans the only significant "export" industries of the country were revenues from the hajj pilgrims to Mecca, and pearls (and the pearl trade was already in decline as the Japanese had started culturing pearls on an industrial scale). The male/female ratio in the workforce of this kingdom where women are kept in subservience by exercise of authority and indoctrination of girls from childhood, is 94:6. No matter the high number of women graduating from Saudi universities, such a workforce ratio, if maintained, would preclude eventual economy-underpinning industrialization. Four or five of Saudi women's present-day six per cent are represented by teachers, doctors, nurses and hospital staff, employed in institutions where the women are corralled in semi-isolation. Such a situation reflects the near-total control exercised by the 250-year-old partnership of the now 6,000-7,000-prince House of Saud – the 50 to 55 sons of serial polygamist Abdul Aziz al-Saud by his 22 to 26 sequenced wives (the record is not clear about these numbers, some sources naming only 37 sons) and their male descendants – and loyal Wahhabis.

The veiling of women needs to be addressed. It has been argued that the veil is symbolic of Arab society's imposing men's insecurities on women, humiliated as women already are by polygamy and the male right to divorce by simple public declaration. The veil is seen by some as symbolic of male mistrust of femininity dressed up as piety. Such reports as the one of the fourteen young girls burned to death in their public intermediary school in Mecca in March 2002, when members of the Committee for the Promotion of Virtue and the Prevention of Vice, the Muttawai'n, blocked the exits from the blazing building preventing escape because the girls were not properly dressed, would seem to give weight to such an interpretation.

The 2004 Jeddah Economic Forum, in which a few Saudi women who were not completely veiled participated with male colleagues, prompted the following outburst from the kingdom's top religious authority (known otherwise as an outspoken critic of Osama bin Laden), Sheikh Abdel Aziz al-Sheikh: "Mixing is the root of all evil... the origin of vice and adultery."

Some Imams of Saudi Arabia preach a gospel of hate against advocates of women's rights, liberals, Christians and Jews. Licensed preachers in some of the largest mosques call openly for the extermination of infidels in the name of God. Some call for the killing of Shias and Sufis. A few of the more fanatical have been dismissed, even jailed, for bringing the kingdom into international disrepute. But little attempt would appear to have been made to cleanse Islamic teaching of the theocratic roots of these incitements. As it was for Europeans five hundred years ago, the unchallengeable commandeering of God's will can be seen as an insuperable obstacle to Arab democracy, modernization and moderation.

Another band of Wahhabis is led or inspired by Osama bin Laden whose purposes are to overthrow the "ungodly" kingdom of the Sauds, to purify Islam sullied by impure rituals, to cleanse the Prophet's land of infidels, and to re-establish the caliphate (all historical examples of which collapsed through dynastic rivalry, sectarianism, corruption and suicidal statecraft) from India to Andalusia, if not further. There is an argument that holy lands are all those that were ever under Islamic rule and all must be restored to the caliphate. Others just as fanatical are dedicated to spreading Islam by jihad "to the four corners of the earth," to use the words of South-east Asia's *Jemaa Islamiya*. Their objectives are shared by those incited by the worldviews of the 7th-8th century Salafis, who include the 9/11 perpetrators and the beheaders and suicide bombers of Bali, Baghdad, Beirut, Tel Aviv, Casablanca, Madrid, London.

17

The Modern State

Defining the Modern State – The Reasons for Western Pre-eminence

Defining the Modern State:
In the view of many people, the modern state uniquely possesses several distinguishing characteristics. All of these originated in the West. It can be argued that they derive from, or at least can be detected within, three events: the Industrial Revolution, beginning in England in the mid to late 18th century; the American Revolution, 1776; and the French Revolution, 1789. All three were born of the changes taking place in European religion, philosophy, science, and people's attitudes from the 14th century onwards, beginning perhaps even earlier. The English issued the Magna Carta in 1215, under which the powers of the monarch were limited, at first through a committee of knights, later through a national representative body, a Parliament, with the attendant development of competing political parties. In the modern state there shines a classical Greek ideal, "democracy", refined by the French in the 18th century. The French moreover developed the ideology of nationalism, the territorial nation-state within defined boundaries, the nation for the first time being identified with its people, not with a ruler, dynasty or religion. The United States – with all its faults the first true democracy – invented several nuclear features of today's modern state: the civil rights of the people, an independent judiciary with appellate review, and federal decentralization. The Americans

also rediscovered the "separation of powers", although separation is often not complete outside the United States and is far from perfect inside. Together, these features provide the foundations of what must be considered as the only true form of democracy, which can be termed "Jeffersonian". (Compare the Democratic People's Republic of [North] Korea and the thankfully departed German Democratic Republic.) In borrowing the term for this summary, one must be acutely conscious of the man's own caveat: "No one nation has a right to sit in judgement over another. But the tribunal of our consciences remains & that also of the opinion of the world." (Memo to President Washington, 1793.)

The modern Western state is distinguished by having a notable proportion of its people believing that they are so closely associated with each other by common descent, language, culture, history, belief system and occupation of the same land that they have to be known as a single nation. Unless some other factors promoting unity are particularly strong, as indeed they are in a few countries such as the USA and Canada, multi-cultural states risk difficulties (as in Iraq, Lebanon, Yugoslavia, Russia, Ukraine, Moldova, Turkey, Rwanda, Burundi, Nigeria, Sierra Leone, Liberia, Ivory Coast, Congo, Sudan, Sri Lanka, Indonesia, India, Burma, Guatemala, Spain, Northern Irleand, England, France and Germany – hardly an exhaustive list).

The modern Jeffersonian state seeks to be secular, meritocratic and liberal. It endeavours to be rationalist and empiricist, aiming to rely upon observation and experience without the aid of scientific specula-tion, or theory, or faith. Even though they may be compelling for a time, the traditional bases for political authority such as royal birth, divine right, religion, ethnicity or caste cannot satisfy the necessary conditions for freedom and progress. Revelation, belief and faith are confined in the modern state to the precious and rewarding yet sepa-rate realm of religion, a private matter, a matter of conscience, separate from political governance. In the modern state civil power is supreme over the ecclesiastical even though the separation of church and state is often not complete. Arguably, as the Church can make significant contributions to human living, separation need not be complete for contentment, progress and stability. Theocracy, however, frozen in the Dark Ages, is incompatible with democracy.

In the modern state, authority resides in the people. Power is exer-cised by the people directly or through their freely elected repre-sentatives. Democracy is the free exercise of choice by the people and reflects their informed and revisable opinions of the principles, policies and alternatives of government. Democracy promotes meritocracy and equal rights among the people and between the sexes. It ignores heredity and religious and ethnic distinctions. While its governance is predominantly secular, the modern state encourages and defends its citizens' freedom of worship and choice of religion or renunciation thereof. Apostasy, still forbidden on pain of fearful penalties under Islam, was a right hard-won in 16th–18th century Europe, a right untouchable now in the West. Islamic countries can thus never be democratic in the Western sense of the term.

The modern state is a polity with effective checks and balances where the majority is prevented from imposing the powers it wins in the polling booth oppressively on the minority. Democracy is tolerant of minority needs and views, and addresses their concerns, including religious, cultural and linguistic concerns, but only to the extent that government policies satisfying such needs or addressing such concerns do not undermine, contrary to the unmistakable will of the majority, the integrity or fundamental character of the state.

The modern state ensures the security of its people. It possesses and nurtures economic sovereignty as a basis for health, education and wealth. It is industrial. It creates conditions ensuring and supporting the essential activities of scientific and technological research and development. It strives to provide conditions facilitating the profitable bringing together of raw materials, capital, ideas, technology, labour, skills, artistry, management, and the rule of law to produce, offer and market a wide variety of goods and services for the benefit of the people. Without the abundant participation of free women in the workforce no democratic, industrially competitive society can be built. Without full and free participation of women a society condemns itself in the long run to backwardness and poverty.

The modern state respects human rights. Because they are a denial of human rights, practices such as bans on alien religions, property dispossession of widows, forced marriage, gender apartheid, female genital mutilation and family "honour killings" are not tolerated. The state that does afflicts itself grievously.

A report by the World Health Organization in October 2002 stated that nearly half of all female victims of murder in the Egyptian city of Alexandria were women who had been raped and as a consequence were murdered by male family members in acts of "family cleansing". With its newfound fragile, dangerous, and debatable freedom, it is reported that Iraq shows signs of readopting this practice, forbidden and severely punished under Saddam Hussein; and with the simultaneous rise of uncompromisingly militant Islam, both Shiite and Sunni, extremists in that country are driving it deeper into medieval barbarity. In 2003 the Jordanian legislature refused to pass into law penalties greater than a slap on the back of the hand for these killings. In Pakistan in 2003, according to Government statistics, 1,300 women were murdered like this. As a consequence the Government passed legislation to combat this scourge, including the death penalty. But the latest reports indicate that the legislation is ineffective, largely ignored by the police and the courts. In June 2002 a young Pakistani woman, Mukhtara Mai (Mukhtaran Bibi), was gang-raped on the orders of tribesmen or a tribal council as punishment for the supposed (and possibly fabricated) sexual misbehaviour of her brother. The international outcry was loud: what makes the case even more disturbing is that the victim was put on Pakistan's Exit-Control List just as she was about to fly to London at the invitation of Amnesty International.

In a case in Afghanistan reported in 2005, one of many such cases, the family of a man accused of murdering another man was able to negotiate settlement of the "blood debt" by handing over two girls aged 8 and 15 to be married without their consent to men of the victim's family. In 2004 a 16-year-old wife was hanged for adultery in Neka, Iran. The man involved received 100 lashes. This is a culture with no place in the modern world or in the world of Allah, the Compassionate, the Merciful, the All-knowing.

The Reasons for Western Pre-eminence:

- The varied natural resources and climatic and ecological advantages of the European continent over many other parts of the world, including the post-10th-century Arab world
- The invaluable corpus of scholarly knowledge, science and technology derived from the Arab, Chinese, Hindu and classical Graeco-Roman worlds
- The macro-economic remodelling of Mediterranean trade at which Westerners were particularly adept after the 12th century
- The individualist market capitalism relying on commercial insurance, bank loans, interest payments and the overstepping of cultural obstacles arising in Europe in the 14th century
- The humanist thinking awakening in some monastic environments

in the 14th and 15th centuries and which began to liberate intellect from the confines of ancient prejudice

- The technological Guns-and-Ships Revolution of the late 15th century launched by the West, and the West's resultant cornering of inter-continental trade

- The spread of knowledge with the mechanical printing press in the later 15th and early 16th century

- The discovery of, and profit from, the Americas, their riches and opportunities

- The Christian religion and its many-faceted Reformation which began early in the 16th century to free Christianity from the hands of corrupt, backward-gazing medievalism

- The Scientific Revolution of the mid-16th to the late 17th century

- The concept of democracy revived by Europeans from ancient roots in the 18th century

- The Enlightenment of the 18th century when reason and free-thinking in art, living and politics came to the fore at the expense of fading tradition

- The Industrial Revolution, with its beginnings in England in the 18th century

- The separation not only of church and state but also of powers within the state: executive, judiciary, and legislature being the most obviously ideally discrete aspects of the state

- The raising of the level of women's rights and freedoms towards that of men.

Progressively, if erratically, after 1100 AD the West rose out of its Dark Age just as the Arab world slipped unknowingly into its own. The West's material circumstances and its more adaptable Christian culture allowed it uniquely to take advantage of changing climates: philosophical, political, environmental. The roots of Western civilization – its underpinnings – are deep and diverse. The coming of Humanism in the West, the Renaissance in art, the Reformation and the Scientific Revolution transformed Europe, spurring it into the future. No such revolutionary initiatives have yet bestirred the Arab world.

Bibliography

Ajram, K., *The Miracle of Islamic Science*. Knowledge House, Cedar Rapids, Iowa 1992

Andromeda Oxford, *The Cassell Atlas of World History*. Cassell, London 1998

Churchill, Winston, *A History of the English-Speaking Peoples*. Cassell, London 1957

Davies, Norman, *Europe – A History*. Pimlico, London 1996/7

El-Hibri, T., *Reinterpreting Islamic Historiography*. Cambridge 1999

Fernandez-Armesto, Filipe, *Civilizations*. Macmillan, London 2000

Finer, S. E., *The History of Government*. OUP, 1997

Fletcher, Richard, *The Cross and the Crescent*. Penguin, London 2003

Gibb, H.A.R., *Mohammedanism*. London 1953

Gibb, H.A.R., *Studies on the Civilization of Islam*. London 1962

Gibbon, Edward., *The Decline and Fall of the Roman Empire*. Penguin, London 1952

Hitti, Philip K., *Makers of Arab History*. Harper, New York 1971

Hosking, Geoffrey, *Russia and the Russians*. Allen Lane, Penguin, London 2001

Hourani, Albert, *A History of the Arab Peoples*. Faber and Faber, London 1991

Issawi, Charles, *An Economic History of the Middle East and North Africa*. New York 1982

Kennedy, Hugh, *The Prophet and the Age of the Caliphates*. Pearson-Longman, London 2004

Kennedy, Paul, *Rise and Fall of the Great Powers*. Unwin Hyman, London 1988

Levey, Michael, *From Giotto to Cézanne*. Thames and Hudson, London 1985

Lewis, Bernard, *The Arabs in History*. OUP, Oxford 1993

Mansfield, Peter, *The Arab World – A Comprehensive History*. Crowell, New York 1976

Merriam-Webster, *Merriam-Webster's Encyclopedia of Literature*. Springfield, Mass. 1995

Holmes, George (Editor), *Oxford Illustrated History of Italy*. OUP, Oxford 1997

Pipes, Richard, *Russia Under the Old Regime*. Charles Scrivener's Sons, New York 1974

Polk, William R., *The United States and the Arab World*. Harvard UP, Cambridge, Mass. 1975

Royal Academy of Arts, (Ed.) Roxburgh, David, *Turks: A Journey of a Thousand Years*. London 2005

Russell, Bertrand, *History of Western Philosophy*. Allen & Unwin, London 1954

Times Books, (Ed.) Overy, R., *Times History of the World*. London 1999

Trevor-Roper, Hugh, *The Rise of Christian Europe*. Thames and Hudson, London 1966

Tuchman, Barbara W., *A Distant Mirror, the Calamitous 14th Century*. Ballantine, NY 1978

Wood, Michael, *Legacy, A Search for the Origins of Civilization*. Network Books, BBC 1992

Index

215

INDEX